not formalist

trope vs. concept — 91, 109
even ambigu[...]

(unannounced reading strategy — intertextuality

1) Winthrop's History in light of Arabella sermon ("model")

2) Johnson's history in light of "edification" literature (p.65)
        (metaphor / trope

3)   Increase Mather —> Habbuk [?] (120)

4) some intertextual reading in ch4 — e.g. 163 / Berkeley book... but
   more explicit negotiation of other interpretations (Bercovitch)

                        |

                    see 192

What does it mean to
    "reauthorize the past" (193)?

(
    Is there a double-meaning to
        "authorize"/ "authorization" here...??

(109)

1. Past illustrates compromise → similar to Henry Clay

Authorizing
the Past

Authorizing the Past

The Rhetoric of History in Seventeenth-Century New England

"revising" Past (149)

Stephen Carl Arch

Northern Illinois

University

Press

DeKalb   1994

© 1994 by Northern Illinois University Press

Published by the Northern Illinois University Press,

DeKalb, Illinois 60115

Manufactured in the United States using acid-free paper

Design by Julia Fauci

Library of Congress Cataloging-in-Publication Data

Arch, Stephen Carl.

Authorizing the past : the rhetoric of history in

seventeenth-century New England / Stephen Carl Arch.

p. cm.

Includes bibliographical references and index.

ISBN 0-87580-188-9

1. Historiography—New England—History—17th

century. 2. New England—History—Colonial period,

ca. 1600-1775—Historiography. I. Title.

F7.A73 1994

907'.2074—dc20   94-8729

CIP

Contents

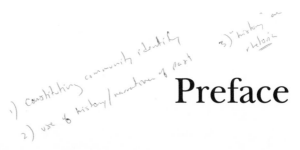

1) constituting community identity
2) use of history / narrative of past
3) history or rhetoric

Preface

I try in this book to understand several colonial and provincial writers who struggled, quite self-consciously, to shape the identity of their community by narrating stories about the past. In my writing, I operated under two convictions that, as they are not universally shared, I wish to underscore here. First, I am convinced that the events of the past are "textualized," that is, they come to us only through the problematic language of texts that are always and already open to interpretation and misinterpretation. Second, I am convinced that writers are human beings who act (that is, write from) within history to understand their relationship to themselves, to other human beings, to historical events, to the future, to their God. Van Wyck Brooks once asserted:

Hayden White

> A literary history confined to 'forms' would perpetuate the fallacy that books breed books by a sort of immaculate conception. In reality books are bred by men [and women], men [and women] by life, and life by books through a constant interrelation and cross-fertilization, so that an element of social history can scarcely be dispensed with in any account of literary phenomena and forces. (qtd. in Nelson 292–93)

Although I acknowledge that, at some level, language does indeed "speak" us, I tend to think that reports of the death of the author have been greatly exaggerated. Certainly, we cannot choose the discourses into which we are born, but we can and do make tremendously important choices, every day of our lives, within those discourses.[2]

on

My goal in this book has been simply to analyze the seventeenth-century histories of New England. If asked to describe my method, I would say that I have tried to trace historical and literary change, analyzing specific, successive texts in order to document a gradual but fundamental shift in the way New England historians understood themselves, their community, and their craft. I have, of

JB White – ish

course, learned much from the work of other scholars on the subject of history and historiography in seventeenth-century New England, scholars like Perry Miller, Sacvan Bercovitch, David Levin, and Cecelia Tichi. However, in the absence of a single authoritative treatment of New England historiography,[3] I was impelled, on one level, simply to describe this small but important body of colonial prose and to account through close textual analysis for its integrity, complexity, and artistry. Hence, given the way in which New England histories have been generally disregarded, my asking the reader to see them as literary texts—worthy of the same sort of analysis as a Dickinson poem or a Twain novel—is itself one of my important arguments.

Beyond that, however, I have at least two specific arguments to make about Puritan historiography in New England. First, I argue that these narratives typify the way in which cultures use the past to generate and regenerate their sense of purpose about themselves and their futures. Cultures are constantly reinventing their stories, their myths, their sense of themselves. I try here to show how one specific culture during one fairly short span of time did just that. Second, I argue that the record of Puritan historiography in the seventeenth century is one of increasing professionalism, to the point at which, by 1700, a "profession" of history, potentially separate from a profession of faith, could even be conceived (though, of course, the development of history into a professional discipline would not occur until the nineteenth century). It is significant that, at the end of the seventeenth century, Cotton Mather saw himself both rhetorically and methodologically as a professional historian, responsible for rescuing the past from the abyss of negligence to which his community had consigned it. In claiming that role for himself, however, and in systematically fulfilling it in his historiographic method, Mather broke with his predecessors: in his view, the historian no longer wrote from within the community but from above or beyond it, a stance that William Bradford and John Winthrop, for example, would not have understood. It is ironic that the very moment at which Puritan historiography achieves its greatest triumph and fulfills its own logic—in Mather's *Magnalia Christi Americana*—is also the moment at which, in a fundamental way, we can imagine it ceasing to be truly Puritan.

I have traced Puritan historiography and developed these arguments through the analysis of specific, successive texts. Each chapter, although it discusses various historians, will focus on one in particular: John Winthrop, Edward Johnson, Increase Mather, and Cotton Mather. I study the way each historian employed a distinctive rhetoric—by which I mean language use (tropes, diction, style), rhetorical strategies, narrative techniques, and evidentiary conventions—to achieve a particular purpose, to create in his audience a particular effect. Understanding the texts as responses both to other texts and to lived experience, I locate the narrative histories both within the context of the developing tradition of New English historiography and within the context of the cultural crises that demarcate seventeenth-century Anglo-American New English history, crises that each historian tried to comprehend, accommodate, revise, even deny. Historical narratives, I argue, are responses to the past, addressed to the future (LaCapra 108, 127).

The dialectic between event and text is crucial in understanding this notion. The Salem witchcraft crisis, for example, was actually first "produced" in 1692—it was a real, and horrible, incident in the lives of many colonists—and was then "reproduced" many times in the following years. Historians had to account for it, not simply as a trope that they could "signify" upon, but as a real and (apparently) unavoidable phenomenon whose meaning had somehow, in communal narratives, to be made consonant with the present-day community's larger purpose. Or (and this proved practically impossible in the case of the Salem crisis, though it was possible in other cases), it had to be forgotten, negated, erased. The crisis helped to change the community's sense of purpose, in other words, even as that sense of purpose was embedded in particular written texts whose meanings were themselves eventually revised, rethought, and reproduced in other texts that embodied a different and revised communal sense of purpose. Event and text, actions and language, deed and thought, are closely intertwined in the drama of life. The past, as William Faulkner had one of his characters say, "is never dead. It's not even past" (Faulkner 92).

Despite the limited number of texts that would seem to fall under the denomination of Seventeenth-Century New England Histories, I have had to make difficult choices about which texts, which words, to analyze in the depth I think many of the texts of the New World—not simply New England—colonists deserve. Although I take as my purview all of the various kinds of history written in seventeenth-century New England, I analyze in detail only these four historians and their writings.[4] Let me explain why.

First, I restricted my focus to New England because its literature is extraordinarily sophisticated for a newly settled colony. Other scholars have pursued the reasons this was so; I do not need to repeat their arguments here. Second, I restricted my focus to the seventeenth century because I was interested in the subtle differences I perceived within the self-conscious tradition of Puritan historiography. That subtlety demanded close attention to the ways in which the tradition developed over a specific and limited span of time. Third, I restricted my focus to "communal" histories because I was interested in public rhetoric and the shaping of social meaning through that rhetoric. Memoirs, personal relations, and diaries also contain public rhetoric, of course, and at times I refer to those sorts of histories; but I am more consistently interested in rhetoric that was designed primarily to address communal, not self, identity. Finally (and here the choice belonged more to the material than to me), I restricted my focus for the most part to works written from within the orthodoxy of the so-called New England Way. I did so because the orthodox authors of these works were, most often, responsible for communal storytelling (and the production and distribution of books); it is significant, but not surprising, that these writers usually had a concomitant interest in advancing and protecting the myth that proclaimed New England "chosen," exclusive, special.[5]

In essence, then, I have tried in this book to trace how cultural power and authority were constituted—and then reconstituted—in a series of texts by self-acknowledged cultural spokesmen in a society that, though vibrant, was yet limited in size of population, geographic extent, and range of dissent. I have not written a history of historical writing in colonial America; I have written a history of a particular kind of rhetoric in seventeenth-century New England. The subtitle of this book refers more to my method of accounting for the relation between history and text than it does to either history or rhetoric as specific disciplines.

At the very least, I hope *Authorizing the Past* will serve as a corrective to the many studies of early America that theorize about Puritan and (more generally) colonial literature without carefully and sympathetically analyzing complete, specific statements of its writers. Such theorizing has led to many distortions: that, for example, the early years of the colony were a "golden age" when "all the cultural norms of the community were fused, for over half a century, with extraordinary success" (Bercovitch, *Puritan Origins* 97), or more to my point, that Puritan historiography was a tragedy and a failure, having in the end, "no history of its own" (Gay 25). The story of Puritan historiography is not that of a "loss of mastery," as has been argued. It is the mastering, by various historians writing in various inventive ways, of communal identity and purpose, a mastering that, because of our insatiable need for myths about ourselves and because of new events and ideas not experienced or comprehended by previous historians, is even still and ever will be in progress, incomplete and ongoing.

Acknowledgments

The idea for this book came to me in 1985 during an independent study directed by Alan Howard at the University of Virginia, and it developed more fully there as a dissertation directed by David Levin. I was fortunate to have two such different but exemplary mentors, and I thank them both for their tough criticism, good advice, and warm friendship. David Levin, in particular, continues to inspire my writing, my teaching, and my intellectual life. Two other teachers, John McCully and Karl Gwiasda at Iowa State University, also deserve my thanks; they gave me a good bit of their time when I was first discovering the world of ideas.

While I was in graduate school, and since, John Ernest and Thomas Prendergast spent many hours patiently listening, disagreeing when necessary, challenging often, and encouraging when things looked the bleakest. They continue to influence my thinking, on art as on life. I would like to thank several colleagues and friends at Michigan State University for their advice and encouragement: A. C. Goodson, Michael Lopez, Bill Penn, Douglas Peterson, and Sheila Teahan. The English Department kindly gave me release time in the spring of 1991 to complete the manuscript.

Parts of chapters 3 and 4 appeared in much revised form as "The Rhetoric of Puritan History" in *Early American Literature* 27: 61–74; chapter 2 appeared in abbreviated form as "The Edifying History of Edward Johnson's *Wonder-Working Providence*" in *Early American Literature* 28: 42–59. I thank the editor of that journal, Philip Gura, for his patience, and its editorial board and readers for their advice. As the book neared completion, Robert Middlekauff, Don Rosenberg, Frank Shuffelton, and an anonymous reader for NIU Press made invaluable criticisms of the manuscript. Their advice made this book much better.

I dedicate this book to my parents, Paul and Mary Louise Arch, who have always been there when I needed them; and to my wife, Kristin Peterson, who entered my life long after the idea for the book was conceived but whose love made its completion possible and, indeed, worthwhile.

Authorizing the Past

Every age makes its own guide-books.

—Herman Melville,
Redburn
(1849)

Each age, it is found, must write its own books;
or, rather, each generation for the next
succeeding.

—Ralph Waldo Emerson,
"The American Scholar"
(1837)

"Scattered Bones"

John Winthrop's
History of New England

1

Sixteenth-century England experienced extensive social and cultural change: the Reformation and Henry VIII's subsequent break with Rome, the advent of Humanism, discoveries in and subsequent explorations of the New World, the rise of nationalism under the relatively stable rule of Elizabeth I, rapid economic growth, and a tremendous increase in literacy and the dissemination of the printed word. The effects of these changes on historical thought have been described by F. J. Levy:

> New ways of writing history were obviously required. The idea of anachronism meant that the whole history of England needed to be rethought. The emphasis on the secular, and especially on the political, meant that standards of accuracy had to be revised. More important still, the techniques of ordering the materials of the past required a total overhaul. The stuffed annals of the old days gradually became unworkable in the new context. (8)

There was, F. Smith Fussner has argued, a revolution in English historical writing in the latter half of Elizabeth's reign, "a whole complex of changes in the purpose, content, method, and style of

Bradford,
of Plymouth
Plantation

historical writing" (300). I do not wish to describe that revolution here, since it has been amply described and documented elsewhere.[1] However, given my focus in this book, it is relevant to note that all of the permanent New World settlements were conceived and organized at this time of heightened historical consciousness, indeed, were both causes and effects of that new historical consciousness. New England's settlers in particular, from the beginning, understood themselves and their settlements in peculiarly historical ways. William Bradford begins his history *Of Plymouth Plantation* by discussing "first . . . the occasion and inducements" of the planting of Plymouth, and then proceeds to detail how Satan had persecuted the true church since the days of "the first Christians" (4–5). That is, Bradford insists that the origins of his little community can be understood only in terms of the larger sweep of human history, within which it is a historically conditioned and situated product. He understood only too well that, though similar in some respects, the present was different from the past.

ok

cf.
Pocock

Given the revolution in historical consciousness, to which the New England settlers—as much as Milton and Hobbes—were heirs, it should come as no surprise that two of the most important literary works written by first-generation settlers of New England were Bradford's *Of Plymouth Plantation* and John Winthrop's *History of New England,* historical accounts of the Plymouth and Massachusetts Bay colonies. Neither history was printed or distributed in the seventeenth century, but many colonists knew of their existence and read them, and several historians consulted them when they wrote their own histories of New England later in the century.[2] Winthrop's *History* was not printed in its entirety until 1825–1826 (though parts of it appeared in print as early as 1790), while Bradford's history, considered lost until the manuscript was found in a private library in England, was not printed until 1856. Despite having remained in manuscript throughout the colonial period, however, the two works are founding documents of New England, and even American, history. They are historiographic repositories of the record of social, political, economic, and quotidian life in the first years of the settlement of New England, and literary accounts of the larger purpose of each colony, its vision of itself and its meaning for human history, as seen through the eyes of its most important leader.

When the two works were rediscovered by nineteenth-century scholars, most readers recognized they were important additions to our knowledge of our Puritan forebears, and historians and antiquarians realized they were gold mines of information about early New England life. Only in recent years, however, have literary critics taken notice of both works, particularly Bradford's *Of Plymouth Plantation.* Alan Howard, for example, has argued that Bradford's narrative moves carefully from peaks, when the pilgrims act out of humility and an awareness of their dependence on God's power and love, to valleys, when their overconfidence in their own abilities and their forsaking of God literally bring them down. Others have recognized that *Of Plymouth Plantation* is really two distinct works, expressive of Bradford's states of mind within two quite different periods of Plymouth's development. Book I, written in 1630 at the outset of the Great Migration to Massachusetts Bay, is a defensive act of self-definition in which Bradford juxtaposes the raising and sustaining hand of God against the repeated act of man's apostasy. This narrative of the emigration and founding is integrated and carefully ordered through the devices of allegory and typology, and Bradford expresses supreme confidence in the meaning and purpose of his band of pilgrims. The tale is mythic, in that Bradford's heroes (the saints who persevere in the face of adversity) serve as primordial types within a primitive view of the world. In Book I, good and evil are clear and distinct entities, and God is without doubt on the side of the emigrants. Book II, written in the troubled years of 1645–1650, is an elegy for the settlement that had become, in Bradford's words, "an ancient mother grown old and forsaken of her children" (334). The narrative of the years from 1620 to 1648 is like an annal in which the record of events spirals down from the communal optimism of the Mayflower Compact to the literal silence—blank entries for 1647 and 1648—of the frustrated historian. Here Bradford works empirically, trying to ascertain the meaning of his colony, and of history itself. He shows little confidence in the relevance of allegory, typology, or myth to his narrative. The tale is prosaic.[3]

This change in narrative tone resulted from Bradford's sad realization, fifteen years after the Great Migration and twenty-five years after his own colony had been settled, that Plymouth Plantation had met neither his nor his society's original expectations. The Mayflower Compact, which begins Book II, set out those expectations publicly:[4]

> for the Glory of God and advancement of the Christian Faith and
> Honour of our King and Country . . . [we] do by these presents
> solemnly and mutually . . . Covenant and Combine ourselves to-
> gether into a Civil Body Politic, for our better ordering and preser-
> vation and furtherance of the ends aforesaid. (76)

Various disappointments in the 1630s and 1640s, such as the desire
of many people in the Plymouth church to leave the "Civil Body
Politic," the outbreak of "wickedness" (316) in 1642 (including
the discovery of the horrible case of bestiality), and the death of
William Brewster, led Bradford in the 1640s to perceive that the
piety evinced in the Compact was no longer the primary shaping
force within his colony.

It seems clear that, as a result of that altered perception, Bradford stopped writing formal history and began to compose dialogues and poetry in which he abandoned the objective stance of
the historian he had used in *Of Plymouth Plantation,* attempting in
these new and more personalized genres to make his audience see,
and perhaps relive, the piety that drove him, Brewster, and the
other Separatist colonists to move through this world as pilgrims,
never citizens of any country, society, or city except heaven, "their
dearest country" (47). Bradford turned away from his relatively
objective recording of communal history and turned toward polemics of various sorts, all of them grounded in a now-idealized
notion of Plymouth's history. He attempted in these later works to
reinvigorate the community's present with the original piety that
had been the driving force behind the settlers' emigration from
the Old World. Hence, for example, in "Some observations of
God's merciful dealing with us in this wilderness," he tries to recall
the community to its original purpose by showing how Israel,
which was blessed with a "golden age" just as New England had
been, degenerated in the years following the deaths of Joshua and
many other elders: "I wish this may not be New England's fate,"
he concludes (477). But this turn toward the idealized rhetoric of
"Some observations" is simply a refiguring of Bradford's discomfort at the end of *Plymouth Plantation:* events were heading in the
wrong direction in the 1640s, and rather than continue faithfully
to record them, as he had promised the readers of his history (3),
Bradford attempts in other genres to redirect them. The silence at
the end of his history of Plymouth Plantation is only the silence of

one sort of historian (and of one sort of history), not of the historian himself or of history itself. His later turn to other genres—and to nostalgia—is revealing, because it indicates that sometime in the late 1640s (as I will argue in chapter 2) the colony's purpose, as well as the historical forms in which that purpose was inscribed, stood desperately in need of reconfiguration.[5]

But while Bradford's *Plymouth Plantation* has in recent years received more critical attention, which now allows us to think about it in these complex ways, John Winthrop's *History of New England* continues to languish in critics' minds as something less than a literary work. I suspect that modern readers have found it an imperfect chronicle, lacking in any saving literary or historiographic characteristics: there is no conscious structure, no theoretical analysis of history, no plain though forceful narrative (as in Bradford's history), not even an eccentric style or narrative stance (such as in Edward Johnson's *Wonder-Working Providence*). The narrative moves abruptly from incident to incident; it reads more as a diary or journal (which is what Winthrop had in mind when he began to write on Easter Monday 1630) than as the more integrated history Bradford presents. In fact, Winthrop's narrator not only lacks an eccentric style, he seems to lack any style at all: the narrative voice, though knowledgeable and highly literate, is almost devoid of character, which derives from Winthrop's conscious attempt to keep his "self" (John Winthrop the private man as opposed to John Winthrop the public figure) out of the *History*. So, although they have turned to it for information, most critics and historians have not considered Winthrop's history worthy of literary analysis.[6]

On an aesthetic level, Winthrop's *History of New England* is not the equal of Bradford's *Of Plymouth Plantation*. It is, however, worthy of much more discussion than it has received. Indeed, it is partly because so much has been said about Bradford's history and so little about Winthrop's that I have chosen the latter to focus on here. From it we can learn a great deal about Winthrop's development as a historian, about his literary attempt to comprehend the past and the future of his colony, and about the ideology of the first-generation settlers of Massachusetts Bay. Additionally, Winthrop's project can be explained, at least in an introductory way, through analogy with Bradford's history as critics have come to understand that history. I begin by recapitulating recent arguments that Bradford's *Of Plymouth Plantation* evinces a split between the "idealism" of 1630 and the "realism" of the 1640s. In

companion to

two

texts

what follows, I argue that a similar relationship exists between Winthrop's 1630 sermon "A Model of Christian Charity" and his *History of New England*, written in the 1630s and 1640s. The second work stands as a sort of photographic negative of the first, inverting its tone, attitude, and assumptions. To pursue this relationship, we must first look more closely at "The Model of Christian Charity."[7]

WINTHROP'S "MODEL"

In 1630, "On Board the Arbella, On the Atlantic Ocean," John Winthrop delivered his famous lay sermon "A Model of Christian Charity." Even more than Book I of William Bradford's *Of Plymouth Plantation*, composed the same year, Winthrop's sermon has served as a starting point for historians, scholars, and rhetoricians of America. It has done so in large part because Winthrop's concise concluding statement is so striking: God, he prophesies, "shall make us a praise and glory, that men shall say of succeeding plantations: the lord make it like that of New England: for we must Consider that we shall be as a City upon a Hill, the eyes of all people are upon us" (295).[8] Since the day Winthrop adopted this image of the "City upon a Hill" from the gospel of Matthew, it has been used by numerous writers to describe American societies, from Edward Johnson, writing of New England in 1653 ("seeing as [we] are to be set as lights upon a Hill," his narrator cries [29]), to Ronald Reagan, speaking of the United States in the 1980s ("America is today . . . what Winthrop said . . . 'We shall be as a shining city for all the world upon the hill' " [980]).[9] Winthrop's sermon introduced an image and a corresponding rhetoric that generations of Americans, colonial and national, have found useful and accessible.[10]

In the tradition of American Puritan studies that has developed since the 1930s, many scholars have turned to Winthrop's sermon to locate the beginnings of American expression; and their scholarship has taught us to better understand Winthrop's sermon, as well as the context within which he delivered it. Two of the most famous readings of Winthrop's sermon have been Perry Miller's and Sacvan Bercovitch's. Miller argued that the "Model" was the reactionary statement of a discontented band of Englishmen on their way to becoming Americanized a generation later. Winthrop's exposition, Miller asserted, was part of the Puritans' attempt to reclaim England: "it was a 'modell' of that to which England might yet be reclaimed. . . . Were [the] model ever to triumph in England, the founders might well go home." Until that time, these settlers promised to provide a living example for the mother country of a thriving, godly society. In Miller's view, the "Model" is practical and this-worldly (*The New England Mind: From Colony to Province* 24–26). Bercovitch, on the other hand, pointed out that the "Model" was a "jeremiad" expressive, even in 1630, of the unique and radical nature of the Massachusetts Bay settlement. For Bercovitch, Winthrop's exposition was a visionary statement that initiated not only America's first indigenous literary genre, but also its preoccupation with social perfection and national destiny (*American Jeremiad* 6–17).[11]

Which is it? Reactionary model or prophetic utterance? My own sense is that we should not force the two readings into an either-or proposition. Like the debate concerning whether Massachusetts Bay was settled for religious or economic reasons, the explanatory models offered by Miller and Bercovitch can be conflated.[12] Winthrop's sermon is both a secular statement of purpose and also a sacred, prophetic vision. The disagreement between Miller and Bercovitch merely helps to reveal how the sermon itself asks to be read in two quite different ways. Repeatedly in "A Model of Christian Charity," Winthrop betrays an ambivalence or tension inherent in both his method and his typically Puritan habit of mind.

"God Almighty," he states in the doctrine, "in his most holy and wise providence hath so disposed of the Condition of mankind, as in all times some must be rich[,] some poor, some high and eminent in power and dignity; others mean and in subjection" (282). A year earlier, when he had first considered removing to New England, Winthrop wrote that man in England had become "more vile and base than the earth we tread upon" (*Winthrop Papers* II: 139).[13] He argued then that the natural hierarchies that defined order in Renaissance England had been called into question by men who did not know or did not accept their own given place in society. In this context, his doctrine in the sermon appears a conservative, even reactionary, statement. It defines the new world sought by these Puritans as a return to the golden age of English history, when each man supposedly knew his appointed place in society.[14]

As Winthrop "opens" it, however, the doctrine contains the promise that the auditors can—if a divinely ordered society is reestablished in the new world—look forward to a time when the charity induced in them by that social framework will gather "together

the scattered bones [of] perfect old man Adam and [knit] them
into one body again in Christ" (290). In the doctrine, Winthrop
asks his audience to look into a future in which man will differ
qualitatively from what he has been since Adam's fall, into an end-
time of individual and social perfection directed by the hand of
God. It is for this reason, as we shall see, that the central images
and references in the "Model" are drawn from the Pentateuch
(particularly from Moses' farewell to the Israelites before they entered the Promised Land); from Samuel and Kings (the reign of
David, when the Jewish nation achieved its greatest glory); and
from Ezekiel (whose prophecies following the fall of Jerusalem
focus on the restoration and rehabilitation of a scattered nation).
In other words, they are drawn from biblical texts that describe or
address particular moments when the entire Jewish nation stood
poised in a delicate balance between failure and success, between
declension and prosperity. By using these images and references,
Winthrop suggests that the group of emigrants before him is similarly poised between the past and the future, between an England
that had declined from its golden age and a community that might
experience the splendor of the millennial restoration of man's
prelapsarian goodness.

The "reasons" section of "A Model of Christian Charity" manifests a slightly different type of ambivalence. Winthrop supports
the doctrine of the sermon with three statements, the first two of
which are Renaissance commonplaces: men are ordered, high to
low, rich to poor, first, "to hold conformity with the rest of [God's]
works," and second, to give God more occasion to manifest His
glory, restraining the wicked from scorning their superiors, preventing the rich from "eating up" the poor, and "exercising his
graces" in the regenerate faithful (282–83). Winthrop spends
merely a brief paragraph defending each of these two reasons. Not
so the third reason. He spends nine (printed) pages—more than
half the sermon—analyzing this third reason, which states that hierarchical societies best serve mankind because, in them, "every
man might have need of [an]other, and from hence they might be
all knit more nearly together in the Bond of brotherly affection"
(283). The difference between the first two reasons and the third
rests in the responsibility inherent in them: God does the work
under the first two; man does the work under the third. Winthrop
takes nine pages to defend this third point because he knows that
his argument must substantiate the claim that fallen man can and

will act charitably in this new world. It was a claim, after all, that ran counter to the insistence of Augustine and Calvin (the tradition that Winthrop knew best) that man was naturally depraved.

Following the basic tenets of Reformed theology, Winthrop begins his defense of the third reason by arguing that two laws regulate man's "conversation one towards another" (283). The first is the law of nature (or the "moral law"), which commands man "to love his neighbor as himself" (283). This law was given to Adam in his "innocency"; it asks each man to recognize "the same flesh and Image of God" in another that is in himself. Adam proved unable to live up to the dictates of the law of nature, however, so God in His mercy decreed a second law, one in which He declared that faith alone could save man from eternal damnation. This law of grace (or "gospel law") asks each *regenerate* man to recognize the saving work of Christ in other regenerate men, thus demanding that those within the "household of faith" be treated differently from and better than the unregenerate people outside that household. Under the law of nature, all men are meant to be friends; all men are meant to be treated equally. Under the gospel law, because the regenerate are isolated from the rest of mankind through the saving intervention of Christ, saints have to deal with "enemies." The law of nature was not, of course, discarded when God provided for a second law that would regulate men's actions; it remained in force as a set of moral guidelines for the regenerate and unregenerate alike, the difference being that regenerate men willingly followed those guidelines, while unregenerate men followed them because they feared divine punishment (283–84).

Now, Winthrop continues, under the law of nature all men and all "seasons and occasions" are the same. Man is always and everywhere to do unto others as he would have them do unto him. The law of nature is a law, essentially, of similarities. The gospel law, on the other hand, is a law of dissimilarities: it derives from God's decision to save a few men and leave the rest to their own futile devices; and it reflects His decision to allow some men to be rich and others poor, to allow some seasons and occasions to be special and others ordinary (284). God, Winthrop assures us, permits these dissimilarities for His own glory and for "the common Good of the Creature, Man" (283). This is an unassailable point not only in this sermon, but for all Puritans in the first half of the seventeenth century: God is infinitely supreme and man is correspondingly debased (Miller, *New England Mind: The Seventeenth Century*

3–34). The gap is measured by God's ability, when He so wishes, to raise and prosper individuals, both in this world and in the next. By exercising that choice, however, God made the world a more complex and confusing place than it was when the law of nature was man's only guide. The gospel law dictates how saints should act amid that complexity.

It is significant that, in this sermon composed and structured in accordance with Ramist doctrine and the Puritan plain style, Winthrop chooses to analyze the gospel law by using the metaphor of a clock. He points out that is not enough in this new world to "love our brother . . . but in regard of the excellency of his parts" (288). In other words, it is not enough to love only those whom we like or find attractive, for that "cause" of action will not always be consistent with the desired effect, "works of mercy." To make those attractions the ground of love would be like manually ringing a clock with the hammer, instead of winding it and letting the mechanism itself produce the desired sound. Winthrop says that his auditors must act, in this new society, not out of worldly emotions or feelings, but out of a prior cause, which will always be consistent with the desired effect, mercy:

> as when we bid one make the clock strike he doth not lay hand on the hammer which is the immediate instrument of the sound but sets on work the first mover or main wheel, knowing that will certainly produce the sound which he intends; so the way to draw men to the works of mercy is not by force of Argument from the goodness or necessity of the work, for though this course may enforce a rational mind to some present Act of mercy as is frequent in experience, yet it cannot work such a habit in a Soul as shall make it prompt upon all occasions to produce the same effect but by framing these affections of love in the heart which will as natively bring forth the other, as any cause doth produce the effect. (288)

What Winthrop has in mind here is that every member of this community be made anew, be revitalized, so that the only cause or motivation for any action is love, or "Christian Charity." The image implies a society in which everyone acts holily, not out of emotion or passion or forethought, but out of a "habit" so ingrained that they must perforce act in that fashion.

This habit of love can only come about through supernatural intervention:

> There is no body but consists of parts and that which knits these
> parts together gives the body its perfection . . . : the several parts of
> this body considered apart before they were united were as dispro-
> portionate and as much disordering as so many contrary qualities
> or elements but when christ comes and by his spirit and love knits
> all these parts to himself and each to other, it is become the most
> perfect and best proportioned body in the world. (288–89)

This second image clarifies what the first leaves vague: that this
new society, this potentially perfect and best-proportioned body,
can be brought about only through Christ's intervention. What
Calvinism says of the individual—that he or she cannot act out of
truly holy impulses without what Jonathan Edwards would later
term the "divine and supernatural light" imparted by God—
Winthrop applies here to society as a whole. He conflates, as Sacvan Bercovitch has shown us, individual and social salvation (*American Jeremiad* 1–30).

Winthrop seems to be aware of that conflation, since his argument includes a scriptural reference that attempts to justify it: "all
true Christians are of one body in Christ I. Cor[inthians] 12.12"
(289). Most commentators in the Reformed tradition saw in this
passage from I Corinthians a reference to the "mystical" church,
pure but invisible, that "included every person living, dead, or yet
to be born, whom God had predestined for salvation" (Morgan,
Visible Saints 3). Calvin, for example, in his commentary on the
passage, remarks that although the word *body* can mean a society
or a city, "among Christians . . . the case is very different; for they
do not constitute a mere political body, but are the spiritual and
mystical body of Christ" (405). However, judging from the size of
Winthrop's audience (there were four hundred emigrants in the
fleet of four ships, but no more than one hundred on the *Arbella*)
and from his rhetoric, Calvin's interpretation seems too broad;
Winthrop's argument is more localized than that. Nor does Winthrop seem to mean the visible body of Christ, the "church living
upon earth" (Ames 178), which is comprised of all professing
Christians in the world at any given moment. His audience was
obviously much narrower than that, too. What he seems to have in
mind, in this reference to the body of Christ, is the "city" or civil
society about to be initiated on the shores of the New World. The
idea derives from William Ames, among others:

> [A] joining together by covenant makes a church only as it looks
> toward the exercising of the communion of saints. For the same

believing men may join themselves in covenant to make a city or
some civil society when their immediate concern is for the common
civil good. . . . The same men may make a city or political society
and not a church. (180)

Winthrop's settlers would eventually form several churches, but on
the *Arbella* he was speaking first and foremost about a civil society.
Floating between two worlds in the middle of the Atlantic Ocean,
Winthrop contrived to make the settlers who would assemble on
the American strand a *civitas dei;* to do so, he extended the work
of salvation from the level of the individual to the level of society.
He blurred the line between elect self and elect community.

In the end, Winthrop insists that the habit of love will necessarily create a perfect society: a "special relation," he says, of "sensi-
bleness and Sympathy of each other's Conditions will *necessarily*
infuse into each part a native desire and endeavour, to strengthen
defend preserve and comfort the other" (289, emphasis added).
Before Adam fell, Winthrop points out, he "was a perfect model
of mankind . . . and in him this love was perfected in regard of the
habit"; but in rebellion, Adam "Rent in himself from his Creator,
rent all his posterity also[,] one from another." The first "model,"
which had defined man's relationship both to God and to his fellow man, had been torn asunder. Since then men had been ruled
by self-love. Until now, that is. Now, Winthrop assured the members of his audience, if they heeded his doctrine, Christ would
come and "[take] possession of [each] soul, and [infuse] another
principle[,] love to God and our brother. And this latter having
continual supply from Christ . . . so by little and little [will expel]
the former" (290). After this happened, the "scattered bones [of]
old man Adam" would be knit together in the perfect unity of
God's chosen society. That chosen society would epitomize the second, and last, model man would ever need: the model of Christian
charity.

Here again, I would argue, Winthrop displays an ambivalence
between his conservative belief in the traditionally ordered distinc-
tions within society and his radical reconception of society: the
"reasons" that he marshals in support of his doctrine combine
traditional Renaissance beliefs and breathtakingly bold assertions
that this community will be unlike any other the world has ever
seen. In this sense, he seems intent on restoring the Old World's

restoration/ creation of something new — page 18

misshapen forms—of man and of society—to their original linea-
ments in the New. It is appropriate, given this goal, that Winthrop
speaks self-consciously as a prophet. I posed the question earlier,
How does the habit of love come about? The "Principal Agent"
is, of course, God or Christ. But the Puritan's God always worked
through material means, through secondary causes that were visible to men and that could be understood rationally by them. Conversion, for example, was always effected through the agency of
the word—sermons, prayer, meditation on biblical passages. In
Winthrop's conception of a converted society, the agency of the
spoken word initiates the habit of love. His words, spoken as prophecy, promise to initiate the new social order. *power of discourse*

Winthrop indicates the prophetic nature of his sermon through
his repeated use of the image of the "scattered bones" that will be
"knit" together again in the future; and through his even more
direct reference to the prophet Ezekiel: "love," Winthrop says at
one point, "works like the Spirit upon the dry bones Ezek[iel]
37.[7] bone came to bone, it gathers together the scattered bones
. . . [and] knits them into one body again in Christ" (290). Or, as
Ezekiel himself wrote, after prophesying, at God's command, upon
a valley of dry bones, "behold . . . the bones came together, bone
to his bone" (Ezekiel 37.7). Without a doubt, Winthrop was aware
of the context from which he drew that quotation. In the Book of
Ezekiel the bones represent the scattered remnants of Israel, and
there is no breath in them after Ezekiel first prophesies upon
them, so God commands him to do so again. The prophet does:

> and the breath came into them, and they lived, and stood up upon
> their feet, an exceeding great army. Then [God] said unto me, Son
> of man, these bones are the whole house of Israel: behold, they say,
> Our bones are dried, and our hope is lost: we are cut off for our
> parts. Therefore prophesy and say unto them, Thus saith the Lord
> God; Behold, O my people, I will open your graves, and cause you
> to come up out of your graves, and bring you into the land of Israel.
> And ye shall know that I am the Lord . . . and I shall place you in
> your own land: then shall ye know that I the Lord have spoken it,
> and performed it. (Ezekiel 37.10–14)

Winthrop has cast himself in the role of prophet in this sermon:
an Ezekiel, he must breathe life into the scattered bones of England that stand before him on the deck of the *Arbella;* he must
voice the words through which the community can redefine and

reshape itself. Then God will place the people in their own land, and then Christ will come in and perfect them. Adam rent the old model, and caused his descendants to become dead to the spirit; Winthrop delivers the new model, revivifying the men and women standing before him. The process will begin in prophecy, and end in timeless perfection.

In this sense, the ambivalence of the "reasons" section of "A Model of Christian Charity" also derives from the fact that Winthrop's words, like all prophecies, operate on two different levels: both human and divine (with reference, that is, to the whole of history as it exists in God's mind). Many scholars of New England's literature have discussed only the divine aspect of Winthrop's sermon, his vision of a New Jerusalem; they have neglected Miller's emphasis on the practical, pragmatic nature of what Winthrop says.[15] Winthrop was a civil leader, remember, who had in England seen signs of man's unwillingness to subject himself to authority. Having been elected governor of this community in 1629 (before he gave this sermon), he was aware that in this new land he would stand at or near the top of a hierarchical structure of authority. Accordingly, the "Model" that he enunciates sets out not only to justify such a hierarchy, but also to inculcate in each and every one of his auditors due "subjection" to authority and charitable behavior to all men. Winthrop wants his audience not merely to submit to his plan, but to embrace it.

His first step in achieving this end was, earlier in the sermon, to blur the distinction between individual salvation and communal success. In doing so, he shifted a heavy burden onto both the regenerate and the unregenerate individuals in his community, for he implied that the outward success of the community could only come about if enough members of the community (who knows how many?) conformed to the "Model." The second step, later in the sermon, is to insist that this community can indeed be perfected, in time, and if men do not try to subvert the basic assumptions—the hierarchy—upon which the society is to be founded. Social perfection, dependent on the charity of society's members, is delayed until some undefined point in the future. Always anticipating the new Canaan, but never quite achieving it: such a conception is an ideal means by which to maintain social order, as we shall see, as long as society's members do not begin to question either what perfection actually is or the assumptions through which that perfection was to be achieved.

In these terms, then, the sermon is both an idealistic, even sacred vision of society and a practical, far-sighted mechanism of social control. Indeed, this practical approach can be seen more clearly in the third section, the application of Winthrop's sermon. God, he says, has given us

> a special Commission. . . . [We] are entered into Covenant with him for this work, we have taken out a Commission, the Lord hath given us leave to draw our own Articles[:] we have professed to enterprise these Actions upon these and these ends. . . . Now if the Lord shall please to hear us, and bring us in peace to the place we desire, then hath he ratified this Covenant and sealed our Commission, [and] will expect a strict performance of the Articles contained in it.

But, he adds carefully, "if we shall neglect the observation of these articles," then "the Lord will surely break out in wrath against us . . . and make us know the price of the breach of such a Covenant" (294). This statement, in which we see Winthrop adopt the familiar language of the covenant, is built upon two conditions, both advantageous to Winthrop. (1) If God brings them to this new land, then He will have ratified the covenant, the terms of which Winthrop himself has laid out in this sermon. Winthrop cannot lose: if the *Arbella* and her fleet do not arrive in the New World—if, perhaps, they are forced to turn back—the point is moot, since nowhere else in the Old World will these emigrants have the freedom to build the sort of society he envisions; even a hospitable Old World location like Holland had circumscribed the dreams of idealistic reformers. If, on the other hand, the fleet does arrive safely, the terms set forth here will implicitly be in effect. (2) If the members of society fail to cohere in an effective way, the enterprise will indeed fail, not because the Lord commands it, necessarily, but because a plantation in the wilderness needs social cohesion in order to succeed. These settlers knew well enough what kinds of problems the Virginia Company had experienced. With one eye on heaven, Winthrop clearly had the other on the community he had been elected to govern.

What Winthrop projects in "A Model of Christian Charity" is the final revolution of mankind. Etymologically, the word *revolution* means both a turning back (from the Latin *revolvo*, "to roll [a thing] back to where it came from") and a turning forward or over (as in the revolution of a wheel or, in modern usage, the overthrow of a government).[16] Both meanings are applicable here. Winthrop's conservative, aristocratic social theory dictates a return to the ordered notion of the cosmos that Elizabethan culture valued, and yet his vision of individual and social perfection anticipates a society unlike any other that man, with or without God's help, had ever managed to create.

Reading the "Model" in this way reveals an important aspect of Puritan thought and rhetoric, one that manifests itself even more clearly in the next several decades of New England's history: success is measured by the ability to keep competing claims in a tenuous but precise balance.[17] In the "Model" itself those claims involve not only these two revolutions but also, for example, Winthrop's claim that men are fundamentally similar (under the law of nature) and dissimilar (under the law of grace). Within New England culture, more generally, the balance involves such competing claims as spirit and mind, democracy and tyranny, enthusiasm and episcopacy. The Puritans walked, as they were proud to point out once they had appropriated the image, a "middle way" between the various dangers to each side.[18] The trope of "balance" was an important aspect of the way they conceived of themselves.

Although he does not specifically appropriate the image of the middle way, Winthrop articulates a similar idea in his sermon, not only in his conception of success as a delicate balance but also in his understanding that success is a process, a way, a model, that is, finally, a method of living within history: "we *shall be* as a City upon a Hill," he says (emphasis added). Even here, ironically, dichotomous views are set in balance: Winthrop is practical enough to realize that man is not going to change his nature immediately upon landing in America, and so perfection must be the result of historical process; at the same time he is idealistic enough to believe that his company will break the discouraging cycle of human history, institute the new Israel there in America, and escape into the end-time purity predicted by the Gospel. Will this community be within history, or will it be outside history? This is not clear, neither here nor in several of the histories of New England written in the first decades of settlement. But the ambivalence does explain why Winthrop chooses, at the end of his sermon, to quote Moses' departing words to the Israelites (Deuteronomy 30.15–20). Even though he has to avoid much that Moses says—that the Word, for example, is not "beyond the sea" (Deuteronomy 30.13), which is exactly where Winthrop's group was going to look for it—what he wants his audience to see, prophet that he is, is that the new Israel is within sight, though not yet within grasp.

In his sweeping assertions and in his self-conscious posing as a prophet in the tradition of Moses and David and Ezekiel, Winthrop employed a mode of prophesying in the "Model" that is different from the still (in 1630) rather ordinary Puritan "art of prophesying" by lay members of the congregation.[19] One effect of reading his sermon—and perhaps of hearing it on the *Arbella*—is to remember most vividly his insistence that the group of settlers gathered before him is "special," "more than ordinary," "extraordinary" (292–94). Renaissance historians had considered England to be special, but they had a protonational story and (especially in Foxe's *Book of Martyrs*) hagiography through which to establish their point.[20] Winthrop did not. They had history; Winthrop did not. He and his companions had only their faith—and the words spoken as they set out on their mission.[21] They had the terms by which Winthrop defends the hierarchy, terms that some colonists in the coming years would seem or try or hope to forget, until, that is, Winthrop or another leader, secular or religious, reviewed those terms in order to remind the people what their forebears had, if only implicitly, approved.

As a prophet, Winthrop conceived of a society that would stand as a beacon for future plantations in America, as the culmination of the Reformation, as the model for the kingdom Christ had promised to institute here on earth. It is a conception that would prove to be an integral part of the rhetoric of New England until events demonstrated, in the 1640s, that the Protestant world could be not only antagonistic to it but, worse, indifferent to it. The need then arose, for the first of several times in the course of the century, to reconceive the history (and the future) of the colony.

But I will return to this point in time. I begin with a brief reading of Winthrop's "A Model of Christian Charity" because the themes, images, and strategy I have located in his sermon recur in historical narratives written later in the century. One strand, at least, of New England's literary history begins with Winthrop's sermon.[22] Prophetlike, he spoke at the founding of what he believed could be a perfect society, and he initiated a tradition in which others asked the same of this relatively isolated and certainly (in 1630) insignificant community clinging to the coast of North America.

He also calls attention to the link between prophecy and history in the Puritan literary imagination. "*Prophesie* is History *antedated,*" the Puritans held, "and History is *Postdated Prophesie*: the same thing is told in both" (Noyes 43). "Reader," Cotton Mather wrote near the end of *Magnalia Christi Americana,* "I call'd these things *Prophecy*; but I wish I be not all this while Writing *History*" (VII: 104). Seventeenth-century histories are always poised, as is the "Model," at the juncture of past and future; after all, history had already in a sense "occurred" in God's mind. Man was simply living and narrating, producing and reproducing, His preconceived plan. Because of this, and because someone somewhere always had to be taught that very lesson in and through a narrative, the histories written by Puritan providential historians are polemical in a way that modern historiography often claims to decry. And it is precisely their polemic that we must analyze to appreciate their worth as literary texts.

THE PROBLEM OF GENRE

I have already mentioned several reasons why critics have been reluctant to read Winthrop's *History of New England* as a literary work. Another reason is that James Kendall Hosmer, the most recent editor of the work (1908), referred to it on the title page of his edition, and elsewhere, as *Winthrop's Journal "History of New England," 1630–1649.* To the reader unfamiliar with the manuscript of the *History* or unfamiliar with the only other complete editions of the work ever published, James Savage's *The History of New England from 1630 to 1649* (1825–1826; 1856), Hosmer's title places the idea of "journal" in the forefront and relegates "history" to a helpful, though perhaps spurious, afterthought. Hosmer, in his introduction, does not say why he chose to refer to Winthrop's work as the *Journal;* he does say that Winthrop's inscription of the "Continuation of the History of New England" at the headings of the second and third notebooks in which he scrawled the history-journal is "a misnomer certainly, for of New England outside of Massachusetts Bay [the *History*] is a most imperfect account" (16). This fact, in conjunction with the dated entries of Winthrop's work, probably led Hosmer to adopt the title of *Journal,* while respect for his predecessor's editions led him to use the more formal designation of *History* as a subtitle.[23]

Winthrop no doubt began the work as a journal—something many seventeenth-century Puritans did, from Thomas Shepard to

Samuel Sewall, in an attempt to ascertain the work and effect of the Spirit in their lives. And as many commentators have noticed, the *History* hews most closely to the journal format during the early entries, recording the progress of the *Arbella* and her fleet across the Atlantic, a number of interesting and (to Winthrop) revealing anecdotes about the developing community, and even occasional personal anecdotes, ranging from Winthrop's calm statement "My son Henry Winthrop was drowned at Salem" to his account of losing his way after dark and spending one night at "a little house of Sagamore John, which stood empty."[24]

Very early in the *History*, however, Winthrop begins to push his work beyond the narrow boundaries of a Puritan journal. He is, for example, seldom concerned with the meaning of his own actions, or with understanding the work of the Spirit in his own life; and the very few personal incidents he does mention are terrifically deemphasized. He records his son's death, for example, not with the coldness of a detached parent, but with the objectivity of an emerging historian. A more obvious example is that he seems to have decided very early in the composition of the work that he would not refer to himself in the first person. In moments of extreme sorrow or anger, he slips—referring to "my" son, for example—but he always recovers his impersonal tone. He makes a conscious choice, I think it is fair to say, that this will not be an autobiographical work.

Other evidence supports this view. As Hosmer pointed out, Winthrop inscribed the second and third notebooks in such a way as to show that, at least as early as 1636, he considered the work to be a history; or, more probably, that he considered the work to be what Francis Bacon would have referred to as the "first or rough draughts of history." The notebooks would serve as the subject matter from which Winthrop would later compose a more formal, unified history. "Memorials, or Preparatory History," Bacon wrote several years before Winthrop began to keep a journal, "set down a continuance of the naked events and actions, without the motives and designs, the counsels, the speeches, the pretexts, the occasions, and other passages of action" (188–89). Winthrop even used marginalia and brief notes to direct the reader to other relevant sections of the *History*, Alan Howard notes, "in what appear to be the first hasty attempts to establish lines of causal or topical relation between individual incidents" ("The Web in the Loom" 341). In addition, Winthrop was certainly aware of his audience in

a way that diarists or journalists are not. He often provides support-
ing documents for his arguments, intending for them to overcome
the reader's skepticism or to locate motivation for questionable
decisions made by Winthrop in his role as governor or by the General Court, motivations that help the reader understand why a particular decision had been made.[25] In the later stages of the *History*
Winthrop even begins to address the reader directly: "And I must
apologize this to the reader" (II: 209).

Finally, the argument for treating Winthrop's work as a history
instead of as a journal is buttressed by Winthrop's heightened concern, as the *History* develops, about the appropriateness or value of
certain events. In the early years he hesitates only a little to report
personal incidents that seem hardly to bear on the larger drama at
hand: "Upon this occasion it is not impertinent (though no credit
or regard to be had of dreams in these days) to report a dream,
which the father of [certain] children had at [this] time" (I: 127).
Maintaining the third-person viewpoint, Winthrop proceeds to interpret what is apparently his own dream as an affirmation that his
children would be made "fellow heirs with Christ in his kingdom"
(I: 127). By 1641 this lack of compunction has been transformed
into a more self-conscious pose. Narrating the account of then-
governor Richard Bellingham's sudden marriage to a woman
"ready to be contracted to a friend of his [that is, Bellingham's]"—an indiscretion that, given the emphasis on social order,
neither New England society nor Winthrop himself took lightly—
Winthrop prefaces his account with these words: "Query, whether
the following be fit to be published. The governor, Mr. Bellingham, was married, (I would not mention such ordinary matters in
our history, but by occasion of some remarkable accidents)" (II:
43). Implicit in this statement is not only Winthrop's growing
awareness of his work as history, but his awareness of the boundaries of that genre. Here history is the province not of the "ordinary," but of the "remarkable," of matters more significant than
everyday incidents. All events, including "acts and incidents of a
meaner nature," are indiscriminatingly entered in a journal,
Bacon wrote in 1605; but only "matters of estate, . . . only matters
of note and greatness," are included in histories (196). Winthrop
has gone far beyond the bounds of a diary or journal by selectively
choosing and arranging events relevant to his sense of the narrative as a public document.

The dated entries in the *History* continue to the end, even though, as Richard Dunn has shown, those entries become progressively longer and more carefully integrated ("John Winthrop"). Early on, Winthrop's technique is to record often but in little detail; as the years pass he writes less often, but in more complex entries that cover longer periods of time, his narrative technique thus mirroring New England's growth in size and complexity, and reflecting Winthrop's own heightened concern with the meaning of New England's history. The *History* never achieves what Bacon called "Perfect History," but neither is it merely a journal. It becomes, as Winthrop composes it, an incomplete but public "History of the Times."[26]

WINTHROP'S METHOD

All histories manifest at least part of their argument in the historian's method, in the chosen "arrangement of selected events . . . into a story" (White, *Metahistory* 7). In the *History,* Winthrop's method is to locate and define a middle way between various extremes. Throughout the narrative, he emphasizes man's reason, his capacity to understand God's intentions for him and to direct his energies toward the fulfillment of His heavenly design. Accordingly, the narrative strives to record a reasonable balance between presbyterianism and enthusiasm in the church, and between arbitrary, tyrannical government and "mere democracy" (II: 118) in the state.[27] Winthrop's story is one of compromise, adaptation, and change.

Puritans held that two elements were necessary to maintain this middle way: Scripture and reason. Scripture is obvious: *sola scriptura* was a central principle of the Reformation. But the Puritans also recognized that Scripture failed to provide specific answers to certain problems, and (even worse) that there was potentially a danger in letting every person be his or her own exegete—the danger of misguided zeal. Reason checked that danger. Puritan theologians argued that when Adam fell, his (and hence all mankind's) ability to reason rightly was impaired; in this life human beings could see but "through a glass, darkly." They were not blind, however:

> tho' God be to be seen by an eye of Faith, yet he must be seen by an eye of Reason too: for tho' Faith sees things above Reason, yet it sees nothing but in a way of Reason, which discerns all things by

> Arguments, which are conceived as distinct from the thing, and
> among themselves. (qtd. in Miller, *The New England Mind: The Seven-*
> *teenth Century* 171)

Faith and right reason complemented each other; the godly man
or woman would, perforce, be a reasonable man or woman. Only
by employing both faith and reason judiciously could he or she
discern the truth.

Just as Puritan theology balanced faith and reason, so does Winthrop's *History* attempt to balance, or reconcile, a series of dichoto-
mies: public and private, society and self, order and disorder,
wealth and poverty, arbitrary power and democratic ideas. Winthrop's emphasis as he narrates the history of the region is on the
various means of reconciliation brought into play in determining
events, petitions, laws, and social behavior, means that include dialogue, argumentation, mediation, and compromise. When, for example, Thomas Hooker and his congregation at Newtown first attempt to remove to Connecticut, they approach the General Court
in 1634 with their "principal reasons for their removal" (I: 140).
The court responds with arguments to the contrary and then votes
on their petition to remove. In what had already by 1634 become
a recurring pattern, most of the deputies support it, while most of
the magistrates (including Winthrop) do not: "Upon this grew a
great difference between the governour and assistants, and the
deputies" (I: 141). Neither will yield, so they agree "to keep a day
of humiliation to seek the Lord" (I: 141), after which John Cotton
preaches on the respective roles of the magistracy, the ministry,
and the people:

> And it pleased the Lord so to assist him, and to bless his own ordi-
> nance, that the affairs of the court went on cheerfully; and although
> all were not satisfied about the negative voice to be left to the magis-
> trates, yet no man moved aught about it, and the congregation of
> Newtown came and accepted of such enlargement as had formerly
> been offered them by Boston and Watertown; and so the fear of
> their removal to Connecticut was removed. (I: 142)

The issue is analyzed, discussed, argued, and lectured upon until
an agreement, however tenuous—the deputies (that is, the "people") and Hooker's congregation are silent—is reached. And
when, two years later, the move to Connecticut is permitted by
the General Court, Winthrop himself remains silent: "Mr. Hooker,

pastor of the church of Newtown, and the most of his congregation, went to Connecticut" (I: 187), he says simply. The other side
of the coin is that even Winthrop must keep silent once a decision
has been shown, through dialogue, mediation, and compromise,
to be in the best interests of the community. *"a gon'*

There is a sense, then, that whereas Bradford's *Of Plymouth Plantation* records the alternate ebbing and flowing of man's faith and
God's grace, Winthrop's *History* records the ebbing and flowing, *interesting*
the rising and falling, of voices. Issues are contended in written *(almost*
and spoken word until truth is realized—and then dissenting *Bakhtinian)*
voices must be silent. Men's judgments are necessary in rightly de-
ciding the boundaries of public issues, but if one's judgment then
falls outside those boundaries set by the dialogic process, one may
continue in it only in silence. The purpose of dialogue—and of
silence—is to keep New England on track: "so shall we keep the
unity of the spirit in the bond of peace," Winthrop had said in "A
Model of Christian Charity," and "the Lord will be our God and
delight to dwell among us" (294). Scripture understood by right
reason kept the fires of radicalism, separation, and antinomianism
from breaking out, just as, in other spheres, it prevented political
and mercantile oppression from gaining the upper hand. Only if
the delicate balance was maintained would New England become
a "City upon a Hill."

We can see a more extensive example of Winthrop's attempt to
balance extremes in his narration of the Antinomian Controversy.[28] He notes the first stirring of controversy in October 1636,
writing that:

> One Mrs. Hutchinson, a member of the church of Boston, a woman
> of a ready wit and bold spirit, brought over with her two dangerous
> errours: 1. That the person of the Holy Ghost dwells in a justified
> person. 2. That no sanctification can help to evidence to us our
> justification. (I: 200)

She had been vaguely encouraged in these opinions by John Cotton, famous pastor of the Boston church, and actively joined in
them by her brother-in-law John Wheelwright, a minister who had
been silenced in England and who had only recently emigrated to
New England. Winthrop's next entry reports that Wheelwright and
Cotton, at a conference of ministers assembled at this time, "gave
satisfaction to [the other ministers], so as [Wheelwright and Cot-
ton] agreed with them all in the point of sanctification . . . [;] they

all did hold, that sanctification did help to evidence justification" (I: 201). However, the third entry in this series provides a new twist on the incident, which at this time still seemed to Winthrop to be relatively minor, although he could already sense its dangerous implications. "Some of the church of Boston, being of the opinion of Mrs. Hutchinson, [labored] to have Mr. Wheelwright to be called to be a teacher there" (I: 202).

It is clear from the narrative that Winthrop had opposed Wheelwright's calling. The historian reports that Winthrop debated the issue with Henry Vane and John Cotton in front of the congregation. In the end, the church gives way, allowing Wheelwright to go to a new church at Braintree. The decision is described as a compromise: Winthrop publicly admits that he might "be content to live under such a ministry; yet, seeing [Wheelwright] was apt to raise doubtful disputations, he could not consent to choose him to that place" (I: 202) in his own church; Vane and some of the congregation must give way and lose the services of their ally Wheelwright, yet they see Wheelwright's opinions vindicated for a second time when he is allowed to assume a ministry within the colony (I: 202). Even now, however, this opening salvo is not quite finished. In arguing against calling Wheelwright, Winthrop had apparently offended "Divers of the brethren" of the church. He is forced to defend "his former speech" to the congregation, and he does so, arguing at the end that "these variances grew . . . from some words and phrases, which were of human invention, and tended to doubtful disputation, rather than to edification, and had no footing in scripture . . . [and asking] that, for the peace of the church, etc. they might be forborn" (I: 203). The church accepts this explanation, significantly, in silence: "no man spake to it" (I: 204).

In this preliminary to the greater "fire" that would soon break out, the historian represents many of the elements by which the Puritans whose story he is narrating tried to maintain social cohesion in the first decades of settlement: a close-knit social and religious order; dissension, arguments, defenses, and counterdefenses in an attempt to locate the truth; and silence. The narration of this prelude to the Antinomian Controversy emphasizes his society's temporarily successful struggle to locate a middle way. The troubles, however, were just beginning: in the next eighteen months the Hutchinsonians called into question each of the elements by which these colonists tried to maintain truth and social order.

Within days of Winthrop's admission of error, the historian notes, the social and religious order is disrupted by "differences and dissensions" (I: 207), "differences and alienations" (I: 209), and "other opinions [breaking] out publickly" (I: 211). Although the questions involved may seem unimportant to us, the historian artfully portrays the extent to which they held his society's imagination:

> A woman of Boston congregation, having been in much trouble of mind about her spiritual estate, at length grew into utter despera-tion, and could not endure to hear of any comfort, etc., so as one day she took her little infant and threw it into a well, and then came into the house and said, now she was sure she should be damned, for she had drowned her child. (I: 236)

This poor woman's confusion is representative of her society's. The historian acknowledges that "no man could tell (except some few, who knew the bottom of the matter) where any difference was" (I: 213) between the position advocated by Wheelwright and Vane, and the one advocated by pastor John Wilson and Winthrop himself. No wonder that the sermon Wheelwright delivers in Janu-ary 1636/37—on a fast day appointed by the Court "as a means of reconciliation of the differences" (I: 215)—only increases conten-tion and alienates more people: neither party, according to Win-throp's account, clearly sees what is at stake in this affair. The histo-rian claims to be one of the few able to see the difference: "the ground of all was found to be assurance by immediate revelation" (I: 211). In reality, Wheelwright, Vane, and Hutchinson probably saw the difference, too, and saw what was at stake. Wheelwright's fast-day sermon, for example, distinguished carefully between those who safely built their assurance on Christ "revealed" to them and those who built it ignorantly on the evidence of "works" (Wheelwright 164). But it is significant that the historian does not say they understand the difference. In his version of the contro-versy, the Antinomians do not see that their belief in immediate assurance undermines the social order enunciated in "A Model of Christian Charity." They do not understand the "words and phrases . . . of human invention" (I: 203) that are being disputed and thus do not understand the consequences of their own beliefs. For the belief that immediate revelation is the ground of one's assurance reduces the value of reason and scripture as tools for analyzing experience, and (theoretically, at least) refashions Winthrop's social order based on interdependence into a social polarity in which people either "are" or "are not" saved. Compromise would have no value in a society based on such "anti-nomian" principles, since truth would be unequivocally understood by all saints; no "Way" would be necessary, since Christ's indwelling presence in saints would be full and complete, not partial and progressive. To help his audience understand this very point, the historian cites John Cotton's characterization of the two parties: "one party seeking to advance the grace of God within us, and the other to advance the grace of God towards us" (I: 213). The grace within leads to social disruption and, eventually, to anarchy; the grace toward, as Winthrop declared in 1630 (indeed, the "Model" is based upon it), leads to a harmonious social order.

Dialogue, argumentation, and compromise proved successful only up to a certain point within Winthrop's account of the Antinomian Controversy. Today, most scholars understand that the differences between the two parties were, to use the Puritan's own term, "fundamental" (Stoever; Caldwell, "Antinomian Language"). No doubt, many people felt that way at the time. But the historian is reluctant to admit that the differences are, finally, irreconcilable. In the same entry that dramatically describes his victory and Vane's defeat in the 1637 court of elections, Winthrop says that the differences between the two parties had been brought so close that "(if men's affections had not been formerly alienated, when the differences were formerly stated as fundamental) they might easily have come to reconciliation" (I: 221). The Court, he notes in approval, even deferred Wheelwright's sentence because "having now power enough to have crushed them, [the Court's] moderation and desire of reconciliation might appear to all" (I: 222). Having consolidated power and reaffirmed the direction society would take, the orthodoxy realizes that to prosecute matters further will only aid Hutchinson's party and continue to disrupt society; if the Hutchinsonians will keep silent, they will be allowed to stay, without punishment. Here the members of the General Court, Winthrop among them, seem to have underestimated the sheer force of enthusiasm, just as the civil leaders of New England were to do again in 1658–1661, when four Quakers met physical punishment and finally death with open arms, witnessing their faith. "For though Mr. Wheelwright and those of his party had been clearly confuted and confounded in the [Synod of 1637],"

the historian remarks, "yet they persisted in their opinions, and were as busy nourishing contentions (the principal of them) as before" (I: 244–45). Thus, and perhaps in contradiction to later accounts, Winthrop insists in the *History* that the mistake of the so-called Antinomians lay not simply in persisting in their opinions, but in persisting in voicing those opinions, once they had been confuted both doctrinally (by the Synod) and politically (by the overwhelming support for Winthrop in the court of elections and, later, by the banishment of Hutchinson and Wheelwright). Scripture and reason had pointed out the correct path for New England, and the Hutchinsonians had not noticed. They "persisted" in giving voice to errors.

Winthrop's language in the two entries that detail Anne Hutchinson's excommunication from the Boston church pulls together these several threads of voice and silence, social order and dialogue, reason and Scripture. Brought before the church, she has her "errours . . . read to her." She maintains the first error, that man's soul is mortal until regeneration makes it immortal, "a long time; but at length she was so clearly convinced by reason and scripture . . . that she yielded she had been in an errour" (I: 254). The method is successful here; consensus is reached through a dialogue in which "errour" is subjected to reasonable and scriptural analysis. Then "they proceeded to three other errours. . . . These were also clearly confuted, but yet [Hutchinson] held her own; so as the church . . . agreed she should be admonished" (I: 254–55). Here, admonishment means that Mrs. Hutchinson would be called to the church again, at a later date, "in regard she had given hope of her repentance" (I: 257). Again, more errors are put to her, "wherein she made a retractation of near all, but with such explanations and circumstances as gave no satisfaction to the church; so as she was required to speak further to them" (I: 257). She does speak further to them, and the church has, again, "good hope of her repentance." But one more time, her answers rebound the other way: she argues against "some particulars" of her indictment, "as that she had denied inherent righteousness. . . . [And] though it was proved by many testimonies, that she had been of that judgment . . . yet she impudently persisted in her affirmation, to the astonishment of all the assembly." It is at this point—when she displays "manifest evil in matter of conversation," the historian says—that she is cast out of the church. Hutchinson's error here is the same as the one Winthrop's *Short Story of the Rise, reign, and ruine of the Antinomians, Familists, and Libertines that infected the Churches of New England* (1644) records her having made at her civil trial: having rejected the orthodoxy's version of truth, she will not keep silent when reason and Scripture—and the majority of ministers and magistrates—show her it is wise to do so. She voices her enthusiasm. In the *History,* the authorities' suspicions of enthusiasm are confirmed when Hutchinson "revived again" upon her sentencing, "saying, that [her banishment] was the greatest happiness, next to Christ, that ever befel her." That disgusts the historian; but he is consoled by the fact that the middle way has been reestablished, and "many poor souls, who had been seduced by [Hutchinson] . . . brought off quite from her errours, and settled again in the truth" (I: 258).

The historian's emphasis on dialogue, mediation, and compromise is quite clear in his treatment of Anne Hutchinson. He argues that the "breeder and nourisher of all these distempers" formed ideas that "either came without a word, or without the sense of the word . . . [and hence stood] above reason and scripture . . . not subject to controll" (Winthrop, *Short Story* 157–58). His rhetoric there and in his description of Hutchinson's "monstrous birth" (I: 271–73) indicates two ways in which he, in particular, tried rhetorically to comprehend Hutchinson: he transformed her into a representative of feminine disorder ("a breeder and nourisher of . . . distempers") whose body, as well as mind, brought forth "misshapen offspring" (Breitwieser 70–73); and he insisted that her ideas were consistently above or beyond or opposed to common social or linguistic comprehension as derived, for the Puritans, from reason and Scripture. She was *anti-nomos,* against the law or word. In the real world of Boston in 1637–1638, the other way of stripping her ideas of any semblance of authority was by excommunicating and banishing her.

Yet it is also important to note that John Wheelwright is the central figure in Winthrop's narration of the Antinomian Controversy in the *History.* Hutchinson comes to the fore in the narrative only after the issue has been decided.[29] Writing contemporaneously with the events themselves, the historian recognizes that it is Wheelwright who represents the greatest threat to the social order. He preached ideas similar to Hutchinson's and could, in effect, give them an authority seemingly derived from reason and Scripture. Wheelwright explained the Word, and thus could challenge, in the pulpit, the social order Winthrop envisioned in the

"Model." Wheelwright—more than Hutchinson, the historian intimates—should have realized that his ideas would set "divisions between husband and wife, and other relations there, till the weaker give place to the stronger," and "all things [be] turned upside down among us" (Winthrop, *Short Story* 177, 141–42). His ideas would, in other words, effect a degeneracy into unstructured social relations—mirroring England's previous degeneracy into social chaos, which Winthrop had remarked upon in 1629 (and fled in 1630).

Indeed, it is for this reason that Winthrop's two accounts of what we have come to know as the Antinomian Controversy—the *History* and the *Short Story*—represent two quite different historiographic efforts. His focus in the *History* is on Wheelwright; in the *Short Story* it is on Hutchinson: the difference in focus reflects different concerns. The *History* is an internal justification, an attempt to explain to those within New England (and perhaps to himself) why the Hutchinsonians had to be dealt with so harshly; the *Short Story* is a more external justification, an attempt to explain to outsiders why such beliefs, which by the early 1640s were becoming acceptable amid the ferment of the Civil War in England, had to be rooted out of New England. From within the covenant, the silencing of a minister of God had to be explained most carefully; from without, the banishment of a sincere, well-learned, and perhaps not-so-radical professor had most to be defended.

In actuality, Hutchinson went much further down the antinomian road than did Wheelwright, as he himself pointed out later in his *Mercurius Americanus* (1645): "she had many strange fancies, and erroneous tenents possest her. . . . [She was] guilty of most of [the] errors" of which she was accused (Wheelwright 197).[30] Both were banished, but Wheelwright refused to follow her to Rhode Island, where she "progressed in her radicalism to a position approximating that of the Seekers" (Gura, *Glimpse* 264). Wheelwright even achieved a reconciliation with the Bay colony in 1643, which Winthrop gladly records—another instance, he suggests, of reason triumphing over unreason, faith over heresy, within the New England Way. More specifically, Wheelwright repents of his adherence "to persons of corrupt judgment" during the controversy and of his use of "unsafe and obscure expressions" in his fast-day sermon: "If," he continues, "it shall appear to me, by scripture light, that in any carriage, word, writing or action, I have walked contrary to rule, I shall be ready, by the grace of God, to give satisfaction" (II: 162–63). Without admitting his error, Winthrop points out, but only by placing himself under the "rule" of language (including behavior) understood by the twin guides of reason and Scripture is Wheelwright freed from his banishment.

The differences between Hutchinson and Wheelwright as each is presented in the *History* help explain the different reason for which each was banished: Hutchinson for more passively conceiving many "errors" (itemized by the Synod's ministers), Wheelwright for more actively delivering a seditious sermon. Winthrop does not really pursue those differences, however. In the end, he is more interested in the danger presented to the community by both figures. Hutchinson, he reports, was "at last . . . so full as she could not contain, but vented her revelations; amongst which this was one, that she had it revealed to her, that she should come into New England, and should here be persecuted, and that God would ruin us and our posterity, and the whole state, for the same" (I: 246–47). She had usurped the role of prophet, which was reserved, in Winthrop's mind, for the socially superior and theologically learned. Similarly, he describes Wheelwright as an incendiary— "he purposely set himself to kindle and increase [disagreements]"—whose ideas were "manifest and dangerous to the state" (I: 214–15). In a sense, he uses Hutchinson and Wheelwright to define the limits of dissension within the New England Way, the boundaries within which mediation can succeed and without which all other unreasonable people must reside: "those . . . [who] were so divided from the rest of the country in their judgment and practice, as it could not stand with the publick peace, that they should continue amongst us . . . must be sent away" (I: 250). Upon the banishment of Hutchinson and Wheelwright, the historian tells us, the "bones" of New England, which Winthrop himself had first breathed upon in 1630, were more firmly set in place.

THE PROBLEM WITH SUCCESS

In many ways, New England flourished in the 1630s. The population grew steadily toward twenty thousand; towns were founded; the economy prospered from the constant infusion of money from new immigrants; Puritans famous in England, like Thomas Shepard, Thomas Hooker, and John Cotton, fled Laud's persecution to settle in Massachusetts. Yet Winthrop's focus in the *History* is often on threats to New England's internal order, threats that range from a "great disorder general through the country in costliness of apparel" (I: 275) to the more disturbing economic inflation that began as early as 1636 and peaked in the depression of 1640–1641, when the Great Migration came to a halt and Winthrop could comment that "now all our money was drained from us" (II: 7). In the course of the narrative, however, the historian discovers that something seemingly as simple as ostentation represents a different problem from Hutchinson's dissent. It raised a new question: What could be done when people simply rejected the social order enunciated in "A Model of Christian Charity," not from religious motives (however misguided), but because it did not fit their own selfish aims? In trying to ease the disorder caused by costly apparel, for example, the court

> sent for the elders of the churches, and conferred with them about it, and laid it upon them, as belonging to them, to redress it, by urging it upon the consciences of their people, which they promised to do. But little was done about it; for divers of the elders' wives, etc., were in some measure partners in this general disorder. (I: 275)

The pun in the choice of the word *redress* may not have been intentional, but the admission probably was: since the ministers have implicitly acquiesced in this small breach of social order, it must be tolerated. Inflation produces the same result:

> One Taylor of Linne, having a milch cow in the ship as he came over, sold the milk to the passengers for 2d the quart, and being after at a sermon wherein oppression was complained of, etc., he fell distracted. . . . This evil ["oppression"] was very notorious among all sorts of people, it being the common rule that most men walked by in all their commerce, to buy as cheap as they could, and to sell as dear. (II: 21–22)

We do not find this idea of buying low and selling high repugnant, but many Puritans did, at least when the profit ratio exceeded certain accepted limits.[31] Theoretically, saints like this "Taylor of Linne" would be affected by the argument laid out in the "Model," and elsewhere, that charity is even more necessary in a "community of perils" (Winthrop, "Model" 284) than it is in a flourishing community. (This is certainly one reason why Winthrop and other leaders during the course of the century continued to claim that New England was degenerating.) But those less affected by the Word or by Winthrop's vision—or those who, perhaps, were simply impoverished—apparently needed to be coerced into selflessness. The historian notes that to avoid the newly imposed laws concerning wages and prices, people simply moved to other towns or "to the south parts" (that is, Virginia), where they could set their wages or the prices of their wares as high as they wished (II: 21–25). "These things," he claims, are a means "whereby God taught us the vanity of all outward things" (II: 21). But not everyone who remained in New England learned that lesson.

After 1640 the historian begins to note a new spirit manifesting itself in the colony. Using a tone and a rhetoric that creep more and more often into the *History,* he can say in 1643: "And indeed it was a very sad thing to see how little of a public spirit appeared in the country, but of self-love too much. Yet there were [still] some here and there, who were men of another spirit, and were willing to abridge themselves, that others might be supplied" (II: 94). Willingness to "abridge" oneself is, of course, at the heart of "A Model of Christian Charity." But, in a comment that serves as an apt metaphor for the way he feels about certain segments of society, he says of a group of "profane" men and women who bewailed their sins to the "magistrates and elders": "Most of them fell back again in time, embracing this present world" (II: 93). The latter half of the *History* is dominated by a spirit of contention, which (the historian tells us) grows out of the love some men and women have for "this present world." Having managed to suppress theological dissent, New England in Winthrop's *History* finds that man's (often) unspoken desires for the present world were much harder to control. The historian certainly found them impossible to understand. The middle way was once again in danger of tipping out of balance.

Winthrop's account of the Hingham affair in 1645 exemplifies the problem. Winthrop, deputy-governor at the time, was charged by the deputies with exceeding his authority when he intervened in a militia election in the town of Hingham. As the historian points out, the petition that charged the deputy-governor with criminally infringing the liberty of the people was the product of a long battle waged by the deputies to gain a greater share of power (II: 230–32). By this point in time, they had made various attempts, several successful, to wrest a greater degree of political power from the magistrates.[32] Throughout those struggles, Winthrop had been the most visible spokesman for the orthodox point of view. He had not hidden his desire to keep power in the hands of those whom he felt were qualified to lead, the nobility of the New World. Perhaps as a result, when the Hingham affair began, the general discontent of some factions of New England society— the historian records one man's haughty question, "what [had] the magistrates . . . to do with [the freemen]?" (II: 221)—was almost immediately focused on Winthrop. Throughout the narration of the events that follow upon the deputies' petition singling Winthrop out for criminal action, the historian emphasizes the same techniques that were at work in the Antinomian Controversy: dialogue, argumentation, mediation, compromise, silence. He describes the petition in familiar terms:

> Two of the magistrates and many of the deputies were of opinion that the magistrates exercised too much power, and that the people's liberty was thereby in danger; and other of the deputies (being about half) and all the rest of the magistrates were of a different judgment, and that authority was overmuch slighted, which, if not timely remedied, would endanger the commonwealth, and bring us to a mere democracy. (II: 226)

Once again, the colony is split in two, and the state is in danger of being subverted. As the historian reconstructs this situation, both the "people" and the authorities fear that New England has slipped to one side of the middle way between "mere democracy" and tyranny.

From the start of his account, the historian artfully portrays Winthrop's confidence in his rectitude as magistrate: the deputy-governor insists on "a public hearing"; he sits "beneath within the bar . . . uncovered" (II:224), like a common defendant; and he forcefully, even dramatically, refutes the grievances filed against him. Yet it is one measure of the direction of events the historian chooses to represent that Winthrop was forced to what was an essentially defensive position. The Antinomian Controversy, at least as the *History* represents it, revealed the opposite: Winthrop as governor, on the offensive, searching out error and cutting it, like a cancer, away from the still-healthy body politic. Not so here. "There was not so orderly carriage at the hearing, as was meet," Winthrop says, "each side striving unseasonably to enforce the evidence, and declaring their judgments thereupon" (II: 226). Indeed, he notes that it took nearly two days for a committee even to be able to state the case to the satisfaction of both parties.

Then "the magistrates and deputies considered [the committee's statement] apart." The deputies, unresolved, send the statement to the magistrates; the magistrates draw out four points, the
two most important being the censure of all who brought the original petition against Winthrop and the full acquittal of Winthrop.
The deputies cannot agree to the censuring of the petitioners, and
send the points back to the magistrates; the magistrates ask for the
elders to be called in as mediators; the deputies refuse, fearful that
the elders will side with the magistrates; and finally, the cause is
referred "to arbitrators, according to an order of the court, when
the magistrates and deputies cannot agree" (II: 227). These actions show that the magistrates were in control throughout; the
deputies were unresolved, unable to agree, and fearful that they
had bitten off more than they could chew in endorsing criminal
accusations against Winthrop. In the dialogue, they must continually give ground; at last they agree to all four of the magistrates'
original points, remaining adamant on only one new point, to
which the magistrates agree: "a promise of silence from the magistrates" at the time the agreement is read in court (II: 228). Chastened for overextending themselves, the deputies fear—or so the
historian draws the picture for us—exactly what in the end hap-
pens: they are rebuked for calling into question the authority of
the magistrates. The rebuke is delivered not by the magistrates,
who promised to keep silent, but by the deputy-governor himself,
the former defendant becoming a righteous and indignant father-
figure to the "troublesome" deputies. Winthrop "desired leave for
a little speech," which the historian then duly records, using it
overtly to link "liberty" with a social order in which the good intentions of magistrates are not questioned by the people (II: 228).
One of the arguments of the "Model" was reasserted with a ven-
geance.

However, if the deputies' willingness to attack Winthrop is read
as a measure of their willingness to call into question Winthrop's
social vision, so can Winthrop's famous lecture on natural and civil
liberty be read as a measure of the lack of progress, in his own
terms and by his own standards, that he perceived in New England
society in the fifteen years since the shipboard sermon. For the
"little speech" is similar in strategy and design to "A Model of
Christian Charity." Certainly, Winthrop's ideas have been refined;
like Peter Bulkeley, John Cotton, and other members of the orthodoxy, he has refined the notion of covenant:

There is a twofold liberty, natural (I mean as our nature is now corrupt) and civil or federal. The first is common to man with beasts and other creatures. By this, man, as he stands in relation to man simply, hath liberty to do what he lists; it is a liberty to evil as well as to good. This liberty is incompatible and inconsistent with authority, and cannot endure the least restraint of the most just authority. . . . The other kind of liberty I call civil or federal . . . in reference to the covenant between God and man . . . and the politic covenants and constitutions, amongst men themselves. This liberty is the proper end and object of authority, and cannot subsist without it. (II: 229)

Within Winthrop's two most famous statements on social order, the natural law of the little speech is essentially the same as the law of nature of the "Model," the civil law of the little speech as the law of grace. But the "Model" emphasizes that when men and women submit themselves to Christ they will then love their fellow members in Christ habitually; the "City upon a Hill" is bound to follow hard upon such individual and social conversion. The little speech, however, is focused more narrowly on the practicalities of this world, on nature instead of supernature. Civil, or federal, liberty "is maintained and exercised in a way of subjection to [civil] authority; it is of the same kind of liberty wherewith Christ hath made us free" (II: 229). The emphasis here is on a lower link in the great chain of being. As represented in the *History*, the deputy-governor understands that the idealistic rhetoric of the "Model" would strike too far from the root of the matter in his chastisement of the deputies.

To the historian, this entire affair represented "the workings of satan to ruin the colonies and churches of Christ in New England." Some people "seriously conceived" that the magistrates "affected an arbitrary government," and that conception "caused them to [mis]interpret all the magistrates' actions and speeches" (II: 230). Here, as in the Antinomian Controversy, misinterpretation of basic principles threatens the state. But the account of the Hingham affair differs from the account of the Antinomian Controversy in two important ways. First (as the historian notes with disgust when he "observes" the incident at its conclusion), the contention arises out of a fundamentally political disagreement about liberty and authority. He presents the opposing faction as consciously challenging his civil authority and through that his social vision; the Hutchinsonians, as the historian presented them, had primarily

challenged the religious order and only secondarily, through that
first challenge as it were, challenged his social vision. They had not
understood the issues involved; the deputies do. Second, although
the incident served as a personal vindication of John Winthrop ("I
am well satisfied," he reports himself as having said, "I was publicly charged, and I am publickly and legally acquitted" [II: 228]),
the historian now understands that the spirit of "open contempt
of authority" evidenced in the affair cannot be legislated out of
existence. In Winthrop's little speech, at least as it is recorded in
the *History,* there is an open admission that, so far, the Model had
not succeeded: this "little speech," he says, "may be of some good
use, to inform and rectify the judgements of some of the people,
and may prevent such distempers as have arisen among us" (II:
228). In Winthrop's eyes, if one's judgment can be rightly informed, then one's interpretation will be correct and the truth—of
God's word or, in this case, of the "Model"—will become clear.
The petitioners in the Hingham affair, as the historian presents
them, are motivated by the same disease as were those people who
insisted on wearing costly apparel: the distemper of self-love.

Seen in this light, the Hingham affair is a watershed in Winthrop's *History.* Winthrop and the magistrates succeeded in what
they set out to do: they humbled those who were contemptuous of
authority. At the same time, however, the amount of opposition at
a fairly high level ("Two of the magistrates and many of the deputies were of the opinion that the magistrates exercised too much
power" [II: 226]) prevented the magistrates from doing anything
but fining those involved and firmly lecturing the deputies. The
little speech itself is an admission that, so far, the "Model" had not
brought into being a charitable populace.

The historian's account of those events emphasizes the rectitude of the magistrates' position and castigates those who disagree
with it. But one senses that Winthrop's relatively long and detailed
defense of the deputy-governor and his investigation of the meaning of the incident (II: 230–33) are meant to dispel not only the
deputies' misinterpretation but also the reader's uncertainty. The
people, the historian notes sadly, "eagerly laid hold on [the Hingham case], and pursued [it] to the utmost" (II: 232). They followed their corrupt instinct—their natural liberty—here as much
as they followed it when they wore costly apparel. The colony was
not progressing. Love had not become habitual. The bones of New
England were rattling.

THE "SCATTERED BONES" OF NEW ENGLAND

Both John Wheelwright and the petitioners in the Hingham affair were charged with sedition. The word is instructive, for by going apart from the social vision that Winthrop enunciated and that many leaders of New England accepted as the norm, these dissenters challenged and thus helped to shape New England's definition of itself (see "sedition," *OED*). The *History*, in other words, reveals a certain flexibility in the orthodoxy's views, a relatively moderate version of the Separatists' insistence that "the Lord hath *more Truth* yet to break forth out of his Holy Word" than He has yet revealed (qtd. in Cotton Mather, *Magnalia* I: 14). Dissent gradually altered John Winthrop's conception and narration of New England's history. The same effects hold true for another series of incidents involving two men, Samuel Gorton and Robert Child, who challenged the authority of the civil and ecclesiastical order of New England in the 1640s.

Gorton's introduction in the *History* is an inauspicious one: "Those of Providence, being all anabaptists, were divided in judgment; some were only against baptizing of infants; others denied all magistracy and churches, etc., of which Gorton, who had lately been whipped at Aquiday . . . was their instructer and captain" (II: 57, 59). At this time, in 1641, Providence was not under the jurisdiction of Massachusetts Bay; accordingly, when "the weaker party"—the faction there that opposed Gorton—complain to the General Court, invoking its aid, they are told, "that except they did submit themselves to some jurisdiction, either Plimouth or [Massachusetts Bay, the General Court] had no calling or warrant to interpose in their contentions" (II: 59). The next year "four of Providence, who could not consort with Gorton and that company, and therefore were continually injured and molested by them, came and offered themselves and their lands, etc., [to the Bay colony], and were accepted under [its] government and protection" (II: 84). As the historian notes in the same entry, motives other than kindness were in play here: "the place was likely to be of use to us [for military affairs], . . . and seeing it came without our seeking, and would be no charge to us, we thought it not wisdom to let it slip" (II: 84–85).[33] In fact, there would be a "charge," though not a financial one, as New England's leaders were soon to find out.

Gorton had been harassed in New England since his arrival.

Seeing what was up now, he moved farther away from the Bay, to Shawomet, where he apparently purchased land from the Indians. The very next year, the two Indian sachems from whom he had bought the land claimed that they had been coerced into selling; they, too, placed themselves under the jurisdiction of the Bay. Before the General Court could proceed in the matter, however, Gorton wrote to it, justifying his purchase of the land and declaring that he and his company would "maintain it to the death" (II: 121). The Court sent for them—"by letter only," the historian notes, and "not in way of command"—but Gorton's company refused to come, sending instead "two letters full of blasphemy against the churches and magistracy" (II: 137). Forty soldiers were dispatched to bring Gorton and his company to Boston. Cornered, the Gortonists asked for arbitration in the case; the Court rejected the proposition for, among other things, "Their blasphemous and reviling writings, etc., were not matters fit to be compounded by arbitrament, but to be purged away only by repentance and public satisfaction, or else by public punishment" (II: 140).

In his account of these events, the historian tries to keep his focus on the land dispute. Again and again, however, he shows that what really rankles him about the Gortonists is that "They were all illiterate men, the ablest of them could not write true English, no not common words, yet they would take upon them the interpretation of the most difficult places of scripture, and wrest them any way to serve their own turns" (II: 145). Here, as in the case of the Antinomians (who could not understand "some words and phrases . . . of human invention" [I: 203] that both parties were using) and in the case of John Wheelwright (who repents in 1643, the historian tells us, for his use of "unsafe and obscure expressions" [II: 162]), the problem turns on language: who is qualified to read and interpret the Word, and hence who is qualified to lead society? In the historian's eyes, Gorton and his men were clearly meant to be in places of "subjection" to authority; they had little or no access either to reason or Scripture, the twin guides of man. The land dispute left behind—since the Gortonists refused to provide witnesses in their own defense, the historian notes, "we need not question them any more about that" (II: 144)—Gorton's blasphemous letters were brought to the fore. Again, language is at the center of the controversy; the Gortonists cannot write well and hence cannot reason well; the Court and the elders spend "near a whole day" trying "to bring [Gorton and the others] to conviction, but . . . They would acknowledge no errour or fault in their writings" (II: 146); part of the initial sentence provides that the Gortonists remain silent, "only with exception for speech with any of the elders" (II: 147). The magistrates and deputies are sharply divided on what sentence to impose on the Gortonists. All of the magistrates except three wish to put Gorton to death; the deputies prevent that degree of "silencing," and the Court finally compromises, providing instead that the Gortonists be separated, put to work, and silenced "upon pain of death" (II: 147).

But the Gortonists were having nothing of silence, that necessary element of the New England Way. The Court learned, very quickly, that they "did corrupt some of our people, especially the women, by their heresies" (II: 148). Sentence being passed, and the deputies' resistance to harsher measures preventing further action, the Gortonists were set free and forbidden upon pain of death to enter Massachusetts territory again. Gorton sailed for England, where his radical religious and social views found a better hearing and where he brought suit against New England. And he won the case: the Commission for Plantations ruled, in 1646, that Gorton's lands in Narragansett Bay were not under the jurisdiction of Massachusetts Bay and that Gorton and his company should be permitted to pass through the Bay colony to reach those lands. The historian's comment on the Commission's decision—they ruled, he says, "generally out of their dislike of us for our late law for banishing anabaptists[; they] seemed to be much offended with us for our rigorous proceeding (as they called it) against [those Anabaptists]" (II: 272)—indicates his growing awareness of the political situation in England. Within that larger context, he realizes that there is little New England can do to correct the Gortonists' misinterpretations. He fulminates against their ignorance and goes into a long defense of New England's actions (II: 295–301), but the fact remains (and is faithfully recorded) that the corrupt opinions of Gorton were not silenced.

Robert Child's entrance into the *History*, in 1646, is less painful than Gorton's. Emboldened by Gorton's success and encouraged by William Vassal, "sometimes one of the assistants of the Massachusetts, but now of Scituate in Plimouth," Child and several others petitioned the government of Massachusetts to open church membership and civil freemanship in the colony to all "free born subjects of England," so that everyone, not just those who had been accepted into the church, "might be wholly governed by the

(Child)

laws of England" (II: 261). Here was a problem for the authorities that arose from the opposite end of the spectrum. Gorton was a radical spiritist, claiming that the dictates of any regenerate soul were above human or man-made laws or authority. His attack on New England came from the same direction as Anne Hutchinson's, and it reflected one type of attack upon established authority generated by the Reformation. Child, on the other hand, was conservative—a Presbyterian—and he argued that English law demanded that all morally upright English Protestants deserved full membership in New England church and society. His attack was actually a counterattack, reflective both of the Church of England's position that ecclesiastical authority be lodged in the king and bishops, not in local congregations, and (ironically) of the Puritans' own crackdown on Gorton. Gorton claimed that authority derived from the Holy Spirit as it was present to each individual believer; Child claimed that authority resided in the Church of England. Neither man believed it resided in Boston.

Winthrop records the events surrounding Child's petition in one of the longest entries in the *History*. The failure to quiet Gorton runs like a theme behind the events at hand, as if the historian can't quite get it out of his mind. Child's petition actually forces Winthrop and the magistrates to revalue New England's purpose. "Then it was propounded to consideration, in what relation we stood to the state of England; whether our government was founded upon our charter, or not; if so, then what subjection we owed to that state" (II: 279). The "Model" had not had to deal with this sort of question, except in the general sense that Winthrop had conceived of his company as separate from but still related to England, and that the company's avowed purpose in the New World was to provide England, and the rest of the Protestant world, with a model for the further reformation of mankind. Here, however, the authorities—including the historian—are forced to clarify their notion of the particular middle way between dependency and independency.

On the one hand, they argue, New England is self-sufficient, "and ergo should not need the help of any superior power" (II: 279); in a phrase that the historian will repeat several times late in the *History*, he says that New England possesses "a perfection of parts, so as we are thereby furnished with all parts of government" (II: 279). In practice and in theory, New England had early begun to distinguish itself from the mother country. Only here, though, is a separation enunciated. The path to Edward Johnson's exuberant revision of New England's purpose and history runs directly through this statement.

On the other hand, the authorities admit that "yet we did owe allegiance and subjection" to England. Or, as the historian defines the relationship, New England is "independent in respect of government," while still dependent "upon the crown" (II: 279). Events in the 1640s in the colonies proved that New England was not an entirely self-directed city upon a hill. The authorities were forced to take on Child's petition precisely as a test case for their redefined, though still intentionally ambiguous, relationship to England.

The Court's first move in the Child affair showed that it had learned an important fact from Gorton's case: it was necessary to preserve the correct image of the colony in England. Edward Winslow was quickly dispatched to England to answer for the colony, before Child or any of his supporters could begin to challenge publicly the orthodoxy's version of events. (Winslow, incidentally, was never to return to New England, one of the sad notes sounded by William Bradford near the end of his history.) Next, the authorities in New England, as they had done in Gorton's case, switched the immediate terms of inquiry: then it had been the land dispute that was bypassed in order to question the social vision inherent in the ideas; here it is the petition itself that is bypassed. Hauled before the General Court in Boston, Child demanded "what should be laid to [the petitioner's] charge, seeing it was no offence to prefer a petition. . . . It was answered, that they were not questioned for petitioning, but for such miscarriage etc. as appeared in their petition and remonstrance" (II: 284).

Having ruled in this way, the authorities formally charged Child "with divers false and scandalous passages . . . against the churches of Christ and the civil government here established, derogating from the honour and authority of the same, and tending to sedition" (II: 285). The charge is familiar—sedition, a turning away from the norm. And once again, the mediating elements of the New England Way are called into play. The petitioners are asked to respond, "to make answer to" the charges; the Court, in turn, counteranswers them. Throughout this dialogue, Child undertakes to prove that New England is subject to the laws of England, while Winthrop and the General Court define New England as subject only to the "general" laws of England, not to specific ones (II:

emerging oxymoron

291). Here, again, is the independent-but-dependent formula-tion—again a middle way.

Like many before them in New England, and even more after, the "petitioners [persist] obstinately and proudly in their evil prac-tice" (II: 291). Again, a familiar charge by the historian—"persisting" in error, persisting in misinterpretation. The heavy fines laid against them are meant to punish that obstinacy, as well as fill the colony's empty coffers (see II: 295) and, one suspects, assuage the Court's feelings at New England's having been de-spised by these petitioners as a "small thing." Yet all the petition-ers need do to have their fines remitted, the historian reminds us, is "ingenuously acknowledge their miscarriage" (II: 292). Child did not. He somehow managed to pay his fine and, at the same time, drew up a new petition, this one signed only by nonfreemen in the colony and designed to be presented to Parliament in En-gland: signed, the historian adds characteristically, by men who lacked understanding of Scripture and "men of no *reason* either" (II: 294; emphasis in the original). This time the Court did not wait to act, illegally searching Child's home to locate incriminating evidence; nor did it, according to Winthrop, discuss the matter with the petitioners in an attempt to show them their errors. Child was apprehended and prevented from going to England, at least until Winslow had arrived and presented the colony's version of events. Child finally did arrive in England, and his brother John immediately took the remonstrants' part in a pamphlet war already engaged in by Gorton and Winslow.

In the *History,* however, Child is ushered out with what, to the Puritan historian, seems equal to damnation: "I must here ob-serve," he says, "a special providence of God, pointing out his dis-pleasure against some profane persons, who took part with Dr. Child etc. against the government and churches here" (II: 305). He goes on to describe how several petitioners lost "a great raft of masts and planks (worth forty or fifty pounds)" at sea; another lost his horse (II: 305). Child's errors are refuted and New England is vindicated by signs of the Lord's displeasure. Like Hutchinson, he is providentially marked by God as an outcast.

signs

Or so the historian wants us to believe. To a reader more re-moved from those events, Winthrop's narrative reveals an inordi-nate level of self-doubt. The account of the rough physical treat-ment of the Gortonists; the determination of the magistrates (and no one else) to kill him; the seizure of Child's papers and the need to prevent him from leaving: these actions were merely corollaries to the historian's refusal to see either man as anything other than ignorant and corrupt, his rising fear that vocal dissent of any kind tends toward sedition, his need to read God's affirmation of New England in such picayune incidents as the loss of a horse. The remonstrant's wife and child, he observes with petty satisfaction, *almost* drowned (II: 305). Compared to the rhetoric in which he described the colonists' victories over Anne Hutchinson and the Hingham petitioners, his language here is pallid, a weak attempt to convince himself that his account is correct. Philip Gura notes:

> In New England the Gortonist episode epitomized a time of communal identity crisis, of profound redefinition and redirection of [the] entire society's belief system; . . . a new "boundary" for acceptable behavior was being established at a point in [New England's] history when [its] members sorely needed such a searching examination of their communal goals. (Gura, *Glimpse* 227)

That crisis was keenly felt by Winthrop in his role as self-appointed historian, and it is most clearly expressed in his record of the events surrounding Gorton and Child.

Several years before the events involving Gorton and Child, in 1639, John Winthrop had received word that the Lord Saye and Sele, a Puritan nobleman living in England, sought to discourage emigrants from settling in New England "by disparaging this country" (I: 333). Saye and Sele had been displeased by New England's rejection of his offer to settle in the colony, an offer that he made contingent upon the creation of a hereditary aristocracy in Massachusetts Bay. He was proceeding with his plans to draw colonists to Providence Island in the West Indies, where he wished to establish a colony directly under his own control. Is it not blasphemous, Saye and Sele wrote to Winthrop the following year, to assume

> that there is the like call from god for your going to that part of America and fixing there, that there was for the Israelites going to the land of promise and fixing there[?] . . . And for you to plant there, and no where else is as much a work of God as his building Jerusalem in that place and no where else[?] . . . Is this to be offered unto men of Judgement? (*Winthrop Papers* IV: 264)

Winthrop had prompted this criticism by sending an apparently stern letter to Saye and Sele in 1639, when he first heard of the nobleman's disparagement of the colony. The original letter is not extant, but Winthrop paraphrased its contents in the *History*, claiming to have shown

> his lordship, how evident it was, that God had chosen this country to plant his people in, and therefore how displeasing it would be to the Lord [God], and dangerous to himself, to hinder this work, or to discourage men from supplying us, by abusing the goodness of the country, which he never saw, and persuading men, that here was no possibility of subsistence. . . . To this letter his lordship returned answer, (not denying that which was reported of him, nor the evidence of the Lord's owning the work, but) alleging, that this was a place appointed only for a present refuge, etc. and that, a better place being found out, we were all called to remove thither. (I: 333)

It would not be surprising if Winthrop had, indeed, favorably compared New England to Israel; he would not have been the only Bay colonist to do so in the 1630s and 1640s.

But for my purposes here what is most revealing in this brief dialogue is the way these two men, both Puritans, understood New England in 1639. Only ten years earlier Winthrop himself, when he first considered removing to New England, had argued along similar lines as did Saye and Sele: "The whole earth is the Lord's garden," he had written, "and he hath given it to the sons of men to be tilled and improved by them" (*Winthrop Papers* II: 115). His position a year later in "A Model of Christian Charity" had not changed; there he focused exclusively on a society, not a place. And that society, he claimed, *will be* chosen by God only in a future brought into being by the auditor's actions in the coming years. In 1630 New England as a location had not been specially chosen by God. But in Winthrop's mind, and in the minds of the other leaders who charted the future of the colony, the purpose and meaning of New England had begun to change by the end of the first decade of settlement (see Delbanco 149–83).

In the *History*, as in his letter to Saye and Sele, Winthrop displays a confident attitude in the late 1630s: there were problems, of course, but heresy had been defeated, the economy prospered, immigration continued apace. The future of the colony looked bright. In the next few years, however, his attitude moves in a descending arc toward extreme self-doubt, both product and representation of the communal identity crisis in the 1640s. In the Hingham episode, the historian realized that men in positions of subjection in New England were for some reason—"self-love," he theorized (II: 94)—unhappy with their lot. For more than ten years some of them had been jockeying for more power; clearly, they lacked those "affections of love in the heart which will as natively bring forth [actions of love], as any cause doth produce the effect" ("Model" 288). They lacked the habit of love. In his account of their petitions and defiance, Winthrop manifests a heightened, almost paranoid, concern for New England's image abroad and at home. The successes of Gorton and Child not only called the city upon a hill into question, they indicated that man's self-love would not and could not be eradicated in the New World.

The ideal and real never meet, of course. It may be unfair to examine Winthrop's social vision in "A Model of Christian Charity," and then point out that his *History* records the unsuccessful effort to implement it, even as the author, apparently, continued to revise the myth he had in part invented. "A Model of Christian Charity," after all, is a hortatory sermon, the *History* an increasingly reflective account of events. Generic difference aside, however, the Puritans themselves insisted that human beings try to live up to certain ideals, even though they knew that they could not do so. Manifested in a variety of ways in the life of each Puritan, this "Puritan dilemma," as Edmund Morgan has so aptly described it, was the lot of all those who desired to live holily. It was, I would argue, John Winthrop's lot once the clarion call of the "Model" had been sounded. As he expressed it in 1630, these Puritan settlers wanted to be a model for all Protestants, they wanted to be the first in a series "of succeeding plantations" that would comprise a new Israel. By the mid 1640s, however, he expressed his awareness that many citizens in both the first and "succeeding" plantations were willing to challenge that model, not tentatively and internally, as did Wheelwright and Hutchinson, but aggressively and externally, by appealing to outside authorities. As governor, Winthrop's response was inevitably to try to hold New England to his model in any way he could: dialogue, mediation, "force of Argument," silence, banishment. In commanding adherence to the social vision, the authorities in the 1640s stopped only short of death, and even then against their wishes, at least in the case of Gorton. As a historian, Winthrop's technique is to investigate the ways in which New England appeared, early on at least, to be on track—then, later, the ways in which it seemed to veer into ordinariness.

Hence, by "real" I do not mean "failure," or even "declension," a favorite word of scholars of seventeenth-century New England. I mean, simply, that events had taken place that ran counter to Winthrop's idealistic social vision of 1630. As a historian, Winthrop tries but is finally unable to make events fit into his prophetic vision of the future. If you bring us to New England, he said to God, then we shall be Your people and we shall thrive; and if You do so and we fail to come up to Your expectations, then "we shall surely perish out of the good land" that You have given us ("Model" 294–95). So the "Model." But amid many hopeful signs that New England had indeed succeeded and was the Lord's stood just as many, if not more—Gorton and Child and the Hingham petitioners and "self-love"—that it had not and was not. Mankind in New England did not differ from mankind anywhere else. And yet New England did not perish. Events did not square with the vision.

Like William Bradford in Book II of his *Of Plymouth Plantation,* Winthrop expressed pain and confusion at the direction events were taking in his colony. In a gloomy effusion in 1642, Winthrop lamented:

> Much disputation there was about liberty of removing [from New England] for outward advantages, and all ways were sought for an open door to get out at; but it is to be feared many crept out at a broken wall. . . . Ask thy conscience, if thou wouldst have plucked up thy stakes, and brought thy family 3000 miles, if thou hadst expected that all, or most, would have forsaken thee there. . . . [For] if one may go, another may, and so the greater part, and so church and commonwealth may be left destitute in a wilderness, exposed to misery and reproach, and all for thy ease and pleasure, whereas these all, being now thy brethren, as near to thee as the Israelites were to Moses, it were much safer for thee, after his example, to choose rather to suffer affliction with thy brethren, than to enlarge thy ease and pleasure by furthering the occasion of their ruin. (II: 87)

The cry is as plaintive as Bradford's when he compares Plymouth, a "poor church," to "an ancient mother grown old and forsaken

of her children" (*Plymouth Plantation* 334). Although both historians use the impersonal third-person voice in their histories, one of
the most striking differences between them is the frequency and
emotional depth of these insights into their character, and their
colonies' character. For just as the New England Way could, ideally,
mute and even silence self-love or passion in the name of maintaining a higher social good, so Winthrop consistently mutes and even
silences displays of self in the *History* in the name of the correct
social order of the New England that he represents in his pages.
Unlike Bradford, he does not wear his emotions on his sleeve.

That such passion shows through at all, in the form of anger or
joy or sadness or even confusion, is a function, then, of his society
having strayed from the path Winthrop had marked out for it. So
it is that, as Winthrop writes and as events under his pen slowly
take a shape he had not expected, he becomes more than a diarist.
He becomes, before our eyes as it were, a chronicler, a historian.
In the latter half of the narrative, even as events become more
confusing and men more selfish, he becomes aware of his audience, of his voice, of the literary creation of New England in his
pages. It took history, in essence, for Winthrop to write a history.
In the "Model" Winthrop had said that, once God brought the
settlers to this new land, their community would be perfected; it
would become the kind of city that existed, according to most Reformed theologians, only after the end of time. History was ab-
jured. In the *History of New England* it was necessarily embraced
again.

But it was embraced with the "Model" as its reference point,
and hence the facts do not fit the assumptions. The *History* grows
out of the tension between the conception of a specific social
order and the realization that mankind often refuses to be purged
of self-love. Winthrop is unable to reconcile those two things; he is
unable either to reconceive his assumptions and the mission behind them or to accept an interpretation that says New England is
just the same as all other human societies. In the terms of the
"Model," the bones that the prophet Ezekiel breathed over have
not come together; Winthrop, as prophet and as historian, was
unable to breathe upon Massachusetts Bay and regenerate "old
man Adam."

His narrative remains as a sometimes-halting but often-eloquent
attempt to comprehend the meaning of the first years of settlement. Winthrop's *History of New England* stands as one colonial artist's attempt to grapple with a society in transition, to fix and hold

the meaning of a culture, an entity that always has resisted and always will resist fixing. Yearning for stability, while determined to record events truthfully as they occurred, Winthrop could in the end narrate only the transformation of his society. To the very end, he remained convinced that authority in the New World—his own, as well as that of his God, his (reading of his) Bible, his tradition, his social hierarchy—should not be problematic. But it was. His use of the impersonal third-person voice is, in this sense, a reflection of the authority of the governor-historian atop the social-interpretive hierarchy, though even in the pages of his *History*, that authority, that voice, did not go unchallenged. Perhaps, then, it was fitting ("providential," he might have felt) that Winthrop died in March 1648/49, after the execution of Charles I but before he heard word of it. His narrative had been struggling since 1630 with a world in which the traditional authority of social standing and the Protestant authority of the trained and blessed intellect were increasingly in conflict. Politically, socially, and theologically, the sources of authority in his world were being refigured. Because of this, by 1650, new conceptions of and new techniques for relating the past in authoritative ways were desperately needed by colonial historians intent on writing New England's past.

Edifying History

Edward Johnson's
Wonder-Working Providence

2

As historians, John Winthrop and William Bradford expressed disillusionment with the history, present state, and apparent future of their communities. In the course of recording events, each began to perceive that history is contingent, that his own best-laid model could not force the community into perfection, could not make it successful in the terms in which the endeavor was originally and ideally couched. In this sense, their histories reveal a complex tension between theory and experience, model and history, hope and reality.

Many writers voice similarly anxious and tension-laden reactions in the first years of settlement in the New England colonies. "Have we not fallen a-dreaming here?" Thomas Shepard wrote in the late 1630s, in the wake of the Antinomian Controversy:

> What meaneth else the delusion of men's brains? What a swarm of strange opinions, which (like flies) have gone to the sores of men's heads and hearts, and these are believed also; and more dreams men have that are never spoken; every man hath some drunken conceit that rocks him asleep: dreams are quite contrary to the truth. (Heimert and Delbanco 174)

The tropes were different, but the experience was similar: these settlers were disillusioned. Perhaps it is ironic, from Massachusetts' point of view, at least, that even John Wheelwright experienced this sort of disillusionment. Why, he asks in *Mercurius Americanus,* did the Hutchinsonians do what they did?

> Alas, we must look at them as men who had left their estates, friends, pleasures of their native soul, spiritual *Chymists,* extracting the sweetnesse of all into freedom of conscience, doubting not but they might find all in that *Elixar,* but as no *Chymist* yet got it, so they were many of them deceived; which when they surveyed, and see the result, it might trouble the weaker, and through melancholy fumes dispose them to strange fancies in Divinity. (Wheelwright 199)

The New World was not what he had imagined, either. Let me propose a Christian riddle, Roger Williams wrote a few years later: "Why is the heart of a David himself (Ps. 30) more apt to decline from God upon the mountain of joy, deliverance, victory, prosperity, than in the dark vale of the shadow of death, persecution, sickness, adversity, etc.?" (Williams 41).[1] It was a riddle many colonists asked themselves.

Not every history written in the early years of settlement expresses such a disjunction or such disillusion. Some, like *Mourt's Relation* (1622) and Francis Higginson's *New England's Plantation* (1630), were designed primarily as promotional tracts, and they sound a fairly consistent note of optimism. Written in the first-person (Higginson, for example, insists that he will "report nothing of *New-England* but what I have . . . seen with mine owne Eyes" [5]), these two narratives are quite hopeful about New England's potential. But they are also too close to the action and ideas they report to evince much of a sense of the past, and too concerned with attracting new settlers to venture into pessimism. Valuable in their own right as immediate perceptions and conceptions of the voyage, the landscape, and the first few months or years of settlement, these narratives tell us relatively little about the effects of social, economic, and intellectual conflict on New England's historical imagination.[2]

Aside from Bradford's *Of Plymouth Plantation* and Winthrop's *History of New England,* other communal histories written in New England prior to 1650 can be grouped, very loosely and with some overlap, in two different categories: relations of specific events, such as the Pequot War; and polemics written overtly to criticize the yet-developing orthodoxy of the New England Way. Texts in both categories are relevant to my argument about disillusionment. The first category would include works like John Winthrop's *A Short Story of the Rise, reign, and ruine of the Antinomians, Familists, and Libertines,* John Wheelwright's *Mercurius Americanus* (1645), Edward Winslow's *Hypocrisie Unmasked* (1646), and John Underhill's *Newes From America* (1638).

Underhill's history, for example, claims to give "a true narration of the warlike proceedings that hath been in New England these two years past [1636–1637]" (1). As one of the commanders of the combined forces of Connecticut, Plymouth, and Massachusetts Bay, Underhill was in an excellent position to tell the story of the Puritans' annihilation of the Pequot tribe.[3] However, he figures the victory in two rather curious ways. First, he insists that his purpose in the history is, in addition to giving a "true narration" of the events, to "discover to the reader divers places in New England, that would afford special accommodations to such persons as will plant upon them" (1). He follows through on this purpose by elaborately describing "the excellence of the whole country," from the new plantations within the Bay colony to the northern plantations of "Puscataway" to the land within the Connecticut valley (which was opened, at least in part, by the victory over the Pequots) (18–20). Like Higginson, Underhill wrote his narrative in order to sell the country to a London audience; his economic motives and his ideological motives are clearly intertwined.

Second, Underhill interrupts his narration just prior to the climactic scene of destruction in the Pequot fort to give a short sermon on faith. The Lord deals with men today, Underhill states, much as He did with David: "The greater the captivities be of his servants, the contentions amongst his churches, the clearer God's presence is amongst his, to pick and cull them out of the fire, and to manifest himself to their souls, and bear them up, as Peter above the water, that they sink not" (31). Do not be so naive as to ask for such afflictions and contentions, he tells us, for "it is against the course of Scripture to wish for evil"; but do not struggle against them, either. The Lord "exercises" His people with troubles and afflictions "that he might appear to them in mercy, and reveal more clearly his free grace unto their souls" (32). *Free grace!* No wonder John Winthrop could report, with scorn, that in one of the aftershocks of the Antinomian Controversy, Underhill told the General Court in 1638 he

> could get no assurance [of his spiritual estate], till at length, as he
> was taking a pipe of tobacco, the Spirit set home an absolute prom-
> ise of free grace with such assurance and joy, as he never since
> doubted of his good estate, neither should he, though he should
> fall into sin. (qtd. in Gura, *Glimpse* 89)

Underhill was an antinomian. Elsewhere in the sermonic inter-
lude in *Newes From America*, for example, we might notice that he
carefully echoes Wheelwright's 1637 fast-day sermon: "Doth not
Christ say, I came not to bring peace, but a sword?" (35). Here, if
not in Wheelwright's fast-day sermon, the sword was intended to
be as real as it was metaphorical, at least if Underhill's actions in
the Pequot War are any indication. Yet "do we not ever find, the
greater the afflictions and troubles of God's people be, the more
eminent is his grace in the souls of his servants? You that intend to
go to New England, fear not a little trouble" (35). This might seem
to us to be an ineffective recruiting pitch; it's like telling potential
servicemen that a charge led by George Pickett in a once-sleepy
Pennsylvania town lies somewhere in their future. But Underhill
quickly subverts any squeamishness his audience might have felt
by questioning their faith and courage:

> he is the most courageous soldier, that sees the battle pitched, the
> drums beat an alarm, and trumpets sound a charge, and yet is not
> afraid to join in the battle. Show not yourselves cowards. . . . Are
> you afraid? . . . What is become of faith? I will not fear that man can
> do unto me, saith David, no, nor what troubles can do, but will trust
> in the Lord, who is my God. (36)

The Pequot War, then, begins to take on both a typological and a
metaphorical meaning in Underhill's narrative. Biblical figures
such as David and Peter are typed as worldly afflicted saints who
consistently trust in the God who has chosen them, even as they
buckle on His armor. In this light, the war is merely another reassuring episode for those who trust in the Lord: "Let the ends and
aims of a man be good, and he may proceed with courage. The
bush may be in the fire, but so long as God appears to Moses out
of the bush, there is no great danger. More good than hurt will
come of it" (36). The war does not point forward in time to yet
another (anti)type within history, as will the typology of writers like
Edward Johnson; it points upward, vertically, toward the spiritual
meaning (Bercovitch, "Typology"). The war figures the difference

between those who, like Underhill, believe in God's free grace and those who (like Winthrop, perhaps) do not. It is probably not co-incidental that Underhill's narrative ends with Massachusetts' troops, "in company with them one Mr. John Wilson" as chaplain, arriving on the scene too late to do battle with the Pequots, except to kill some few "distressed" refugees who remained (44). Wilson was one of the most vigorous opponents of the Antinomians during the Antinomian Controversy.[4]

Underhill's use of a particular branch of typology—Bercovitch traces it back to Augustine—may help to explain why his narrative contains so few temporal markers: what is important is not the forward movement of time, but the sharp infusion, at any moment, of God's free grace. Hence, specific dates of any sort are not mentioned; and transitions are figured in terms that are purely relative to other internal markers ("The next morning . . ."), and so cannot be pinpointed. Also, the narrative thrust is interrupted by minisermons and propaganda tracts, because what is important is not the events as they occur over time and within history, but the sharp "light" that God bestowed in the entire "proceedings" (40).

For all its differences, however, Underhill's *Newes From America* is similar to the latter half of Winthrop's history in the way it figures the early experience of New England as "troubling." Expect trouble if you come to New England, Underhill suggests; you can't escape it in the New World. Simply be aware, he argues, that an extrahistorical meaning is available in incidents like the Pequot War to those who submit themselves to Christ's free grace. Amid the troubling events of the New World one can only hope for the sharp infusion of grace that shatters time and transcends those troubles. Like Winthrop, Underhill lacks a coherent sense of New England's purpose within history; but, then again, having apparently received Christ's free grace, he does not need or desire that coherence.

The other texts that I have grouped as polemics written to oppose the orthodoxy also figure the early colonial experience as "troubling." Here I would include such works as Thomas Morton's *New English Canaan* (1637), John Child's *New-England's Jonas cast up at London* (1647), and Thomas Lechford's *Plain Dealing: Or, Newes from New-England* (1641).

Like Underhill, Lechford speaks from personal experience: he is "plain dealing" because he has lived in New England and because he is "impartiall" (79). His account of Massachusetts Bay's early years is quite critical of the orthodoxy: church members have too much power, the demand for public conversion narratives inhibits many persons from joining the church, the Indians are not being instructed in the faith, the courts do not keep adequate records, and so on. Indeed, in hindsight, many of his criticisms appear perspicuous. The problem, he summarizes, is not only that New England has slighted "all former laws of the Church or State, cases of experience and precedents, to go hammer out new, according to severall exigencies; upon pretence that the Word of God is sufficient to rule us" (28). As a lawyer and a supporter of episcopacy, Lechford might be expected to criticize the "innovations" of the settlers' new government and churches. The problem is also that the "experimentall footsteps" of New England are "inconstant," wavering, almost drunken (70, 79). His experience in the colony, Lechford claims, taught him the correctness of episcopacy, tradition, the law. He, like the other early historians of the New England colonies, is troubled by events in the New World. However, whereas Winthrop fell into the contingency of history and Bradford tried to retreat from it, Lechford, like many other critics of the orthodoxy, simply left New England in disgust. *Plain Dealing* remains to attest, concisely and eloquently, to his (and others') disillusionment with the troubling history and ambiguous possibilities of that place called New England.

A New Past

There are moments in his *History of New England* when John Winthrop wrote as if he did not understand how men and women in New England could be so greedy, so obstinate, so evil—even though the sermons he heard on Thursdays and Sundays continued to remind him that little more could be expected from them in this fallen world. He had changed, and so perhaps had they. Yet, according to all available evidence, New England colonists did not become more evil in the 1640s. Winthrop, measuring their desire for certain freedoms against the idealism of "A Model of Christian Charity," simply began to conceive of declension as a way of understanding what was happening to his community. As a historian, his dilemma was caused at least in part by his proximity to his material: he was intimately involved in every important crisis and controversy that affected Massachusetts Bay and the United Colonies from 1629 to 1649. "The *Eye*," Cotton Mather wrote later in the century, "sees not those Objects which are applied close unto it, and even lye upon it; but when the Objects are to some distance removed, it clearly discerns them" (*Magnalia* II: 70).

A new perspective on New England's past came from what seemed an unlikely perspective. Edward Johnson was born in Canterbury in 1598, was (according to some sources) brought up to the trade of joiner, and emigrated to New England in 1630 (probably on the *Arbella*, where he might very well have listened to Winthrop's sermon). He went back to England in the early 1630s and returned to New England with his wife and children in 1636 in the midst of the Antinomian Controversy, an experience he recounts in a fictionalized version in his history. He settled first at Charlestown, but in 1640 he became a founder of Woburn. He lived there until his death in 1672, serving as town clerk, selectman, deputy to the General Court, and militia captain. Little in the sparse biographical information available about Johnson would indicate his abilities either as historian or poet.[5] Sometime in 1649 or 1650, however, he set himself the task of composing a history of New England. Internal evidence indicates that the manuscript was completed no later than December 1651. It was published in London in 1653.[6]

Wonder-Working Providence of Sions Saviour in New England seems to depart dramatically from Bradford's and Winthrop's histories. Divided into three books, each spanning a seven-year interval, the history is a vibrant, carefully structured defense of New England's mission, which in the context of Johnson's postmillennial vision is to battle and ultimately defeat the Antichrist. The narrative is consistently overlaid with typological and numerological significance, giving it an internal sense of order and external allusiveness that Winthrop's *History of New England* and Book II of Bradford's *Of Plymouth Plantation* lack. It is laced with poems, usually set in iambic pentameter with an alternating rhyme scheme, but also sonorous "fourteeners" of the sort Michael Wigglesworth would later employ in his *Day of Doom*. The prose is often exuberant, sometimes swaggering.

Yet Johnson's history is, in several senses at least, not so very different from Bradford's and Winthrop's. As its title indicates, the history is providential. Johnson, like his predecessors, believed that God's providence directed every action, even to the fall of a sparrow; his narrative insists that His providence, manifested in "wonders," is especially directed on behalf of this particular community. In addition, the prose is not always exuberant; Johnson sometimes adopts a plain style of his own, as when he describes the founding of Woburn. Even the poems, most of them biographies, "penned of purpose to keepe in memory the Names of such worthies as Christ made strong for himselfe" (44), simply serve the same purpose as did Bradford's touching vignette of William Brewster in *Of Plymouth Plantation*—to "say something" of the lives of men and women who "had done and suffered much for the Lord Jesus and the gospel's sake" (324–25).

However, not surprisingly, the narrative's supposed shortcomings relative to Bradford's history dominated the criticism of Johnson's history for many years. J. Franklin Jameson, in the introduction to his edition of the history, described *Wonder-Working Providence* as the work of an "organization man" who was "quite incapable of understanding the subtilties of theology," and so adhered instinctively though ardently to the orthodox cause (17). That same ardor, Kenneth Murdock believed, "led [Johnson] to play the sedulous ape to better artists and spotted his pages with travesties of the ornateness and elegance and pattern of prose writers who were bred to their art" ("Colonial Historians" 8). Perry Miller was no more sensitive than Jameson and Murdock: "The historian Edward Johnson . . . attempted in *The Wonder-Working Providence of Sions Saviour in New England* to write with a copious use of rhetorical flowers, though hardly with what we can call artistic success" (*Seventeenth Century* 352). And, more recently, Peter Gay continued this scholarly line of literary judgment by curtly dismissing the history as "that naive military bulletin reporting Christ's victories against Satan in America" (53).

Fortunately, in several studies published since the late 1960s, scholars have begun to revise the critical status of Johnson's history. Sacvan Bercovitch has explained the relevance of linear typology in the history and argued that, by its attempt to define New England, *Wonder-Working Providence* established "a pattern which may be traced in secular form through many of the subsequent urgent and obsessive definitions of the meaning of America" ("Historiography" 161). Edward Gallagher, in a series of articles on the history, has contended that Johnson used three basic methods—spiritual biography, typology, and rhetoric—to revive his audience's lagging faith in the idea of New England as a holy commonwealth. And, more recently, Dennis R. Perry has traced the series of autobiographical masks that Johnson adopted from his own life and incorporated into the history, attempting to write New

England's "composite autobiography." What these articles have in common is an insistence that *Wonder-Working Providence* be read as a complex literary work that brilliantly addresses the crisis New England faced in the late 1640s and early 1650s. Alan Heimert's and Andrew Delbanco's recent revaluation of Johnson's history—"it is perhaps the literary masterpiece of first-generation New England" (113)—is a recognition of this new understanding.[7]

I intend to expand on those revaluations, first by reading Johnson's history as a rhetorical strategy, and then by placing his narrative more squarely in the cultural context within which it was written. *Wonder-Working Providence*, I shall argue, represents the first of several histories in seventeenth-century New England that revise the past in order to appeal to the future. It is the first of several histories written in seventeenth-century New England that attempt to "rehabilitate" the past in order to "inhabit" the future. "I see in the plots we invent," Paul Ricoeur has written, "the privileged means by which we re-configure our confused, unformed, and at the limit mute temporal experience" (xi).

Johnson opens *Wonder-Working Providence*, just as William Bradford does his *Of Plymouth Plantation*, by describing "a touch of the time when this worke [of settlement] began" (Johnson 23). In 1630 Bradford consciously reached back to the early centuries of Christianity to provide a context for his pilgrims.[8] Johnson instead reaches back less than fifty years to provide a context for his "souldiers." He begins by referring to the time

> When England began to decline in Religion, like lukewarm Laodicea, and instead of purging out Popery, a farther compliance was sought not only in vaine Idolatrous Ceremonies, but also in prophaning the Sabbath, and by Proclamation throughout their Parish churches, exasperating lewd and prophane persons to celebrate a Sabbath like the Heathen to Venus, Baccus and Ceres; in so much that the multitude of irreligious and popish affected persons spred the whole land like Grashoppers. (23)

The allusions here are to the reign of King James when, from the Puritan point of view, England lost all hope of becoming the pure and godly commonwealth that Henry, Edward, and even Elizabeth had apparently intended.[9] The difference is important: Bradford immediately and appropriately establishes his plantation within the context of the new dispensation wrought by Christ's death; his story is, after all, one of individuals who wander the earth as pilgrims and witnesses, having severed their ties to all nations and all places. Johnson's context is post-Elizabethan England, which had been given the opportunity to purge out popery, but which chose instead to comply with "vaine Idolatrous Ceremonies" and laws encouraging the profanation of the Sabbath. England during the reigns of James and Charles, like Laodicea in the time of John (Revelation 3.14–16), proved to be "neither cold or hot" toward the establishment of a pure and godly commonwealth. Hence (the narrator informs us), Christ raised "an Army out of our English Nation" and created "a New England to muster up the first of his forces in" (23). In that long opening sentence of the history, Johnson establishes early seventeenth-century England as the backdrop to his story, painting it as an antitype of Old Testament Egypt, puffed up with "pride" and overrun by "Grashoppers." Through a typological shorthand, which draws on ideas such as "Popery," "Prelacy" (23), and "Idolatrous Ceremonies" to trace God's progressive unfolding of meaning within history, Johnson dismisses England as the oppressor of God's chosen people, presents the chosen emigrants as the typological extension of the Israelites, and defines New England as the typological extension of Canaan, the place where Christ will establish that newly chosen people in His church.[10] Having failed to become a holy land, England will be transformed on the shores of the New World, made new through the agency of this chosen remnant.

Johnson amplifies that opening paragraph, with its description of England as a type both of Old Testament paganism (Egypt) and New Testament spiritual insufficiency (Laodicea), by re-creating for his audience the exact moment when this work of Christ began. In what is perhaps the boldest rhetorical move devised by a seventeenth-century writer in New England, the historian's voice gives way to that of Christ's "Herald" at arms, who makes "this proclamation for Voluntiers" in 1628:

> Oh yes! oh yes! oh yes! All you the people of Christ that are here Oppressed, Imprisoned and scurrilously derided, gather yourselves together, your Wives and little ones, and answer to your several Names as you shall be shipped for his service, in the Westerne World, and more especially for planting the united Collonies of new England; Where you are to attend the service of the King of Kings. (24)

The word has real power in Johnson's narrative, as it did in Winthrop's "Model": later in the history, for example, he points out (in the voice of the herald) that Christ's final victory will be achieved "by the word of his Mouth, audibly spoken the World throughout" (35). By adopting the "divinely given" word of Christ's herald here at the beginning of *Wonder-Working Providence*, Johnson establishes not only the authority of his position as historian, a scribe of God's providences, but also the whole structure of New England society as it appears in 1653. Winthrop's struggles with the deputies and with Gorton can and will be elided in Johnson's narrative, since, from the beginning, authority is refigured (and enunciated) as divine. For, as the herald further proclaims, the "Commission" to be shipped for Christ's service in America involves the establishment of Congregational churches, which the herald describes in detail (25–30), and a "Civill Government" capable of protecting "the peace of [those] churches" (30–32). The herald even goes on to defend intolerance, to predict the rise of "silly Women laden with diverse lusts" (28), to define those sects that will arise in New England and challenge the authority of church and state, and to reassert in the strongest possible terms of encouragement the value of New England: "the Lord Christ," he says, "intends to atchieve greater matters by this little handfull then the World is aware of" (33).

The herald's proclamation is a measure of New England's psychological needs in the early 1650s.[11] Attacked by English Presbyterians and Independents because they insisted that intolerance is necessary for a church to remain pure, and confused by their feeling that history—in the form of the Puritan victory in the Civil War—had somehow passed them by, New England's settlers seemed by 1650 to have lost the sense of mission that John Winthrop and the other founders of the colony had provided in the early years of settlement. That feeling of loss was compounded, according to contemporary accounts at least, by the economic crisis of the early 1640s, by Gorton's and Child's (and others') attacks, by the deaths of such founding fathers as Thomas Hooker (1647), Winthrop (1649), and Thomas Shepard (1649). Johnson's prophecy, spoken by Christ's own messenger, serves to reaffirm New England's value. By 1653 the colonists had indeed seen intolerance, withstood the rise of a "silly" Woman (Anne Hutchinson), and survived the disturbances caused by the very sects the herald describes. With their confidence in the narrative buttressed by the obvious truth of those sections of the herald's "prophecy," Johnson's audience is then urged to believe a corollary: that "this little handfull" of "souldiers" will not merely achieve great things, but will fight as Christ's main troops in the final battle against Satan. And they will win! They will defeat the Antichrist, and thus put an end to history itself, as Winthrop had hinted in his shipboard sermon twenty years earlier.

One specific example of Johnson's strategy within this "Commission" is his reinterpretation of New England's settlers, who he claims were "Oppressed, Imprisoned, and scurrilously derided" in England (24). Neither Winthrop nor Bradford had been so harsh on England: Winthrop's settlers had left willingly to found a new city, just as Bradford's settlers had willingly embarked on a pilgrimage to the New World. Johnson's herald proclaims New England's settlers "souldiers of Christ," instead of founders or pilgrims. Usually, the military metaphors in *Wonder-Working Providence* are interpreted as reflections of Johnson's own role as militia captain of Woburn. But it is important to note that a number of settlers left New England in the 1640s to take part in the Civil War, and that those who remained felt no small measure of guilt at not returning to fight.[12] Johnson simply translates what some in England perceive as meanness, and what some in New England fear is cowardice, into a highly exalted purpose:

> for although it may seeme a meane thing to be a New England Souldier, yet some of you [in New England] shall have the battering and beating down, scaling, winning and wasting the over-topping Towers of the Hierarchy. . . . And then shall the time be of breaking Speares into Mattocks, and Swordes into Sithes; and this to remaine to [Christ's] last comming. (34–35)

Those who have not returned to England, he suggests, are also soldiers. The Civil War in England is not the most important historical fact of the Reformation or even of seventeenth-century England: there is another war yet to be fought, the cosmic battle between good and evil preceding the millennium. That war, the herald proclaims, will be fought by the New English settlers—in which case, of course, there is no need to feel bad about the New Model Army temporarily doing all of the fighting.

Another example of Johnson's strategy in this appropriation of the divine Word is his reinterpretation of the colony's purpose. In

"A Model of Christian Charity," Winthrop had used the typological identification of New England with Israel to establish for his audience the relevance of their mission: the creation of a model for succeeding plantations, pointing the way to the final and complete reformation of society and mankind. Winthrop's focus is on the community, the city upon a hill, which the people before him can bring into being; he is not as interested in why New England has been chosen to be a people set apart as in how they are to act once they have established themselves in the New World. Johnson's herald is also interested in how the mission is to be fulfilled; but he is at the same time quite interested in answering the question Why should these particular men and women ship for the New World, and remain there not only when their spiritual brethren begin to criticize them for their harsh intolerance, but also when those brethren desperately need their help in overthrowing episcopacy in England? The answer is that the settlement is now to be seen as a refuge or a retreat: "of purpose [Christ] caused such instruments to retreate as he hath made strong for himselfe: that so his adversaries glorying in the pride of their power, insulting over the little remnant remaining, Christ causeth them to be cast downe suddenly forever" (240). In Johnson's vision of the past— his revision of New England's history—New England is conceived as a specific "retreate" into the wilderness for Christ, a retreat that He will use to deceive and then conquer the forces of the Antichrist. Although his terminology is slightly different from that of later expositors like Samuel Danforth, Johnson is the first New Englander to conceive of the mission as an "errand into the wilderness."

The military metaphors and the idea of errand are fused in the millennial images that pervade the herald's proclamation: references to Exodus (typologically, the first escape from bondage into purity), to Revelation, to an end-time purity predicted by the New Testament, to the conversion of the Jews. More explicitly, the herald makes the prediction, quoted earlier, that New England's soldiers will overthrow the "Hierarchy" and usher in the age when spears shall be turned into "Mattocks," and "Swordes into Sithes":

> Not that [Christ] shall come personally to Reigne upon Earth (as some vainly imagine) but his powerful Presence and Glorious brightnesse of his Gospell both to Jew and Gentile, shall . . . cause the Churches of Christ to grow beyond number . . . [and] the whole

civill Government of people upon Earth [to] become his . . . and this to remaine to his last comming, which will be personally to overcome the last enemies of the Saints, even death. (34–35)

In his final admonition to New England's soldiers, however, the herald indicates that although Christ *intends* to do these things, the fulfillment of them depends on New England: "the great day of [Antichrist's] final overthrow shall not come till the bright Sonne of that one cleare truth of Christ, stand still in the Gentile Churches" (36). Given an errand, the purpose of which is to usher in the millennium (and that, Johnson feels, ought to quiet all criticism from abroad and reassure his audience of their value), New England must, as of 1628, yet fulfill certain covenant conditions.

Johnson has the herald lay out a three-part plan of "purity, peace, and plenty," which corresponds, appropriately, to the three-part history he himself narrates. The first stage involves the establishment of a primitive "purity" in the churches—by refusing to tolerate all "unsound and undeceivable Doctrines, together with the people that hold them," (36) and by rejecting all forms of covetousness, such as that displayed by Achan in the days prior to Israel's destruction of the walls of Jericho. The model for this religious purity is, typologically, the "temple" in Jerusalem, and New England's settlers are the "stones" with which it is to be rebuilt in this new Sion (25, 28). Second, once purity is achieved, the civil government must marshall its power so as to be able to maintain "peace" within the commonwealth, so "that the people of and under [New England's] Government . . . may live a quiet and peaceable life in all godliness and honesty" (32). The magistrates of the godly, civil government will become "the Eyes of Restraint set up for Walles and Bulwarkes, to surround the Sion of God" (32). They will, like a walled medieval city, defend purity from outside attack. Third, with purity established and the walls of a new city built to protect it, the soldiers of Christ must be wary of misusing the material abundance the Lord will provide in the New World. Christ has promised, the herald says, to transform the howling wilderness into a land of plenty, but "so soon as you shall seeke to ingrosse the Lords wast into your hands, he will ease you of your burden by making stay of any farther resort unto you and then be sure you shall have wast land enough" (35). Once established in their new Canaan, the settlers must resist the indolence that destroyed its Old Testament type, Israel. This final injunction is presented just prior to the herald's closing words, which reemphasize the fact—and the typological implications could not have been lost on Johnson's audience—that if these three steps are followed "the Sun may stand still in Gibeon" (36).

Rhetorically, then, Johnson establishes New England's settlers as the new Israelites. His immediate context is the England of the Stuarts, but by identifying the settlement as the antitype of Israel (and, implicitly, as the Church in Revelation) his context is more accurately the final days—the thousand-year reign of the saints prior to Christ's "last comming" (35), His defeat of the Antichrist, and the final day of judgment. If New England meets the requirements set out in 1628, and recorded and presented again by the historian, its future as God's chosen people will be assured.

EDIFICATION

Johnson is aware that his history encompasses a strategy for dealing with New England's recent problems. "I doubt not," he remarks at one point, "but this History will take of[f] that unjust accusation, and slanderous imputation of the rise of that floud of errors and false Doctrines sprung up of late, as flowing from the Independent or rather congregational Churches" (99). He is not ashamed to be writing a party platform that is the historiographic counterpart of contemporaneous attempts to define New England in terms of church polity (*The Cambridge Platform* [1648]) and civil law (*The Book of the General Lawes and Libertyes* [1648]), as well as other attempts to define New England literarily and imaginatively, as in Nathaniel Ward's satire, *The Simple Cobler of Aggawam in America* (1647). The purpose of Johnson's history is exactly the same as that of those texts: to provide "publicke edification" concerning New England's mission in the New World and to describe the "harmony" of and "unity" within New England (*Cambridge Platform* 194). Along those lines, Johnson's many references to "edifying" the temple of Christ can be seen as representative of a larger, culture-wide refiguration of identity.

Ward notes in *The Simpler Cobler*, for example, that New Englanders "have been reputed a Colluvies of wild Opinionists, swarmed into a remote wilderness to find elbow-roome for our phanatick Doctrines and practises" (6). Like Johnson, he begins in a defensive posture: New England is not a colluvium (that is, a loose deposit of rock debris), though it is indeed intolerant of heretical ideas. Tolerance in matters of religion and of state, Ward goes on to argue, merely means that a society "either doubts" its own beliefs or is "not sincere" in them. Ward's rhetorical strategy as a "cobler" is to repair Old England's "upper-Leather and sole" by lecturing both King and Parliament on just this fact—and, then, on their respective duties in light of it. "For England," he says, "however the upper Stories are [maliciously] shattered; yet the foundations and frame being good or mendable by the Architectors now at worke, there is good hope, when peace is settled, people shall dwell more wind-tight and water-tight than formerly" (34).

Ward conceives of England as a building being reconstructed. Asked why New England's settlers have not returned to England "to helpe the Lord against the Mighty" (24), to help reconstruct that building, the cobbler responds they are too busy praying that England will follow the example (of intolerance and, therefore, peace) being set for them in the New World. This seeming confidence about New England's purpose in the mid 1640s results from two factors. First, New England's spokesmen throughout that decade tried to present a united public front to England and Europe: when, for example, attacks on the Congregational Way came fast and furious in the early 1640s, individual spokesmen were assigned the task of responding to the charges, providing the illusion of cohesiveness in their "monologic" response. Ward's confidence, in other words, is partly bluster. Second, although Ward was engaged in a debate that had been heating up since 1640, he wrote at a moment (in 1645) when the internecine conflict in England had yet to be decided in favor of the Independents. Although heavily criticized by both Presbyterians and Independents, New England felt as late as 1647 that, should King and Parliament come to their senses, the New England Way might yet serve as the model for England's future. Ward's imagery, then, focuses only briefly on New England's identity (it is not a "colluvium") and much more on England's (it is a razed building that can yet be reconstructed, preferably now in imitation of New England). Implicitly, then, New England has succeeded in constructing a building—or at least in writing the blueprints for such a building. Ward's satire is very much a product of the New England imagination prior to Charles's death and the rise of the Commonwealth; but the trope of edification with which Johnson will refigure New England's purpose is already in play in his text.

In *The Cambridge Platform*—a joint effort that carried no author's name, only the imprimatur of "The Synod at Cambridge in New

England" (194)—we can see how, several years later, New England began to turn that trope of construction toward itself. The *Platform*'s spokesmen begin by confessing their subordination to England: "wee hope . . . that as wee are a remnant of the people of [England]: so wee are professors of the same common faith, and fellow-heyres of the same common salvation. . . . [even] though wee are forced to dissent from them in matters of church-discipline" (195). The exigencies of the Civil War had forced the Independents in England to become tolerant of dissenting views; New England—unwilling to tolerate dissent either in church discipline or, as various events had shown, in civil discipline—was left to defend a "Way" that, clearly, Cromwell's England, no more than Charles's, was not interested in pursuing. Accordingly, *The Cambridge Platform* quickly turns from the topic of New England's subordination to imagery of the reconstruction of New England:

> The setting forth of [this] Publick Confession of the Faith of Churches hath a double end, and both tending to publicke edification: first the maintenance of the faith entire within it self: secondly the holding forth of Unity and Harmony, both amongst us, and with other Churches. (194)

The word *edification* means enlightenment, but for the seventeenth century the word had other implications deriving from the Latin *aedes* ("dwelling") plus *ficare* ("to make"), thus meaning "building" (both concretely and figuratively); and, in religious use, "the building up the church . . . in faith and holiness" (see "edification," *OED*). All three uses are in play here. The *Platform* (itself, significantly, a ground plan or representation of a structure) was meant to enlighten skeptics of the New England Way, build up its adherents' faith, and construct the religious and civil polity—the "building"—represented by the platform itself. Not surprisingly, all three epigraphs to the document refer to "the house of the Lord"; and the document itself speaks, at various times, of how much easier it is to build an "edifice" if "rough and unhewen stones" are squared "before they be layed into the building" (200).

Johnson apparently adopted the figure of edification from these other texts; just so, he adopts a method that derived from the wider culture. Like Bradford, like Wheelwright, like nearly everyone writing in the seventeenth century, Johnson was constrained by his belief that truth was transcendent, knowable, and enforce-able. At one point in the history, describing a barber-surgeon who, it was thought, drew men to sinful errors, Johnson remarks:

> He having fit opportunity [to corrupt men], by reason of his trade, so soone as any were set downe in his chair, he would commonly be cutting of theire haire and the truth together; notwithstanding some report better of the man, the example is for the living, the dead is judged of the Lord alone. (191–92)

The "example" lies in the barber's death: Johnson goes on to report that he froze to death in a snowstorm, having lost his "way" in the New England wilderness (191), which, in *Wonder-Working Providence*, is both metaphorical and real. Stripped of all unnecessary facts, the "example" is instructive for the reader of the history: the truth that New England is harmonious and unified in one faith and in one purpose ("the example . . . for the living") is more important than any details—such as the man's innocence—that judged from a higher perspective ("of the Lord") may or may not be true. "Justice and Equity were before time," Ward wrote in *The Simple Cobler*, "and will be after it: Time hath neither Politicks nor Ethicks, good nor evil in it; it is an empty thing, as empty as a *New-English* purse, and emptier it cannot be" (49). Truth ("Justice and Equity") is indeed transcendent, Johnson claims; but narratives describing or defending the providence of God and the actions of men have necessary shapes, are in essence edifices constructed within history and designed to be inhabited by the living. Truth exists outside history; man and his narratives do not.

THE STRUCTURE OF PROVIDENCE

Providential historians, as much as Progressive historians or Marxist historians, must choose their material, emphasize certain events and people over other events and people, figure events in specific ways, begin and end with the illusion of origin and closure, and so on. They must, in other words, make use of a method more particular and specific than the one we denominate providential. They must methodize providence itself. Johnson's method is to bend providence to the rhythms of a threefold movement in time: the three stages of purity, peace, and plenty enunciated by Christ's herald in the opening pages. Book I, the longest of the three books, traces God's "preparation" of the land for settlement, the establishment of the first fourteen churches in the colony, and the gradual transformation of the "poore barren Wildernesse [into] a fruitfull Land" (108). Throughout this section, Johnson focuses on the "Temple," the pure and unified religion that these soldiers of Christ had not been able to establish in England: "I am now prest for the service of our Lord Christ," he has one soldier say, "to rebuild the most glorious Edifice of Mount Sion in a Wildernesse" (52). He records New England's attempts to establish the indivisible truth of congregational polity, and then to keep it pure. Narrating the history of the drought of 1633, for example, he paraphrases the New England settlers' prayers, in which they begged mercy of the Lord, "urging this as a chiefe argument, that the malignant adversary would rejoyce in their destruction, and blaspheme the pure Ordinances of Christ, trampling down his Kingly Commands with their own inventions" (86). They do not need to ask for rain itself; they need only plead that a lack of rain will lead to impure worship. Not surprisingly, "the Lord showred down water on their Gardens and Fields" even before their prayer had ended (86–87).

Johnson draws attention to this three-part structure even as he develops it. Midway through Book I he tells us that the description of "the manner of [New England's] Government is by the Author deferred till the year 1637, where the Reader may behold Government both in Churches and Common-wealth, to be an institution of the Lord" (87). The year 1637 is the transition year from Book I to Book II. "Peace," the focus of Book II, can only be established—and its progress narrated—once purity is. Again, twenty pages later, he argues that, "could Purity, Peace and Plenty run all in one channell, Gods people here should sure have met with none other, but the still waters of Peace and Plenty for back and belly soone contract much mudde, as you shall heare (God willing) in the following History" (101–2). "Peace and Plenty" will be established ("cleaned," in this image) later, in the order that Christ's herald predicted—that is, in the order that Johnson himself imposes on the history.

The purity of religion established in New England is a reaction to England's (Laodicea's) spiritual lukewarmness. The temple Johnson's soldiers establish is at one and the same time the "Edifice of Mount Sion" and a refuge or a retreat from those in England who refuse to establish such purity. The mission has two

goals. Through most of Book I, Johnson tries to buttress his audience's confidence in the success of the quest for purity. In a long
chapter that describes the settlement of the town of Concord, he
celebrates the triumph of purity through "a short Epitome of the
manner how" (111) Christ's New English "souldiers" were able to
establish towns and churches. Johnson focuses his narration here
on the settlers wandering confusedly in the woods, "sadly search-
[ing] up and down for a known way" (113) in the "howling Desart" (115), unable to locate the correct way to the place where
the Lord intends that they settle. Their wanderings are as metaphorical as they are real; and their subsequent success in establishing this particular plantation and church symbolizes New England's larger success in establishing purity and uniformity out of
the swamps and thickets and woods of human error (111–15).

But, almost as if He had waited for religion in New England to
become strong enough or pure enough to be tested, God now
allows "enemies to Reformation" to infiltrate the churches and
"oppose the pure and perfect truth of Christ" (121). The remaining pages of Book I are taken up with the spiritual battle between
those who are "for" purity and uniformity and those who are "for"
Satan's "deceaveible Doctrines" and "divisions." Johnson describes Satan's policy as "that machevillian Principle, divide and
overcome" (124), and he locates it in the public utterances of the
"Erronists," the followers of Anne Hutchinson. He understands
their goal to be the infiltration of the temple; here, as elsewhere,
Johnson conceives truth to be enclosed and self-contained, errors
to be dashing, "flowing" (130), "beating" (133), or "sliding"
(131) against that enclosed space. The Erronists are, of course,
unsuccessful: "the Churches of Christ in New England . . . have
hitherto been so far from imbracing the erronious Doctrines of
these times, that through the powers of Christ they have valiantly
defended the truth, and cut down all deceivable Doctrine" (137).

To assure his audience that he is right, Johnson then adds a
short narrative, another "epitome," that imaginatively supports his
assertion. This time, a "poore Soul" lands in New England in 1636,
wanders down "a narrow Indian path" where he loses his way in
what is clearly a wilderness of error, and is finally steered into the
"broade beaten way" by Thomas Shepard's sermon (134, 135).
After listening for two hours, the man is "metamorphosed": "now
he resolves (the Lord willing) to live and die" for the truth in all
its purity (136). He has been, like the wilderness itself and all other
godly soldiers shipped for America, transformed.

With purity secure, Johnson insists that now New England can withstand direct assaults on its mission. Hence, in the opening lines of the final chapter of Book I he carefully begins to shift his focus: "The vernall of the yeare 1637 . . . being now in his prime, and as the season of the yeare grew hotter, so the minds of many were hot in the eager pursuite of their selfe conceited opinions" (139). Book I represented New England's seven-year response to spiritual lukewarmness; this brief reference to summer points ahead to the fact that Book II will be New England's seven-year response to "heat," to the lust for liberty, for freedom from authority, for the desire to pursue any "selfe conceited opinion" that runs counter to truth's purity and unity. These "lusts" will prove to be much different from, say, the errors of the Hutchinsonians. Those were described as "fogs" (132), "bastardly brats" (125), a "darkness" in which Satan could divide and overcome the truth (131); these are consistently described in terms of heat. Such "hot" desires can only be defeated by the civil government, whose job it is—as the herald has proclaimed—to serve as the "Walles and Bulworkes . . . [of] Jerusalem" (32), to envelope truth so that the errors that dash against it, the "darkness" in which Satan tries to subvert it, and the "hot" lust of those within it cannot succeed. Book I closes with an account of New England's civil government, an account that Johnson had intentionally delayed until this point.

The civil government actually faces two kinds of threats in Book II of *Wonder-Working Providence.* The first threat is a series of attacks by opponents of New England. The book opens with four such "calamities," described once again as forces "breaking in" upon truth, forces that have hedged the colonists in:

> As the Lord surrounded his chosen Israel with dangers deepe to make his miraculous deliverance famous throughout, and to the end of the world, so here behold the Lord Christ, having egged a small handful of his people forth in a forlorne Wildernesse, stripping them naked from all humane helps, plunging them in a gulph of miseries, that they may swim for their lives through the Ocean of his Mercies, and land themselves safe in the armes of his compassion. (151)

Here, as elsewhere, Johnson is confident that God's providence has directed these settlers to New England, and that in doing so He has tested them, as metals are tested in the fire. Bradford and Winthrop began to write their histories with such confidence, but the experience of the New World confused them. Johnson has found a way to convert into metaphors of New England's mission signs that Bradford and Winthrop had read negatively or ambiguously. None of these four calamities—Erronists, episcopacy in England, the wilderness, and the threat of Indian attack—is confusing to Johnson. They all feed into the second stage of New England's three-stage mission. When the settlers have established purity then a civil government capable of resolving these calamities will be put into place. New England, the historian explains, has by 1637 the strength to "warre with the weapons [Christ] had furnished them" (174), real weapons to defeat the wilderness and the Indians, spiritual weapons to defeat episcopacy, legal weapons to defeat the Erronists. Peace is maintained, and New England saved from Satan's attempt to "choke" it off.

Most of Book II focuses on the civil government "looking after such as were like to disturb the peace of this new erected government; some persons being so hot headed for maintaining . . . sinfull opinions, that [the government] feared breach of peace" (175). As in Book I, when the people thought purity established only to see it attacked from within New England, so Johnson in this book describes how the people thought the "peace of this little Common-wealth [was] now in great measure settled" (182)—but it isn't. He makes the preceding statement under the heading of the year 1638, after the Pequot War and the Synod of 1637—the two crisis points of the 1630s—had been resolved. The New England settlers seem at that time to have achieved the peace that Christ's herald had proclaimed would be theirs, but immediately, a number of them become disenchanted with the "moderate" seasons of New England's climate:

> Then they wanted a warmer country, and every Northwest [winter] wind that blew, they crept into some odd chimney-corner or other, to discourse of the diversity of Climates in the Southerne parts, but chiefly of a thing very sweet to the palate of the flesh, called liberty, which they supposed might be very easily attain'd, could they but once come into a place where all men were chosen to the office of a Magistrate, and all were preachers of the Word, and no hearers, then it would be all Summer and no Winter. (207–8)

The problem here is not, as in the previous calamities faced by the government, that the settlers are besieged by external forces of evil; the problem is that some settlers mistake the moderate authority of ecclesiastical and civil polity for unnatural constraints, and they strive to break loose. (The urge is one that Winthrop identified as a product of man's corrupt, natural liberty.)

Johnson's "epitome," through which he resolves this crisis, once again turns landscape—"climate," more accurately, in this case—into metaphor. A company of settlers seeking this lawless liberty voyage to the (appropriately named) Summer Islands in the West Indies. There they are attacked by Spaniards who so harass them that "some of them returned back again for New England, being sore abashed at this providence that befel them, that they would never seek to be governed by liberty again to this very day" (208). They return to the self-contained shell of New England's truth. Others, "strongly bent for the heat of liberty," continue on to another island and institute there a colony whose charter establishes religious freedom for all: they nearly starve to death before God saves them by providentially sending a ship to take them off the island (209). The lesson is clear: "hot" liberty leads to toleration, which in turn leads to physical and spiritual starvation; "moderate" life under the New England government leads to intolerance (that is, purity), which in turn leads to peace and, as we shall soon see, plenty. The Summer Islands—or any other place where it is always summer—is unhealthy; so, too (the imagery implies), is any place where it is always winter: but the forty-second parallel, where New England lies, is perfect. "Upon this the Winters discourse ceased, and projects for a warmer Country were husht and done" (209).[13]

Book II ends in similar fashion to Book I. First, Johnson describes the planting of "a Town and Church . . . called Wooburn" (212). The focus now is not, as it was in his description of Concord in Book I, on the settlers as they stumble through real and metaphorical wilds in search of purity; it is on the establishment of a town and church that are both pure and peaceful. Accordingly, Johnson emphasizes the equitable distribution of land, the harmonious church covenant, and the peaceful welcoming of any settlers "willing to take up their dwellings within the said precinct"— except, he adds carefully, "such as [are] exorbitant, and of a turbulent spirit, unfit for a civil society, [whom] they would reject, till they came to mend their manners" (213). Woburn is an "epitome" of peace. Book II ends with another long concluding chapter, in which Johnson elaborates the military affairs of New England. Although these settlers had been soldiers of Christ from the beginning, "yet they knew right well the Temple was surrounded with walls and bulworks, and the people of God in re-edifying the same, did prepare to resist their enemies with weapons of war, even while they continued building" (227). Less directly than at the end of Book I, Johnson at the end of Book II orients us toward the theme of Book III. These military preparations reflect New England's condition in 1644, the year that ends Book II: "These souldiers of Christ Jesus, having made a fair retreat from their Native country hither, and now being come to a convenient station, resolved to stand it out . . . against all such as should come to rob them of their priviledges" (227). This statement seems merely to repeat ideas we heard before in Johnson's history. But two points are important: the heightened condition of military preparedness, which looks forward to the millennial pronouncements in Book III; and the fact that "now" New England has achieved "a convenient station." What awaits the reader in Book III are the consequences of that comfortable existence.

Book III describes a series of internalized failings produced by a life that is too easy. These failings are represented in some people by a "suddain forgetfulness of the Lords former received mercy" (254); in others by "frozen affections, and . . . barren breasts, that began to dry up with a lazy lethargy" (238); and in many by a "fulness" of spirit that causes them "even to loath the very honey-comb, insomuch that good wholesome truths would not down" (252–53). With the same care as he displays elsewhere, Johnson locates this coldness not just in the settlers but also in the landscape: "an Army of caterpillars," he says, fell upon the trees and "left them like winter-wasting cold, bare and naked" (253). Worse, this deadness of spirit and environment has a physical correlative in the population itself: "the death of divers personages, who were in great esteem with the people of New-England, famous for their godliness, and eminent parts, both for Magistracy and Ministery" (252)—John Winthrop, Thomas Shepard, Thomas Hooker, and many others. As he lists the leaders who have died, Johnson emphasizes not the passing of the first generation (which is, after all, his own), but merely the sense that New England needs to be brought back from those frozen regions by "the correcting hand of the Lord" (252). There is no declension here of the sort that ministers will decry in the 1660s and 1670s; Johnson transforms the loss of these beloved leaders into another necessary step within New England's progress toward perfection. Those deaths will be a positive experience, if God "shall once again be pleased to refine them in [that] furnace of his" (256) and if those "with more warmer affections exhort" (253) those who have become spiritually cold. Warmth is needed.

Johnson ends this shortest book of *Wonder-Working Providence* as he did the previous two, with a search for historical and imaginative resolution. He attempts to draw the third book as well as the history to their conclusion by two distinct steps, which both reaffirm the theme of Book III. First, he narrates a long poem that retells the sad facts of Book III. At the end of the poem, the historian cites these facts to prove "that either the Lord will raise up another people to himself to do his work, or raise [New England] up by his Rod to a more eager pursuit of his work" (261). Given the pattern of *Wonder-Working Providence* to this point, and given his reduction of the possible readings of New England's history to one negative and one affirmative reading, Johnson could probably rest assured of his reader's response. Christ's own herald had assured his audience, many pages and "years" earlier, that perseverance for only a little while longer—once this purity, peace, and plenty had been achieved—would bring down Antichrist and usher in the millennium.

Johnson's second step in the conclusion shows that New England is consciously reforming itself, putting off its worldliness, "warming" itself. He insists that the full purpose of New England is finally being fulfilled. That purpose, remember, was to provide a refuge for "such instruments [of Christ] to retreate as hee hath made strong for himself; that so [Christ's] adversaries glorying in the pride of their power . . . Christ causeth them to be cast downe suddenly forever" (24). So the herald had said, indicating that these soldiers would then be called back to England—or to wherever Christ "thinks meete to make use of" (25) them—in order to fight the battle of battles at the end of time. New England is both a military training ground and a refuge that will fool Satan into thinking Christ's forces debilitated. Hence, as if in atonement for their lethargic backsliding in Book III, the settlers "now endeavor to be assisting to others" (262). Some ministers are sent to England, John Eliot and others take pains to convert the Indians, other ministers are sent to Virginia, and still others pursue the work of Christ in Bermuda. Having served as a refuge for Christ's remnant, New England is now sending His soldiers back out into the larger world to fight His wars.

Remember, too, that as each Book is brought to this kind of narrative closure, Johnson points forward to what would come next: at the end of Book I, a chapter describing the civil government points to peace in Book II; in Book II, a chapter describing New England's "convenient station" points to plenty in Book III. Here Johnson points to the millennium:

> But to come to the time of Antichrist's fall . . .: yea it may be boldly said that the time has come, and all may see the dawning of the day. . . . Now the Lord will come and not tarry. As it was necessary that there should be a Moses and Aaron, before the Lord would deliver his people and destroy Pharaoh lest they should be wildred indeed in the Wilderness; so now it was needfull, that the Churches of Christ should first obtain their purity, and the civil government its power to defend them, before Antichrist come to his finall ruine: and because you shall be sure the day is come indeed, behold the Lord Christ marshalling of his invincible Army to the battell. (269–70)

Wonder-Working Providence is a cry of encouragement to New England's troops at the exact moment when it looked to everyone— England, Europe, Satan, even themselves—that such a "retreate" was a waste, an abysmal failure. In order to make that cry, Johnson has taken Winthrop's conception of this society as an exemplary city upon a hill and Bradford's conception of a pilgrimage and has consciously reworked them into the idea of a "retreate" that is strategic, not exemplary:

> the Forlorne hopes of Antichrists Army, were the proud Prelates of England; the Forlorne of Christs Armies, were these N.E. people, who are the subject of this History, which encountring each other for some space of time, ours being overpowered with multitude were forced to retreat to a place of greater safety, where they waited for a fresh opportunity to ingage with the main battel of Antichrist, so soon as the Lord shall be pleased to give a word of Command. (271)

The errand is to wait patiently for Christ's Word, which has not come yet. The "battel," Johnson says, has already begun—the right wing of Christ's army has been, and still is, fighting in England. But New England will not be needed until the crucial moment; it will be needed not for a mere civil "battel" between episcopacy and Independency but for the larger, more important battle between Babylon and Sion.

In order to revise New England's understanding of itself and its mission, Johnson restructures its history, shaping the twenty-one years from 1629 to 1651 into a progressive movement from purity to peace to plenty to participation in Armageddon. Out of a similar urge, the General Court had written to Parliament in 1651, humbly reminding them of what the colonists were up to:

> Let it therefore pleas you, most honourable, we humbly entreat, to take notice, hereby, what were our orders, upon what conditions and with what authority we came hither, and what we have done since our coming. We were the first moovers and undertakers of soe great an attempt, being men able enough to live in England with our neighbors, and being helpfull to others, and not needing the help of any for outward things, about three or four and twenty years since, seeing just cause to feare the persecution of the then bishops and high commission, for not conforming to the ceremonies then pressed upon the consciences of those under their power, we thought it our safest course to get to this outside of the world, out of their view and beyond their reach. ("Copy of a Petition" 428)

Johnson's history is an elaboration of and answer to the General Court's lament and confusion in that petition. *Wonder-Working Providence* is a myth about the construction of a community there at the "outside of the world."

Winthrop's image of the city upon the hill is still very much in play: at one point, Johnson has the herald prophesy that Christ's soldiers in New England "are to be set as lights upon a Hill more obvious than the highest Mountaine in the world" (29). Winthrop's model of man and society in the New World is still valuable: like Winthrop in his sermon, Johnson sees that Christ may very well perfect man in this new society; that New England's identity ideally lies in the future, in what this society will be and what it will do; and that New England's relevance lies outside the place itself, in the role that it will play in the final reformation of mankind. For Winthrop, however, that relevance hinged on the hope that men throughout the world might see and imitate the new society he envisioned. For Johnson—and herein lies the difference between the two conceptions—that relevance lies in New England's status as a refuge for soldiers, out of the ranks of which Christ will draw the saints he needs to defeat Satan's forces.[14] Johnson has revised both the history and the purpose of New England.

THE PROBLEM OF AUTHORITY

One major problem Johnson faced in his revision of the past was textual authority: how to ground his history in an authoritative form and narrate it in an authoritative voice. To authorize the structure of the past, he employs Christ's messenger at the beginning of the narrative; the messenger announces the three-part plan that the colonists are to follow and that Johnson himself transcribes. To authorize his own narrative voice, following the herald's injunction, he employs two biblical figures as types of himself. The first is David, whose story serves as a thematic touchstone at key points in the history and resembles New England's in its general outlines; in addition, David is a warrior-poet who, like Edward Johnson, first makes his nation's history and then sings of it.[15] The otherwise inexplicable presence of several dozen poems in Johnson's history becomes more purposeful when seen in this light. The history that both David and Edward Johnson make or sing is of "the glorious days" (183) of their nation, which had been chosen by God to fulfill his providential plans. Accordingly, the last line of *Wonder-Working Providence* is a fitting way to end this poetic history: "For thy words sake," Johnson quotes David, "and according to thine own heart, hast thou done all these great things, to make thy servant know them, 2 Sam[uel] 7.21" (275). David says this after God, through another herald Jonathan, has promised to "appoint a place for [His] people Israel. . . . And thine house [David] and thy kingdom shall be established for ever before thee: thy throne shall be established forever" (II Samuel 7.10, 16). The parallels with the history of New England as Johnson has written it are clear. David's voice is meant to lend credence to Johnson's.

The second figure is John, whose voice suffuses the narrative in references to the millennial landscape of his Revelation: "a new Heaven and new Earth" (25; Revelation 21.1), for example, or the "golden candlesticks" (239; Revelation 1.12–16).[16] Here too, however, Johnson refers even more explicitly to the authorizing presence of this other visionary:

> Oh you proud Bishops, that would have all the World stoope to your Lordly power, the heathen Romans your predecessors, after they

had banished John to the Isle of Pathmos, suffered him quietly to injoy the Revelation of Jesus Christ there; here is a people that have betaken themselves to a newfound World, distanced from you with the widest Ocean the World affords, and yet you grudge them the purity of Christs Ordinances there. (157)

The parallel here could be between John and the soldiers of New England, since they too are in exile and may also (according to Johnson's narration) "see" the millennial splendor of the final revelation; but Johnson must have been aware of the more obvious parallel between himself and John, and between *Wonder-Working Providence* and Revelation. For, like Revelation, this history opens with the speaking of God's word (Revelation 1.11–3.22), moves on to recount what the exilic writer has "seen," and ends with the promise that "the time is at hand" when Satan shall be bound and the new Jerusalem established on earth. Indeed, there is even the sense, as Johnson ends Book III with the proof that the "refuge" in America is now sending soldiers to fight that last battle elsewhere, that the Revelation of John stands as the already-written Book IV of *Wonder-Working Providence*. Just as "the Lord Christ will overturn, overturn, overturn [the civil government in England], till he hath caused such a Government to be set up, as shall become nursing fathers to his new-planted Churches" (262), so Johnson the historian "overturns, overturns, overturns" New England—through lukewarmness, heat, and cold—until the perfect "refuge" created in America proves itself worthy and ready to serve in the battles prophesied by John.

With his authority figured in the structure announced by the herald and in his voice as prophet-historian, Johnson is able to reconstruct New England's history into a progressive movement from purity to peace to plenty to—in the space beyond Book III— participation in Armageddon. Rhetorically, the history attempts to redeem New England: for outsiders, Johnson tries to lift New England to a preeminent position in world affairs; for insiders, he revises the meaning and purpose of the settlement itself. It is due in part, I suspect, to this double vision that Johnson's trope of "retreate" contains a certain ambiguity.

Let me explain. Johnson begins by asserting that New England is a type of Israel, which implies that these settlers have left England/Egypt to locate their permanent home on the other side of the Atlantic Ocean/Red Sea. Then, he augments this metaphor of "retreate" by implying that the emigration is temporary and strategic, that it is merely a tactical ploy within a larger military strategy. Home? or flanking maneuver? The ambiguity is pervasive: "Could Caesar," the herald asks,

> so suddenly fetch over fresh forces from Europe to Asia, Pompy to foyle? How much more shall Christ who createth all power, call over this 900 league Ocean at his pleasure, such instruments as he thinks meete to make use of in this place, from whence you are now to depart, but further that you not delay the Voyage intended, for your full satisfaction know *this is the place* where the Lord will create a new heaven, and a new Earth in new Churches, and a new Commonwealth together. (24–25, emphasis added)

Is England to be the place where God creates a new heaven, after the main battle is fought there by New England's soldiers? Or is New England to be the new heaven, though its soldiers may fight on a battlefront established in the old country? Johnson seems to mean England, a reading that squares with his revision of New England's mission as a temporary retreat. But his comment that "this is the place" can also be read as a reference to New England. The historian, like many of his contemporaries, was leaving his options open in 1651. And to read his history as *either* triumphant *or* enervated is to miss the tremendous ambiguity at the center of Johnson's revision of the past.[17] His history allows for two widely divergent readings on the meaning of New England as a place. He was, for the time being at least, hedging his bets.

In a general sense, Johnson, like many other colonial writers, is simply well aware of the different ways in which "margin" and "center" will read his work. The fear of being forgotten, ignored, mistreated, or abused is inherent in the colonial condition; colonial historians like Cotton Mather, Robert Beverley, and William Byrd will continue to be fascinated by the same theme well into the eighteenth century. In a narrower sense, Johnson's ambiguity reflects New England's cultural anxiety in the 1640s and 1650s. After all, the return migration in the 1640s indicated that many New Englanders cared little about where the New Jerusalem was; they simply wanted to help bring it into being (Delbanco 184–214). Johnson was trying to speak both to those who stayed and to those who left. His solution is ambiguous to the very end because the "home" he describes may, indeed, be only temporary. Such ambiguity was not necessarily problematic, evidently, since it was and would continue to be an integral part, in various ways, of New England's sense of itself./ "Errand," we learned long ago, can mean at least two different things (Miller *Errand* 1–15); so can Johnson's "refuge." Culture does not need to be logical./

And yet, even as Johnson appropriates this divine, prophetic authority and constructs his revision of the past, he alludes to the fact that his narrative is not essentially truthful. The aside in reference to the barber that I cited earlier—"the example is for the living, the dead is judged of the Lord alone" (192)—discloses a conviction that examples for the living are more important than, let's say, the debate over who is and who is not a saint that annoyed the Synod of 1646–1648. Johnson reveals in his brief comment on the barber a larger impatience with other means of addressing New England's cultural uncertainty in the late 1640s, means that may well have included *The Cambridge Platform*, pasted together by the Synod of 1646–1648. We "stand at a stay," he remarks bitterly near the end of the narrative, "as if the Lord had no farther work for his people to do, but every bird to feather his own nest" (260). He sees here what Winthrop saw in the 1640s: the people have lost a sense of purpose in the mission; they are merely looking out for themselves. Winthrop's charity has not proved a tie that binds, and neither has Bradford's notion of pilgrimage. In such a vacuum, what is needed is a way for the community to feather its own nest, a way for the community to understand itself as a community. The people need a "home," a convincing story about themselves.

Johnson's narrative is designed to provide just such a feathering, a reconstructed narrative that makes the New England of 1653 into a nest. The impulse is the same impulse as lies behind Bradford's retreat from history at the end of *Plymouth Plantation*—the blank entries for 1647 and 1648 (347)—and his advance into the genres of poetry and dialogue to reconfigure the meaning and purpose of New England (Sargent; Arch). Hence, in one of his later poems, "Some observations of God's merciful dealing with us," Bradford tries to recall his community to its original purpose by showing how Israel, which was blessed with a "golden age" just as New England had been, "degenerated" in the years following the deaths of Joshua and many other "elders":

> Yet [Israel] did soon forget and turn aside,
> And in his truth and ways did not abide;

But i'the next age they did degenerate;
I wish this may not be New England's fate. (477)

This turn toward typology and the rhetoric of nostalgia he had so
often eschewed in *Of Plymouth Plantation* is simply a refiguring of
his discomfort at the direction events were heading in the 1640s;
rather than continue faithfully to record those events, as he had
promised his readers, Bradford attempts in other genres to redirect them. To writers other than Johnson, in the late 1640s and
1650s, the colony's purpose, as well as the historical forms in which
that purpose was inscribed, seemed desperately in need of reconfiguration.

Johnson's *Wonder-Working Providence* not only addresses a cultural crisis, it does so in a self-consciously fictive way. Let me give
one more brief example of this self-conscious artifice, one to which
I alluded earlier. Book I closes with an account of New England's
civil government, an account that the narrator says has been "deferred till [the end of Book I]" (81) precisely because the seven-
year stage of peace, which that government initiates, can only be
recounted once the seven-year stage of purity is established and
recounted.[18] In other words, the narrative is an admittedly self-
conscious construction of reality: the cycle of purity-peace-plenty
itself is not necessarily true, though it may indeed be useful. The
narrative is—and knows itself to be—a "construction," which is
itself simply part of the larger process of "re-constructing" and
"re-edifying" (227) its audience. Examples for the living must be
"made" to be useful; the events of the past must be "made" to fit
a useful purpose. New England must be "made." The historian's
job is to construct the past. The reader's job is to "dwell" within
that construction, to be edified by and assumed into it much as is
the settler who hears Thomas Shepard's sermon in Book I (a fact
that in itself helps explain why Johnson must bring so much rhetorical authority to bear in his narrative), much as are the "stones"
or settlers who are the heroes of Johnson's narrative. Edification,
it seems clear, is Johnson's tropical solution to the problem that
confronted Winthrop in the 1640s.

In this sense, Johnson's history, though often seen as anoma-
lous, accurately reflects the urge in New England in the late 1640s
and later to revise the meaning and purpose of the corporate enterprise. Rhetorically—and somewhat illogically it might seem to

us—his history both records and tries itself to achieve the edification of New England, much as *The Cambridge Platform* tried at the same time both to "maintain" the community's faith and establish unity within that same community by public edification (194), and much as Bradford's late sermons in prose and poetry were designed both to prove and to teach the rising generation about the intellectual and moral foundations of New England.[19] Johnson, like these other authors, was striving to construct in words what the Pilgrims had constructed in wood and mud on that Christmas Day in 1620, "the first house for common use to receive them" (*Plymouth Plantation* 72). The stories that had carried them from England no longer served their purpose; new stories, like Johnson's, had to be constructed.

TRANSFORMING SOCIETY

Wonder-Working Providence is similar in tone, design, and purpose to many polemical tracts that flowed from New England's pens in the 1640s and 1650s. In those years the entire New England orthodoxy began to reconceive the mission along the same lines as Johnson's history; events "seemed to conspire to cause New England to reconceive itself as a 'peculiar and separate people' like the tribes of Israel" (Heimert and Delbanco 195). Johnson attempts to reshape cultural confusion into an organized, coherent myth of settlement in which the colonists are exalted, raised to a preeminent position in the history of God's providence to man, constructing a coherent and powerful myth with which to "edify" his community. The confused man who disembarks in New England at the height of the Antinomian Controversy wanders in an actual wilderness that is an analogue of his mental state: "Oh, woe is mee," he moans as he passes among the "sencelesse Trees and eccohing [*sic*] Rocks," that no one can "shew me a way" among these errors (134). Thomas Shepard does show him the "broade beaten way"—in Johnson's New England the straight and narrow path is trod by many—and "the man [is] metamorphosed" (136).[20] Just so does Johnson intend his narrative to convert his audience, not to transcendent truths, as it were, but to useful action.

Indeed, Johnson consistently describes the experience of the New World as a transforming force on people, business, ideas, farming, even nature. Transformation is a central trope in *Wonder-Working Providence*. The historian begins to emphasize it almost immediately after he has the herald finish his proclamation: Christ, he says, "prepared [the country] for his peoples arrivall" by "smiting" the local Indian tribes with a plague; "by this means [He] . . . not only made roome for his people to plant; but also tamed the hard and cruell hearts of these barbarous Indians" (41). A "warlike people" (41) was temporarily reduced to meekness, allowing Christ's soldiers just enough time to gain a foothold on the coast. "And now let every . . . heart admire," Johnson cries, "and inlarge itself to the astonishment of the whole man at this wonderous work of the great Jehovah . . . that wrought such . . . wonderfull Alterations . . . in this dismal Desart" (48).

Throughout the history he returns to this idea that the land itself has been transformed: "a desolate and barren Wildernesse . . . which the Lord in his wonderfull mercy hath turned to fruitfull fields" (68); a "poore barren Wildernesse become a fruitfull land" (108); "this remote, rocky, barren, bushy, wild-woody wildernesse . . . become a second England for fertilnes in so short a space, that it is indeed the wonder of the world" (210). Of course, Bradford and Winthrop had described the settlement of the land, too. But Johnson organizes the pattern of settlement into an orderly and progressive expansion from the temple (purity) to the walls of the city (the civil government enforcing peace) to the land itself (plenty). Man and nature, society and wilderness, are transformed. "Thus hath the Lord been pleased," he says near the end of the history, "to turn one of the most hideous, boundless, and unknown Wildernesses in the world in an instant, as 'twere . . . to a well-ordered Commonwealth" (248). In this sense, the commonwealth serves as a metaphor for man's ability to achieve purity and peace, while the wilderness metaphorically represents his sinful, fallen nature. It comes as no surprise, then, that in Johnson's history the wilderness is a real and appropriate dwelling place not only for Satan (a common notion in the seventeenth century), but also for the Hutchinsonians and Samuel Gorton. Those who espouse errors live in the "Thickets" (112); Christ's "souldiers" live in a "well-ordered Commonwealth" (248).

Johnson's history, though certainly a defense of the purity of the New England Way, is at the same time—and less consciously so, I believe—a defense of New England as a specific place with a specific history that has for the first time been identified, in literary terms, as belonging to a particular people. In short, unlike Bradford's and Winthrop's histories, *Wonder-Working Providence* is patriotic. The defense is of the refuge itself, not simply the act of seeking refuge; it is a defense of the land, and of the people who have cut out of the wilderness a self-sufficient, orderly, productive community. Johnson develops it through a series of descriptions of the country:

> [Whereas] at their first comming it was a rare matter for a man to have foure or five Acres of Corne, now many have four or five score, and [they] . . . labour with more ease: to great admiration also inlarg'd it, for it was with sore labour that one man could Plant and tend foure Acres of Indians Graine, and now with two Oxen hee can Plant and tend 30. (154)
>
> . . . The scituation of this Colledg [Harvard] is very pleasant, at the end of a spacious plain, more like a bowling green then a Wilderness, neer a fair navigable river, environed with many Neighbouring Towns of note, being so neer, that their houses joyn with her Suburbs; the building thought by some to be too gorgeous for a Wilderness. . . . This hath been a place certainly more free from temptations to lewdness then ordinarily England hath been. (201–2)
>
> . . . [Now] good white and wheaten bread is no dainty, but even ordinary man hath his choice, if gay clothing, and a liquerish tooth after sack, sugar, and plums lick not away his bread too fast, all which are but ordinary . . . the poorest person in [the land] hath a house and land of his own, and bread of his own growing, if not some cattel: beside, flesh is now no rare food, beef, pork, and mutton being frequent in many houses, so that this poor Wilderness hath not onely equalized England in food, but goes beyond it in some places for the great plenty of wine and sugar . . . apples, pears, and quince tarts. . . . Poultry they have plenty. (210)

The lists of lavish plenty, of the self-subsistent economy, of occupations held and products marketed, of the towns, the homes, and the university that is founded: Johnson insists that, in the changeable air of the New World, society and even nature might—if man is not "of a turbulent spirit" (213)—be made anew. Mankind and society, fragmented in the Old World, has been refashioned in the new. The lists, the catalogues, and the rhapsodies do not indicate, as has been wrongly asserted, the declension of second-generation New England; they indicate the desire to encompass the tremendous plenty of a new world.[21]

They are part and parcel of the myth Edward Johnson constructs. Of course, it is the very need to mythologize, to turn formerly confusing events into a recognizable narrative, that records the growing distance between England and New England in the 1640s and 1650s: settlers, even those in exile, do not need myths that differ from the myths of their homeland until they begin to see themselves as unique. Johnson's *Wonder-Working Providence* marks the moment in the seventeenth century when the distance between home and colony had grown to be critical. As a historian, Johnson does more than express New England's superiority to England and the Old World; he expresses its emotional and spiritual independence from it. He constructs a new version of the past out of confusing events that Winthrop and Bradford failed to understand. In his history, each event takes on a new meaning, in which New England is invariably recast, not just as a city upon a hill, but as a place where Christ's soldiers can find a refuge or can "re-treate" from the "tyranny of Antichrist," "re-edify" the temple and city of God, and usher in the millennium. Winthrop could not revitalize the "scattered bones" of New England; in Johnson's history, they are revivified:

> Bright shining shall [the] Gospel come,
>   Oh glorious King of Saints,
> Thy blessed breath confounds thy foes,
>   all mortal power faints,
> The ratling bones together run
>   with self-same breath that blows,
> Of Israels sons long dead and dry,
>   each joynt their sinew grows,
> Fair flesh doth cover them, and veins
>   (lifes fountain) takes there place. (203)

Where Winthrop and Bradford could in the end find only confusion and fragmentation, Johnson finds significance and creates social order and communal purpose out of it.

Rhetorically, Johnson refigured Winthrop's *History of New England* and Bradford's *Of Plymouth Plantation;* methodologically, he comprehended or grasped the meaning of events they were unable to grasp. Johnson spoke in 1651 in a new way and with a new authority because he perceived that New England in the early years of the Puritan Commonwealth was faced with a set of problems that the early idealism of Winthrop could not solve, problems that were both internal (such as the people's resistance to authority) and external (such as England's attitude toward the colonies). Hence, my title to this chapter is intended to suggest one way Johnson addresses those problems. His history "edifies"; it teaches his audience about the meaning and purpose of New England. That is, Johnson tries to provide a new way to understand the corporate enterprise, a way that in the course of things necessitated a particular sort of revision of the past. Johnson fills what Nathaniel Ward referred to as that "empty thing" called time (Ward 49), makes the events of the past into a new, yet recognizable, story, and offers the resulting narrative to his audience as a description of the past, present, and future that will, with their cooperation, become a lived, not simply a linguistic, structure. His narrative revolves around the trope of edification, making it a central theme, because both the audience reading the narrative and the past itself are being edified or structured. In *Wonder-Working Providence,* history is being built, fortified, defended, and—sometime in the future that, from God's point of view, had already happened—enjoyed in a timeless, perfect place called Sion.

My title to this chapter also suggests, a bit more obliquely, the way Johnson addresses the more general problem that all New England historians had to face: how to bring authority to bear in and upon the narrative. His history is edified, is a structure to be inhabited, is external to his audience and his audience's previous experience. Accordingly, he must appeal to the highest authority possible in his world—Christ the Savior, and through Him, two of his most visionary spokesmen—in order to "authorize" that external edifice. Johnson must, like Milton several years later in *Paradise Lost,* claim in essence that the story is not "his." His appeal to Christ's herald early in the narrative is thus much more than simply a way into the story; it is the strategy through which a simple "stone"—no matter whether a "joiner," a militia captain, or a university-trained aristocrat—can speak at all, much less speak with the authority of those other figures, Christ and David and John, who foresaw the glorious future, at the end of human history, of Sion—or, if you preferred, of New England.

History in Pieces

Increase Mather
and the New England Past

3

Edward Johnson's *Wonder-Working Providence* was not printed in New England until William Poole's edition of 1867, more than two hundred years after its first printing in England. But later generations' lack of interest in such an important work of colonial historiography should not obscure the fact that the historical imagination flourished in New England in the 1650s and 1660s. The execution of Charles I in January 1648/49 had quite obviously marked the end of an era, even the end of a world view. Some American Puritans reacted to it in confusion ("a very solemn and strange act," John Hull wrote in his diary, "and God alone can work good by so great a change" [qtd. in Dunn, *Puritans* 55]) but they soon turned their attention to the future—and to the past. Until the Restoration in 1660 many continued to imagine New England as a "model" for the Old World, issuing strident instructions to their former Independent allies in England about the proper institution and administration of a godly commonwealth. This supreme, though naive, self-confidence manifested itself not simply in works like Thomas Cobbett's *The Civil Magistrate's Power* (1653) and John Eliot's *The Christian Commonwealth* (1660; written ca. 1651), which contained specific advice for Cromwell's England, but also in Massachusetts' severe intolerance in the 1650s. With the exception of Rhode Island, New England colonies had never tolerated a very wide range of dissent, but in the 1650s the orthodoxy's insistence on uniformity reached an almost hysterical pitch. John Clarke, an Anabaptist from Rhode Island, vividly recounted his persecution at the hands of Massachusetts Bay authorities in 1651; his was only one of many stories involving harassment, whippings, fines, banishment, and eventually capital punishment. In 1658 the General Court of Massachusetts Bay attempted to stem a perceptibly growing tide of Quakerism by banishing all Quakers from the colony, and promising death to those who returned. As the orthodox might have suspected—had they still been able to read Foxe's *Book of Martyrs* from the point of view from which it had been written—the Quakers did return. Four of them were hanged in the next two years. Upon his restoration, Charles II demanded that Massachusetts put an end to such executions.[1]

Massachusetts' harsh treatment of these more radical Protestants was a result of its having codified intolerance in the 1640s, and then, of its frustration at the way people—Anabaptists, Quakers, all of England, it seemed—misunderstood the logic of such a position. Willfully, perhaps wishfully, New England continued to insist upon a narrowly defined uniformity, to punish dissent, and to believe that these aspects of the New England Way would be adopted by the Lord Protector. One senses, here, the importance of the tremendous distance between London and Boston in the seventeenth century: New England was so far removed from the exigencies of the Civil War and of its aftermath that it was unable to comprehend the need for toleration (to form a working political coalition in the late 1640s) and, a decade later, the desire for toleration (to end twenty years of enervating and demoralizing strife). In 1662 the Crown followed its demand that Massachusetts stop hanging Quakers by issuing a more general demand that it become more tolerant. Off and on for nearly thirty years, until the series of toleration acts adopted in England after the Glorious Revolution, Boston continued to receive such demands. They were, for the most part, ignored. The level of toleration apparently did increase in New England in those years, but it did so more as a result of slowly evolving public opinion within the United Colonies than pressure from London (see Holifield).

Because many New Englanders had continued to imagine their society as the model for England's reformation, the Restoration itself came as a shock, jolting Massachusetts into a conception of itself, after 1660, as the last, isolated outpost of light in a world of darkness. That shock was only intensified by conditions within the colonies in the late 1650s and early 1660s: the original leaders of the various enterprises to settle New England continued to die, leading Michael Wigglesworth to comment, in 1662, that "The brightest of our morning stars / Did wholly disappeare" (lines 137–38); a severe drought in 1661–1662 punished the land and the economy; and even worse, the issues clustered around the settlement that eventually became known as the Halfway Covenant were raised, debated (sometimes acrimoniously), and settled (rather uncomfortably as it turned out) in the Synod of 1662.

Wigglesworth's long narrative history poem "God's Controversy with New England" attempts to fit the changed circumstances of New England in the early 1660s into a framework derived from Johnson's *Wonder-Working Providence*. Like Johnson, Wigglesworth conceives of New England as a "hiding place" that God had provided for His "redeemed ones," and of the covenant He made with His redeemed settlers as a guarantee that both "temp'rall blessings" and "spiritual good things" would abound to those settlers: "God's throne was here set up," he says, echoing Johnson, "This was the place" (lines 76–78, 117–18, 121–23). But this prosperity soon gives way in the poem to "a strange and suddain change," the deaths of New England's leaders; "And those that tarried behind / With sack-cloth covered were" (lines 135, 139–40). Such deaths are obviously external signs of internal failings, as God Himself takes time to point out in the lines that follow: how is it, He asks, that in New England He finds

> In stead of holiness Carnality,
> In stead of heavenly frames an Earthly mind,
> For burning zeal luke-warm Indifferency,
> For flaming Love, key-cold Dead-heartedness,
> For temperance (in meat, and drinke, and cloaths) excess? (lines
>   210–14)

Wigglesworth seems to be alluding to one of the systems of tropes (lukewarmness, heat, and cold) that organizes Johnson's history. But whereas Johnson turned these failings in the settlers into a vision of historical progress and millennial triumph, Wigglesworth is hardly so sure of success. Running through a lengthy and more detailed list of New England's failures, God goes on to point out that He has refrained from destroying the community only for the sakes of "some there be that still retain / Their ancient vigour and sincerity" (lines 239–40). The allusion to Genesis 18.16–33, where God agrees to spare Sodom and Gomorrah for the sake of ten righteous men, could hardly have been comforting to Wigglesworth's audience; they would have known all too well how that particular story ended. And not surprisingly, God has nothing good to say about Wigglesworth's contemporaries, "the Generation that [has succeeded] / The men, whose eyes have seen my great and awfull deeds" (lines 327–28). He promises to destroy it if it does not repent of its too-sensual life. When finally, after more than one hundred lines, God has finished speaking, the stunned narrator stands in isolation, surveying New England: all he sees in the span of time since God spoke is sickness, famine, illness, and disease. There is no hope, he assures us, seconding God's own argument, unless the present generation reforms.

The logic of Wigglesworth's poem indicates that something dramatic has changed in the writing of New England's history: God speaks here not at the beginning of the venture, sanctioning it, giving rise to it, but in the midst of it, shattering the illusion of blessed beginnings and of the continuity of time. He splits the community's history into two parts: the "first" times, and the present day. There is no doubt that "God's Controversy" is one of the texts from which scholars have derived the notion of "generations" in seventeenth-century New England; but we should remember that the so-called second generation (Wigglesworth, Danforth, Increase Mather et al.) actually invented it, and invented it for a reason. The trope of declension was a way during the Restoration to account for New England's isolation, its ambivalences, its confusions, not simply to describe them. On a small scale, then, Wigglesworth's poem can be seen as a revision of Johnson's history, merely one in a series of tentative revisions that would be more fully elaborated in Increase Mather's historical narratives in the 1670s and 1680s.

It is interesting to note that, again within the logic of Wigglesworth's poem, the cited causes of God's controversy with the country do not really "cause" God's anger. For example, the historian begins the poem by speaking of the glorious days of settlement; then, quite suddenly, he notices that "The brightest of our morning starrs / Did wholly disappeare." Nothing else seems wrong, until this point in the poem. Now, however, God begins to speak, angrily accusing the settlers of backsliding. The historian meekly follows His tirade with the remark that from "that day forward hath the Lord / Apparently contended / With us in Anger, and in Wrath: / But we have not amended" (lines 347–50). Thus, whereas in *Wonder-Working Providence* God (through His herald) initiates New England's history and then permits the historian to control the narrative, here in "God's Controversy" He narrates it Himself. Rhetorically, the historian depends on God to tell the sad story of the past. "And though we may be cast out by men," John Norton remarked in an election-day sermon in 1661, "yet may we hope that God will look after his outcasts, and care for us, being outcasts for the truth" ("Sion" 15). Wigglesworth needs Him to do more than look after them; he needs Him to tell them what, exactly, they have been doing wrong, for although he knows something is wrong, the historian-poet does not know what that something is. He, like the community figured in the poem, is confused.

REFIGURING

It is no coincidence that the genre of biography is first put to use in New England at this cultural moment. John Norton's *Abel Being Dead, Yet Speaketh; or, The Life and Death of . . . John Cotton*, published in 1658, is one attempt to bring order out of the apparent cultural chaos signified by the deaths of leaders like Hooker, Shepard, and Cotton. Norton, accordingly, figures Cotton as a survivor: Cotton survives in his Lincolnshire pulpit because, due to various lobbying efforts on his behalf in the courts, he is "treated . . . as if he were a conformable man" (17); before emigrating to New England, he escapes imprisonment by hiding out in London, much as Moses, David, and Jesus Christ hid themselves before withdrawing "from the lust of [their] Persecutors" (20–21); he survives the Antinomian Controversy (unnamed in the text) unscathed by offering such "eminent behaviour throughout, as argued in the conscience of the spectators singular patience" (34); he even "survives" his own death to speak to the "generation present, and to many an one that is to come" (4).[2] As Edward Gallagher has noted, Cotton's long-suffering patience, persecutions, and afflictions, not his piety or his doctrine or his writings, dominate Norton's narrative (Introduction xxiv–xxv).

Cotton is a survivor because he is passive. He refuses to attack others, including the oppressive High Church party of William Laud, preferring to enjoy the "desarts" of the American wilderness rather than openly resist those oppressions. "The non-resistance and softness of the Wooll breaks the force of the Cannon, and so saveth both the bullett and it self," Norton explains (34). Throughout the narrative, Cotton is wool, if not woolly. (Or, as Don Rosenberg waggishly suggested to me, Norton's Cotton is indeed "cottony.") He gives, never breaking, always absorbing the criticisms of his enemies. Emigration itself, Norton goes on to say,

> was not a flight from duty, but from evident, and regularly evitable danger; not from the evil of persecution, but from the evil of obstruction unto servicableness. It was not a flight from duty, but unto duty; not from the profession of the Truth, but unto a more opportune place for the profession of it. (21)

As David D. Hall has pointed out, Norton's defense of Cotton in this manner reflects the crisis of legitimacy New England's ministers, especially, felt during the Civil War and the Protectorate. Giles Firmin, Hugh Peters, and a dozen others returned to England in the 1640s to take part in events there; "another dozen either planned or executed a withdrawal from the colonies" in the 1650s, including a young and idealistic Increase Mather (Hall, *Faithful* 171).[3] Norton was among those who planned to withdraw. But his biography of Cotton apparently came on the heels of his decision to stay in New England and, as such, attempts to bridge the darkness of the present moment—the deaths of leaders like Cotton, as well as the sense of missing the history being made in England—and the uncertain future. He concludes the biography by referring to that darkness: "Now our Candlesticks cannot but lament in darkness, when their Lights are gone" (46). This image of himself and his contemporaries having been stranded harks back to an earlier image of the "first" and "second" times:

> So God disposeth of the hearts of hearers, as that generally they are all open and loving to their Preachers in their first times: Trials are often reserved until afterwards. . . . The Disciples in their first mission want nothing, and return all safe; but after [Christ's] death they met with other entertainment, and come short home. Young *Peter* girdeth himself and walks whither he will; but Old *Peter* is girded by another, and carried whither he would not. (16)

Although Norton is here referring to Cotton's separate experiences in Lincolnshire and in Boston, the relevance of this passage to his contemporary audience should be clear. Having lost its leaders, New England has now but "very few [sons] that take her by the hand of all the sons which she hath brought up" (46). It is now experiencing the "Trials" reserved until "afterwards" when the clear light of truth has become darkened (16).

Norton's solution in the narrative has to do with perspective. "The fixing of a Beleevers eye aright, hath a vivifical and marvellous influence upon his heart. . . . A Christian runneth cheerfully and indefiledly, over the foulest part of the race set before him, looking into Jesus" (50). He asks his readers to ignore the darkness of the times and to focus their attention on the eternal goal of redemption. What this means, as Heimert and Delbanco have recently pointed out, is "that what one does matters less than the spirit in which one does it" (211). Indeed, Cotton's passivity, as figured by Norton, is just such an example of focusing on the result (redemption) not on the race itself (life, lived events, history). Retreat to New England is not important in the sense that Edward Johnson had figured it (as a strategic military mission); it is important because, no matter what anyone else thought it meant, it was done in a spirit of faith—"not a flight from duty, but unto duty"— even though that duty is never explicitly defined in the narrative itself.

In this sense, the specific events of history are not important in Norton's narrative: his argument insists that darkness and trials and tribulations are merely part of the "normal" spiritual race, and must be endured (that is, ignored). There is, in fact, no need for the biographer even to name the Antinomian Controversy: the specifics of the case are unimportant. In this sense Norton's method, as Underhill's in *Newes From America*, denies the relevancy of the specifics of history. Specific events or lives do not point forward in time; they point upward, out of linear time and toward the unchanging realm of the Christic self. If one has faith in Christ— the goal—one will triumph, just as Cotton did, through a precise mixture of doctrine, example, and discipline (8).

But what if a person, or a community, did not have faith? Of what use was Cotton's example if doctrine and discipline and faith itself were uncertain? Norton's method was not appealing to people who were even less certain than he was that God's purposes, or even John Cotton's, were self-evidently clear.

The orthodox faith was attacked in a number of treatises that
have been largely forgotten by scholars and critics: John Clarke's *Ill
Newes From New England* (1652), Samuel Gorton's *Simplicities Defence
Against Seven-Headed Policy* (1646), William Pynchon's *The Meritorious Price of Our Redemption* (1650), William Aspinwall's several
works on the Fifth Monarchy.[4] But that much was to be expected.
What was more disconcerting—and what is key to many of the historical narratives written in New England between the Restoration
and the Glorious Revolution—was the feeling that something was
not quite right within the orthodox position. The Halfway Covenant of 1662 is not the only expression of this feeling; it is merely
symptomatic. The dilemma over whether to extend church membership to as-yet-unregenerate descendants of the saints or to restrict it to those who themselves could convincingly demonstrate
that they had experienced saving faith gave rise to the same sort
of confusion as Wigglesworth's narrator expresses in "God's Controversy." In both cases, what was at stake was nothing less than
the definition of a Puritan commonwealth—of the community itself. This confusion also manifests itself in the Third Church controversy, in debates about New England's relationship to England,
and in the turmoil of King Philip's War. These incidents were all
symptomatic of a general cultural confusion. To many of its members, the community seemed unfocused and misdirected.

Nathaniel Morton's history of Plymouth, *New Englands Memoriall*
(1669), is another historical text that tries to deal with this confusion. Working directly out of Book II of his uncle's *Of Plymouth
Plantation*, Morton organizes his history in the form of annals; his
narrative claims to be a yearly catalogue of God's "gracious dispensations" to the "first Beginners of this Plantation in New-England," written for the benefit of those beginners' children ("To
the Christian Reader" [xviii-xix]). Transcribing from Bradford's
manuscript entries, Morton is able to lift his narrative almost directly from Bradford's pages. Until he reached the pages for 1647,
when Bradford lapsed into silence, Morton had to write little new
text.

What is most interesting in this use of Bradford's history is Morton's omission of those very incidents that I and others have found
central to understanding Bradford's historiographic enterprise—
the horrible case of bestiality, Bradford's melancholy at the disper-
sion of the community, Uncas's murder of Miantonomo.[5] It is significant that Morton retains the account of Brewster's death; he

even uses it to launch a series of short elegies, which in effect constitute the latter half of *New Englands Memoriall*, when he no longer has his uncle's manuscript to direct him. Hooker, Winthrop, Cotton, Dudley, Winslow, Standish, Bradford, Partridge, Norton, Stone, Endicott, Wilson, and Mitchell are just some of the figures "commemorized" ("To the Christian Reader" n.p.) there. In this half of the narrative, too, omissions are obvious: for example, the Halfway Covenant is not mentioned under the entries for 1660–1662. The deaths of New England's leaders fill the pages, crowding out the rest of history. Without the template of Bradford's history, Morton sees nothing but death in New England's history. But like Wigglesworth's narrator in "God's Controversy," Morton is unable to say, exactly, what those deaths signify. At one point, he states: "This year [1668] it pleased'God to visit *New-England* with the manifestation of his displeasure, by the death of three Eminent Instruments" (190), but he does not then tell his audience what those deaths mean. God's displeasure is inscrutable. Remember these men, he insists, for "if yet notwithstanding afterwards [the people] forget, and not regard those [of God's] great Works presented [here]," then God "will destroy [the people], and not build them up" (198). Within this catalogue of deaths, Morton reveals neither a sense of history nor a strategy for dealing with the confusion generated by those deaths. Like Wigglesworth, he does not have an effective way to explain what is happening to New England. Memory, the ritual of remembering, has taken on a life of its own in his narrative.

Increase Mather came into his own in the 1660s, when Morton and Norton and Wigglesworth were struggling with the ambiguity of New England's history and purpose. He was born in 1639, at the height of the economic prosperity of the young Massachusetts Bay colony—his father, Richard Mather, named him Increase because of the "never-to-be-forgotten *Increase*, of every sort, wherewith God favoured the Country, about the time of his Nativity" (Scheick 87)—and he lived long enough to engage in a bitter public debate over smallpox inoculation with Benjamin Franklin's brother James, in the pages of the *New England Courant* and the *Boston Gazette*. He died two years after that incident, having been, his old opponent Benjamin Colman observed, "a Father to us all" (qtd. in Miller, *From Colony to Province* 481).

Throughout his life, Mather would struggle against what he perceived as the forces of evil in the world: those New Englanders who wished to open churches to the children of halfway members in the 1660s; apostates from the New England Way in the 1670s; the agents of the Crown in the 1680s; opponents of the new Massachusetts Bay charter in the 1690s; the French during Queen Anne's War in the early years of the next century. But although he insisted throughout his life on splitting the world into absolutes—in this, perhaps, he was a typical Calvinist—he was not the harsh and unyielding fanatic some critics have made him (and his son) out to be.[6] Studying his life, one finds numerous instances of his resilient character: although, for example, he helped to lead the opposition to the Halfway Covenant in the 1660s, he later reversed his position and argued publicly for wider acceptance of the covenant in New England's churches; although for most of his life he railed against all kinds of apostasy from the New England Way, he helped to ordain a Baptist minister in Boston in 1718.

In this sense Increase Mather's life, as his most recent biographer has observed, can be read as a synecdoche for New England history in the years from the Halfway Covenant (1660) to those of the furor over smallpox inoculation in Boston (1721) (M. Hall xiv–xv, 361–63). In his life, one can trace the movement from colony to province in the community's affairs, from narrow theological concerns to a broad pietism in the church's affairs, and from medieval constructs to Enlightenment empiricism in the realm of science. Mather's career as a historian is best understood in the same way, as a reflection of the larger historical situation of New England in the late seventeenth century. For Mather (unlike Winthrop, Bradford, and Johnson) wrote a considerable number of historical works, ranging from biography to social history to providential history to rudimentary theory. Significantly, however, his interest in writing and commenting upon history lasted only from 1670, the year he published a biography of his father, to 1692, when he returned from London bearing a charter that did away with the old Puritan commonwealth and established in its place a royal province under the direct control of the Crown. From 1692 until his death, he did not write history. Thomas Holmes's bibliography of his works lists 102 separate titles and, even accounting for the seventeenth century's more fluid notion of the genre, not one written after 1691 is historically oriented—there are no "relations," "accounts," "histories," "narratives," "biographies," whatever. His historical narratives were dependent upon a certain vision of New England's past; when that vision was obviated by

William's imposition of a new charter in 1691, Mather lost his willingness, perhaps even his ability, to write history.

Yet in the years from 1670 to 1692, Increase Mather was New England's most prolific theologian, historian, and public spokesman. As the most powerful minister in Boston, he helped to shape public policy on nearly every important question involving both church and state; and as the foremost historian of the time, he helped to shape the ways that colonists thought about themselves, their society, and their future. A close reading of his several historical narratives reveals two important patterns, one concerning Mather himself and one concerning Mather's relationship to New England in the 1670s and 1680s.

First, Mather's histories, though they vary in approach and method, share a rhetorical strategy that urges and a formal thesis that argues for consensus and compromise: consensus in that his narratives ask the audience to agree with the historian's understanding of a current crisis, and to submit to his plan for resolving it; compromise in that his narrative strategies urge readers to subordinate their selfish desires to the needs of the community, as those needs are defined by the historian. The explanatory power of this urge to negotiate and to agree—an urge that eventually takes shape in his narratives as the argument for covenant renewal—can be traced to Mather's own psychological needs in the wake of his disappointments in social reform in the 1650s (in England) and the 1660s (in New England).

Second, Mather is finally unable to triumph over his materials, to write a comprehensive account of New England's past and its present purpose. He does find answers where Wigglesworth and Morton found only questions, but those answers prove to be only temporary stopgap measures in a world that Mather felt sliding away from him. Accordingly, as my analysis of his narratives will show, he always wrote history in response to specific events, as polemics in what he took to be skirmishes with New England's enemies. In the 1660s he responds to the Halfway Covenant; in the 1670s to King Philip's War; in the 1680s to the revocation of the charter; and in the 1690s to the debate over the colony's new charter. But his vision never crystallized; it never managed to comprehend the whole of his culture's experience and hopes. Hence in the end he, too, epitomizes New England's cultural confusion in the 1670s and 1680s, and his many and varied historical narratives symbolize the fragmented nature of a society that has no convincing "historical explanation" (Wise 50–53) to tell about itself. In his career as a historian, Increase Mather was able to authorize the past only in piecemeal fashion. Even after Mather had written a half-dozen historical narratives, New England's past still lay in pieces, waiting for the community itself or for one individual to refashion it into a convincing myth.

FINDING ANSWERS

Increase Mather was one of the leaders who insisted, throughout the 1670s and 1680s, that New England was undergoing a "great degeneracy" (*Discourse* 50). Although several godly people yet remain in the land, he cried in 1679, "there is doleful degeneracy appearing in the face of this generation, and no man can say, but that the body of the present generation will perish both temporally and eternally" (*Call* 19). This type of rhetoric can be traced back to the dilemma of the Halfway Covenant and to works like Wigglesworth's "God's Controversy with New England"; but it can also be traced back to Mather's experiences in England in the waning years of the Republic. Having graduated from Harvard in 1656, Mather sailed for England the next year; he planned to take the masters degree at the University of Dublin and then stay in England to minister to a congregation, as two of his older brothers and a handful of other ministers from New England had done. Although it had supposedly provided England with the model of a godly commonwealth, New England appeared to him now to be a small and insignificant outpost. The future of Protestantism lay in England. Despite his ties to his family and to the colony, he did not plan to return to New England.[7]

At Dublin, Mather distinguished himself as an ultra-orthodox believer; years later, even he would refer to himself in those years as a "precisian" (*Autobiography* 281). Reading Mather's comments on this phase of his life, one senses that this son of one of the founders of the Puritan commonwealth in New England felt a need to stand out among the Puritans of the English Republic: after all, hadn't New England shown England the way, and wasn't his own father one of the founders and still one of the leaders of New England? His over-precise tenets were part of an attempt to mold his self-identity.

But by the time Mather had taken his degree and found a ministerial position the Puritan revolution in England was nearly over. Oliver Cromwell died in 1658, and his son and successor, Richard, resigned from the Protectorship in May 1659. A new Parliament was called that summer, and it favored a restoration of the monarchy. Charles II assumed the throne in 1660, and the Puritan revolution in England was over. Mather watched the collapse of the revolution from three different English parishes. Twice he was asked or forced to leave a parish because of his uncompromising religious views. In both places he refused to conform either to the Church of England or to rapidly changing public sentiment. "When the King was proclaimed," he wrote in his memoirs, "I did out of conscience openly refuse to drink his Health . . . I refuse[d] to subscribe to some papers . . . that [said] now we beleeved the Times were and would be happy" (*Autobiography* 284). They might have been happy, at least financially, for Mather had he not been a "precisian": in 1660 he was offered a position worth 400 pounds a year if he would conform to the Church of England. He refused. With the failed coup of the Fifth Monarchy Men in January 1660/ 61, and the election of the vengeful Cavalier Parliament in May 1661, England became a dangerous place for a nonconformist as unyielding as he. Increase Mather set sail for New England in August. He was twenty-two years old.

His four-year stay in England had changed him dramatically. It was with grim satisfaction that he later remarked: "Thus was I persecuted out of two [parishes in England], before I was 22 years of age" (*Autobiography* 285). Those experiences were a mark of distinction for a young man reentering a society that was becoming dominated by the ghosts and the deeds of a heroic past, captured in works with such funereal titles and subject matter as Norton's *Abel Being Dead* and Morton's *New Englands Memoriall.* Now he, too, had been tested by the temptation to conform; and he, too, had resisted. As his father, Richard, and as (at least some of) his cultural forefathers, men who had been harried out of England because of their beliefs, he had passed through fire. Leaving behind a country that he had wanted to make his home—and to which, because of its cultural and intellectual impact on him, he would for the rest of his life yearn to return—Mather crossed the ocean to start a new life in America. But, ironically, he returned to find that the very fathers he had been trying to imitate were prepared to alter one of the fundamental concepts of Congregational polity. The Halfway Covenant was not conformity to the Church of England, but it was almost as bad. It was definitely not the sort of backsliding one expected from New England. "Degeneracy," Increase Mather once wrote, voicing a commonly held sentiment in

recurrent fear—

New England, is "a greater Evil in us, than in any People" ("Epistle Dedicatory" 161).

In the Synod of 1662, Richard Mather led the drive to extend baptism, and hence church membership, to children of parents who were baptized but unconverted. His youngest son was in the small but vocal minority that opposed any loosening of the criteria. The vote was not close: the Synod overwhelmingly favored the Halfway Covenant. But the minority opposition did come away with a victory of sorts: permission from the General Court to publish arguments opposed to the decision of the Synod. John Winthrop reports that he had demanded silence—and had even been forced into it himself—in the 1630s and 1640s whenever the majority of church members or magistrates had decided a question, even in cases that deeply divided the church or the country. This freedom to dissent in 1662 was not, then, a sign of how deeply the issue of baptism had divided the colony: other issues had caused deep antagonisms without requiring the concession of this privilege. It was, at least from our point of view, a sign of toleration, a recognition that dissent might serve a useful purpose in a community. Traditionalists like John Davenport and Increase Mather may not have had many votes in the Synod itself, but their supporters among the laymen were many; and New England's leaders could see that ending debate on this issue the way Winthrop had ended debate on the Antinomian issue after his election in 1637 might cause more harm than good. In this limited sense, the court's decision was an early sign of the stirring of a new spirit in the colony, one of pluralism and toleration—and a sign of the orthodoxy's realization that dissent could not continue to be legislated or forced out of existence. But to a "precisian" like young Increase Mather, and to many other New Englanders, the Halfway Covenant itself was a sign, no matter how one painted it, of weakness, of apostasy from the fundamental truths of Congregational polity, of a falling away from the clear light of truth. One year after returning home, Increase Mather found himself exiled not only from England but, in a sense, also from his own country. He was caught between two worlds: on one side he saw an England that had totally spurned the revolution of the saints; on the other, a New England that was threatening to follow suit. He immediately set out to resolve this dilemma by returning New England to the original ways of the founders.

There was one problem: young enough to be idealistic, Mather apparently did not feel old enough or mature enough—"tested" enough, perhaps—to attack the Synod's decision in the press. Instead, he signed Charles Chauncy's essay against the Halfway Covenant, *Anti-Synodalia Scripta Americana* (1662), and urged John Davenport to write another. Davenport did, and Mather wrote the unsigned "Apologetical Preface" for *Another Essay for the Investigation of Truth* (1663). That preface, Increase Mather's first published work, represented his only contemporary contribution to the heated public debate over baptism that continued throughout the 1660s.[8] When Mather next appeared in print, in *The Mystery of Israel's Salvation* (1669), it was to argue that the conversion of the Jews and, hence, the second coming of Christ were near. Heavily annotated, as if in composing them Mather had retreated from the public controversy into the privacy of his study (where he signs the "Author's Preface"), the four sermons comprising *The Mystery of Israel's Salvation* are abstract and otherworldly. Mather studiously avoids the subjects of baptism and of New England, presenting instead his contemplations on the millennium when, in some vague though not-too-distant future, the troubles of this world will be forgiven and forgotten. Surely, he concludes, "the day will not be long before the Lord appear[s] in glory to build up Sion" (181). Indeed, the millennium that he imagined in *The Mystery of Israel's Salvation* was the world precisians like himself had tried, and failed, to bring about in both England and New England. In the wake of those failures, Mather fashioned in *The Mystery of Israel's Salvation* a spiritual and mystical realm, separate from this lower world, in which the politics of baptism and other divisive issues were irrelevant.

The date of publication of Mather's first full-length work is deceptive, since he finished *The Mystery of Israel's Salvation* and sent it to London in the summer of 1667. In the interval between the completion of the manuscript and the publication of the finished work, Mather experienced two setbacks, one public and one private, that changed his view of New England and gave rise to his desire to reconstruct both its history and its future. The public disappointment involved John Davenport, one of the bulwarks against "innovation" in the controversy over baptism. In 1668 Davenport forged several documents in order to force his New Haven congregation to release him as their minister; and then he accepted what, it was learned, had been a previously arranged call to the ministry of Boston's First Church. Davenport clearly wanted to move to a pulpit of greater power and influence within the colony, a pulpit from which he could urge the colony to revoke its stance on the Halfway Covenant. If the First Church had been unanimous in its wish to call Davenport, the affair might have blown over; but it was not. The lay members were deeply divided over Davenport's fitness, not simply because some of them favored the Halfway Covenant and Davenport did not, but because most Congregationalists did not condone the luring of ministers from their pulpits. The First Church split into two factions, the minority members who dissented from the decision to call Davenport eventually forming the Third Church of Boston (see Simmons). For Increase Mather, it was a disappointment to see that one of his allies, one of the members of New England's revered first generation, could adopt such tactics, even in a cause as important as this one; on a less personal level, the affair was a lesson in the practical consequences of taking a stand that opposed the consensus of society's leaders. The First Church controversy demonstrated the disruptive effect on individual and social morality that uncompromising stands, such as Davenport's, could have.

Perhaps more significant in terms of Mather's career was his father's death, and the circumstances surrounding it, in April 1669. In early April, Richard Mather had been chosen to be the moderator of a council formed to resolve the differences between the two contending factions in the First Church. On April 16, Davenport refused to meet either with the council or with the elder Mather. Exhausted by his efforts to achieve harmony on the issue, Richard Mather returned to Increase's house in Boston that night and collapsed. He died a week later. The "circumstances of his collapse made it seem that his death was brought on directly by the crisis over Davenport's appointment and indirectly by the argument over the halfway covenant" (Hall, *Last* 80). To a Puritan like Increase Mather, convinced that "the Lord speaketh by his Works" (*Times* 20), these events clearly indicated that something was wrong. To make matters worse, one of Increase's elder brothers, Eleazar, unexpectedly died in July of the same year. After crossing the colony to be with his brother's family in Northampton, Increase himself collapsed from exhaustion and lay near death for a week. He was not able to make the journey back to Boston until November. He apparently spent that fall and winter rethinking not just his attitude toward the Halfway Covenant, but his attitude toward his father, toward the cultural fathers whose original vision he admired, and toward the future of the colony itself.

Mather's changed attitudes are expressed in the first history he wrote, *The Life and Death of that Reverend Man of God, Mr. Richard Mather,* the biography of his father written in the summer of 1670 and published later that year. Mather published the biography anonymously, a common practice in the seventeenth century; he did so also, I suspect, in an attempt to deflect any criticism that it was too laudatory.[9] (As we shall see, his own role in the biography is as a mute or silent son, that is, the author-protagonist himself does not appear to praise Richard Mather.) In publishing the biography anonymously, however, Increase had yet another rhetorical purpose, one more in keeping with the larger public goals he set for himself here, and elsewhere, in the early 1670s: to show, and perhaps put his reader into, the place of a cultural son of a generation of fathers who, having themselves been tested by fire, had the wisdom and foresight to prepare for their children's future.

Accordingly, Mather opens the biography by showing Richard Mather as a son. "His parents *Thomas* and *Margarite Mather* were of Ancient Families in *Lowton,* . . . but by reason of some unhappy Mortgages they were reduced unto a low condition as to the World. Nevertheless, God so disposed their hearts, that they were willing to Educate this their Son in good Learning" (2). Although brought low in the world, the parents do not lose sight of important values (like education), a fact that Mather is quick to dramatize for the reader. At school, the master would beat the young Richard "eight times in a day whether in fault or in no fault: The like Magisterial harshness caused [Richard to] earnestly desire that his Father would take him from School, and dispose of him to some other Calling." His father knew best, however, as Richard could later admit: "*God intended better for me,*" Increase has him say, "*then I would have chosen for myself; and therefore my Father, though in other things indulgent enough, yet in this would never condescend to my request*" (3; the italics indicate that Mather is letting his father speak his own words). He stayed in school; and his father, having appointed himself mediator in the conflict, spoke privately to the master about the mistreatment.

He apparently spoke well, an element of the story that Increase uses to expand its significance. For later, when his "Estate was so decayed, that he almost despaired of bringing up [Richard] as he had intended," Richard's father very nearly apprentices him to "some Popish merchants." Now it is the master's turn "to be importunate with [the] Father still to keep him at School, professing that it was great pity that a Wit so prone to Learning should be taken from it, (as indeed it was) or that he should be undone by Popish education" (4). Providence had clarified matters: the future is safe when it is placed in the hands of father figures; sons should be guided by the wisdom of an older and more godly generation.

The biography ends with the same type of incident, although now, as the narrative comes full circle, the obedient son has become the knowing father. This father, too, has been brought low in the world, not simply in that his material comforts in the "Wilderness" of New England are few, but in that he has chosen to be humbled before men: "Some have thought that [Richard Mather's] greatest errour was, that he did not magnifie his Office, as he might and sometimes should have done. *Humble enough, and good enough,* was the frequent saying of that Divine" (34). The advice from father to son at the end of the biography is contained in Richard Mather's last will and testament, in which his "*serious and solemn charge* [as] *a Dying Father* [is], *That none of* [my sons] *presume after my decease to walk in any way of sin and wickedness in one kind or another, or in a careless neglect of God, and the things of God, and of their own Salvation by Christ*" (37). The next generation of sons has been shown the way to the future, and that way involves conformity to the decisions of the fathers, decisions like the Halfway Covenant.

Isolated like this, Richard Mather's dying charge to his sons may seem platitudinous, a stock element of the seventeenth-century spiritual biography. But Increase is careful to ground it in a series of dramatically rendered scenes, each of which hammers home the point of his father's "charge" and of the biography itself. One such scene, apparently taken directly from Richard's journal, centers on Richard's turbulent voyage across the Atlantic. As his ship approaches the end of the journey, it encounters a fierce storm. Too near New England's coast to let the ship drift with the storm, the crew cast three anchors, losing them all; they hoist sail, but the wind rips the sails to shreds; finally, the ship is driven full force toward a "mighty rock": "*In this extremity and appearance of Death, as distress and distraction would suffer us, we cried to the Lord, and he was pleased to have compassion on us: for by his over-ruling Providence, and his own immediate good hand, he guided the Ship past the Rock, assuaged the violence of the Sea and of the Wind*" (21–22). The lesson is to submit to the will of God as father who gave us, Richard says in the journal from which Increase in quoting, "*hearts contented and willing that he should do with us and ours what he pleased . . . and in that we rested ourselves"* (22).

"Hearts contented," in *The Life and Death of . . . Richard Mather* the central scene, the father's dramatic deathbed request to his son, indicates how that contentedness is to be achieved. Increase notes first the conditions under which his father became ill:

> There being some Differences in *Boston,* Counsel from Neighbour-Churches was by some desired, to direct them in the Lord what should be done. . . . [Richard] was, because of his Age, Gravity, Grace and Wisdome wherewith the Lord had endowed and Adorned him, chosen the *Moderator* in that *Reverend Assembly.* [Three days later, he becomes ill, and Increase comments:] Great was the favour of god towards [him], that he should be *found about such a blessed Work* as then he was ingaged in, for the Lord found him sincerely and earnestly endeavouring to be a Peace-maker. (26)

The allusion, of course, is to another Son who went "about [His] Father's business" (Luke 2.49). The fact is that Richard tried to repair the breach in New England's churches: he died trying to forge a consensus among a divided people. And on his deathbed he transfers the responsibility for continuing that "blessed Work" to the next generation: "*A speciall thing which I would commend to you,*" he tells the nameless silent son who sits with him, "*is, Care concerning the Rising Generation in this Country, that they be brought under the Government of Christ in his Church; and that when grown up and qualified, they have Baptism for their Children.*" In these last words, Richard admits that "the Dissenting of some in our Church discouraged me. . . . [Yet] I see no cause to alter my judgement as to that particular" (27). The battle against "Dissenters" from the majority opinion—the agreement on the Halfway Covenant—has been put into the hands of the next generation.

Having almost completed this literary journey through his father's life, Mather pauses near the end of the biography to highlight his father's value to New England: "Because he was esteemed eminently *Judicious,* therefore amongst the Reverend Elders in *New-England,* he was much improved in Managing the Controversies then under Debate about Church-Government" (32). In at least three instances, he notes, his father was called in to mediate disputes or "manage controversies." His father seemed to be saying through his "Workes," his actions in this life, that communal harmony on divisive issues was the particular "way" in which the sons should try to "walk" (37).

Chastened by the events of 1669, Increase Mather prepared himself for his change of mind on the issue of the Halfway Covenant by writing this narrative of the past, allowing his father, through the trope of prosopopoeia, to speak for the biographer's own mute self. The biography of his father provided him with a way to make the transition from son to father, from follower to leader, from idealism to practical experience. It is in this sense that Mather's writing of his father's life can be seen as a sort of psychotherapy, a process of psychological healing and ideological accommodation by which he steadied himself to assume the symbolic and cultural role of the father.

His newfound realization of the need for consensus on divisive issues illuminates *The First Principles of New-England,* a work he wrote in 1671 but did not publish until 1675.[10] From the writings of the founders, particularly John Cotton, John Norton, and Richard Mather, Mather gathered statements that had anticipated the decisions of the Synod of 1662, and he printed them here in defense of the Halfway Covenant. Taken together, he says, these statements prove that the "*Inlargement of Baptism . . .* is not Apostasy from the first Principles of *New-England,* nor yet any declension from the *Congregational way.*"[11] Revising not the past but the perception of the present as a time of doctrinal apostasy (a perception he had helped to foster ten years earlier in his criticisms of the Halfway Covenant), Mather urges all Halfway Covenant holdouts to conform to the wishes of the fathers, not necessarily to their practices, which for whatever reasons may not have included the enlargement of baptism. As in the biography, the father's wishes have become the way in which the sons should walk.

In *The Life and Death of . . . Richard Mather* and *The First Principles of New England,* Increase Mather introduced several themes that were to distinguish his writings: filial piety, the need for personal and social reformation, the purity of church and society in the early years of the colony. Those themes were, even then, only means to an end: social harmony. The composition of the biography of his father marked the moment in his life when he began to believe that, in the small but increasingly diversified world of seventeenth-century New England, consensus was better than disagreement, uniformity better than divisiveness, conformity better than difference. That conception and the social vision inherent in

it determined his historiographic method for the next twenty
years. Mather became a historian of compromise and consensus,
whose only authority for speaking could be, in the end, the actual
production of social compromise and consensus within his community. And because of this urge, at least in part, his career as a
historian became limited by the need to respond to every divisive
issue and every disagreement, usually through the argument that
the people should reform themselves, an argument that his audience found less and less compelling as the years went by.

COMPREHENDING THE 1670s

From the very beginning the founders of the Bay colony, having
read the early reports from Virginia, insisted on a strong central
authority in their colony, and they did all they could to make both
the godly and the unconverted conform to the decisions of that
authority. In his *History of New England* John Winthrop recorded
the community's various struggles to reach those decisions, enforce them, and if need be silence any who opposed them. Truth
for him was coherent, knowable, and enforceable, even if people
and events did not always subordinate themselves to it. Responding to events in the 1640s, including more vocal and more successful attacks on the governor and General Court, Edward Johnson
conceived a history of New England in which an even greater authority—the Word of Christ as announced by His herald—molded
society into a unified and purposeful whole. Within the narrative,
dissent was either excised or silenced so that Christ's army in New
England might be ready for its triumphant entrance into history
to put history to an end.

To Increase Mather, and other leaders in the 1660s and 1670s,
the selfish, anti-authoritarian "impulses" noted by Winthrop,
Bradford, and Johnson seemed still to be on the rise. "But who is
there left among you that saw those churches in their first glory
and how do you see [those churches] now?" Samuel Danforth
asked in 1670:

> Pride, contention, worldliness, covetousness, luxury, drunkenness,
> and uncleanness break in like a flood upon us and good men grow
> cold in their love to God and to one another. . . . What then is the
> cause of our coolings, faintings, and languishings? The grand and
> principal cause is our unbelief . . . [as well as] inordinate worldly

cares, predominant lusts, and malignant passions and distempers. (68–70)

New England's spokesmen refined in these years the rhetorical device of lists of sins that not only seemed to offer control over their environment (if you can name it, you can do something about it), but which also had the potential to goad people into changing their behavior. Most often, ministers employed the device, incorporating it into numerous sermons and lectures that both honed the sharpness of the attacks and expanded the list of potential sins; but even the General Court published them. This passion for cataloguing society's sins eventually culminated in *The Necessity for Reformation*, the official agreement of the Reforming Synod of 1679–1680; there, New England's "Elders and Messengers" pinpoint, first, what the "Evils" were that "provoked the Lord to bring his Judgments on New-England" and, second, "What is to be done that so those Evils may be Reformed" (423).

These lists—and the concept of declension from the purity of the founding fathers to the sinfulness of later generations that went hand in hand with them—were part of an attempt in the 1670s to prod an oft-quarrelling and ever-diversifying citizenry into a more unified whole. They were strategies designed to impose a reconfigured social authority on the people. In the biography of his father, Increase Mather had come to understand the value of communal agreement; and he began there to fashion a concept of history that would emphasize the necessity of such agreement and to imagine an audience that would allow itself to be controlled by it. The two histories he wrote in the 1670s are attempts to extend his discovery of the importance of compromise and consensus to other problems, other events. He authorizes the past as a series of arguments designed to prove the value of communal agreement, and to induce it within his audience.

Mather began *A Brief History of the Warr With the Indians in New England* in May 1676, just as the tide of that war had turned in favor of the colonists, and he completed it in August, after Philip had been killed. As the history of a war still in progress, the narrative would be an untrustworthy record of facts. But not for that reason alone is it untrustworthy on the "facts." More than other colonial historians of the war such as William Hubbard, Daniel Gookin, and Nathaniel Saltonstall, Mather wrote history hoping to effect certain specific changes in his audience, and he consistently made use of specific rhetorical strategies to bring about those changes. In much the same way as Edward Johnson's "epitomes" sometimes isolate spiritual or rhetorical truth at the cost of historical veracity, Mather's overall design of the history was designed to be more important than the "facts" that comprised it.

In the later stages of the *Brief History*, Mather emphasizes the symmetrical structure of King Philip's War:

> Whereas this very day of the Month (*viz. June 29*) was kept as a day of publick *Humiliation* the last year . . . God hath so ordered, as that the same day of the month was in the year after set apart to magnifie his name on the account of mercies received, being the first publick day of Thanksgiving, which hath been attended throughout this Colony since the *War* began. (37)

Philip's death is another instance of this symmetry: "And in that very place where [Philip] first contrived and began his mischief, was he taken and destroyed." Temporally and geographically, Mather perceives a pattern of reversals in the events of King Philip's War: "humiliation" one year becomes "thanksgiving" the next; Philip alive and uncontrollable one year becomes, a year later, Philip "cut into four quarters, and . . . hanged up as a monument of revenging Justice" (47) the next.

To highlight this symmetry, Mather opens the narrative by defining the spiritual and social condition of the colonists at the start of the war. One soldier, "a stout man," seeing his Indian guide slain, hearing his fellow soldiers swear oaths, and "considering the unseasonableness of the weather . . . was possessed with a strong conceit that God was against the english, whereupon he immediately ran distracted, and so was returned home a lamentable Spectacle" (4). In another instance, Mather records the devastation of a family, the parents killed and the children led into captivity; he remembers that the father, old man Wakely:

> would sometimes say with tears, that he believed God was angry with him, because although he came into *New-England* for the Gospels sake, yet he had left another place in this Country, where there was a Church of Christ, which he once was in Communion with, and had lived many years in a Plantation where was no *Church, nor Instituted Worship*. (12)

These stories are synecdochic: it is New England that is distracted and divided; the colonists have lost faith in God and in themselves.

Eventually, Mather lays out these problems in what is by 1676 a
conventional catalogue of sins (18); but his method is more effective when it remains metaphoric:

> Our Army pursued *Philip* who fled unto a dismal Swamp for refuge.
> . . . The Swamp was so Boggy and thick of Bushes, as that it was
> judged to proceed further therein would be but to throw away Mens
> lives. It could not there be descerned who were *English* and who the
> *Indians.* Our Men when in that hideous place if they did but see a
> Bush stir would fire presently, whereby 'tis verily feared, that they
> did sometimes unhappily shoot *English men* instead of *Indians.* (5)

At the start of the war, the colonists were indistinguishable from
the Indians.

The seventeenth century could never quite decide exactly who,
or what, the Indians were. In 1674 Daniel Gookin, the Indian su-
perintendent in Massachusetts Bay, wrote:

> Some conceive that this people are of the race of the ten tribes of
> Israel that Salmanasser carried captive out of their own country . . .
> and that God has, by some means or another, not yet discovered,
> brought into America. . . . Another apprehension is that the original
> of these Americans is from the Tartars, or Scythians, that live in the
> north-east parts of Asia, which some geographers conceive is nearly
> joined to the northwest parts of America. . . . A third conjecture of
> the original of these Indians is that some of the tawny Moors of
> Africa . . . have put off to sea, and been transported over . . . unto
> the south parts of America, where the two continents of Africa and
> America are nearest. (*Historical Collections* 4–7)

Gookin's focus in this particular passage is on how the Indians
reached America, but behind that interest lies the question of who
they were. "The native cultures of [America] could not be recognized and respected in their own right," Edmundo O'Gorman
wrote, "as an original way of realizing human ideals and values,
but only for the meaning they might have in relation to European
Christian culture" (qtd. in McQuade 59; see also Pearce 3–49; and
Todorov). The meaning most New England colonists brought with
them, and the one they implicitly agreed to apply to the natives,
was that they were essentially "uncivilized." We may see, Gookin
wrote:

> as in a mirror . . . the woful, miserable, and deplorable estate, that
> sin hath reduced mankind unto naturally, and especially without
> means of cultivating and civilizing, [in] these poor, brutish barbar-
> ians [that is, the natives]; for these . . . are like unto the wild ass's
> colt, and not many degrees above beasts in matters of fact. (*Histori-
> cal Collections* 83)

Settlers were quick to point out that the system of hierarchies by
which Renaissance Europe conceived of order—the chain of being
that put master over slave, husband over wife, king over subjects,
and God over man—was absent in Indian society. In this sense
Mather's history begins, as does *Hamlet*, when "The time is out of
joint" (I.v.188); the natural order of things was inverted in Anglo-
American society in New England in 1675. The settlers had become uncivilized, "Indianized."

Midway through the narrative, Mather provides another example that locates this problem in more familiar terms for the colonists:

> And soon after [Lieutenant Adams] was killed, his Wife was casually
> slain by an *English-man,* whose Gun discharged before he was aware,
> and the Bullet therein passed through the boards overhead, and
> mortally wounded Lieutenant *Adam's* wife. It is a sign God is angry,
> when he turns our Weapons against our selves. (23)

The main question Mather asks in this history is how the colonists'
guns can be turned away from themselves and toward their real
enemies, how, in effect, God's favor can be restored to New England. The expected answer, both for Mather and his audience, is
"reformation." This was what Norton, Wigglesworth, Morton, and
countless ministers in the pulpit had asked for in recent years. But
reformation does not work. "We have often carried it before the
Lord," Mather wrote at one point, "as if we could *Reform* our
wayes, and yet when it hath come to, we have done nothing: So
hath the Lord carried toward us, as if he would deliver us, and yet
hath deferred our *Salvation,* as we our selves have delayed *Reformation*" (22).

Again and again, like a haunting melody, Mather records New
England's failed attempts to reform itself during the war. June 24,
1675, is a day of "solemn Humiliation throughout [the] colony,"
but at the end of the day the colonists are attacked by the Indians
and sustain their first casualties of the war. "The Providence of

God," Mather wrote, "is deeply to be observed, that the sword should be first drawn upon a day of Humiliation, the Lord thereby declaring from heaven that he expects something else from his People *besides* fasting and prayer" (3; emphasis added). In October, another day of humiliation is appointed and "solemnly observed: yet attended with awfull testemonyes of divine displeasure. The very next day . . . was that dismal and fatal blow, when Captain *Lothrop* and his company . . . were slaughtered" (16). The colonists try all of the old methods of reform—humiliation, prayer, fasting—but all are met by defeats (see 3, 7, 19, and 27). The historian, for one, is not surprised: the people have not completely and correctly reformed themselves. In a sense, they are still their own worst enemy, and it is entirely appropriate that they shoot each other, not Philip's men. Even when the colonists gain a great victory at Hadley, Mather is careful to point out that the battle ends on a negative note: "God saw that if things had ended thus [another] and not Christ would have had the Glory of this Victory" (30). The times are still out of joint.

These failures force Mather into a predicament as New England begins to gain control of the war in the spring of 1676. As a passionate believer in a certain sort of cause and effect—if New England correctly reforms itself, then God will give it the victory— Mather must locate the proper technique or method of reform that explains or accounts for the colonists' shift in fortune. At one point, he describes yet another "day of Humiliation by Fasting and Prayer"—this one on May 9, 1676—that seems to hold the key to New England's ascendancy in the war: "Although many such solemn occasions have at times been attended in former years, yet it hath been observed by some, that God did alwayes signally own his Servants, upon their being before him in such a way and manner: And so it was now." The very next day Boston receives word that the Mohawks have turned against Philip. This incident should surprise any discerning reader of *Brief History:* how was this day of humiliation any different from the four or five such days recorded here that preceded it? Mather does not say. Later in the passage, though, he tries to qualify the significance of that day. "There are [those]," he says, "who have dated the turn of Providence towards us in this Colony, and against the Enemy in a wonderful manner, from this day forward" (29). Some people have done so; but not the historian. He immediately describes an attack on Plymouth that takes place two days later. Simple humiliation, as Mather has insisted throughout the narrative, cannot save New England.

In late June 1676, New England's leaders changed their strategy: they appointed a day of thanksgiving, not humiliation, in an attempt to restore God's favor. Increase Mather had, in reality, vehemently opposed this decision, but he gives no indication of that opposition here. He records, instead, a long list of reasons why thanksgiving was in order, at the end of which he finds "two things . . . observable": first, this day of thanksgiving fell on the same day in 1676 as a day of humiliation in 1675; second, the act of giving thanks had immediate effects both on the colonists and on the Indians (37–38). The effects seem to suggest that the narrative is being brought full circle: captives are returned to the colonists, intimating society's movement toward health and reunification, and the Indians begin to turn on each other, indicating that they are returning to their own (appropriately) disjointed, uncivilized ways. Here too, however, Mather is reluctant to declare thanksgiving the cause of this reversal of fortune. "The Lord from Heaven smiled upon us," he wrote, by returning the captives to them; but "there is [still] cause for Humiliation before the Lord" (36). The next day the army marches "out of *Boston* towards the place, where *Philip* was supposed to be. But when they came thither, they found that he was newly gone" (38). This day of "publick Thanksgiving" was simply another date that some people, again, considered the "turn of Providence" (29). But not the historian. Philip's absence in this latter scene serves as an apt metaphor for the effect thanksgiving has on the colony in *Brief History*: it didn't do the colonists any harm, but neither did it gain them a tangible victory.[12]

Not until late July does Mather link the colonists' improved fortunes in the war to their new method of reforming themselves:

> there is of late such a strange *turn of providence* (especially in *Plimouth* Colony, since the Churches in that Colony . . . did solemnly *renew their Covenant with God and one another*) as the like hath rarely been heard of in any age. Whereas formerly almost every week did conclude with sad tydings, now the Lord sends us good news weekly. (42)

The town of Bridgewater likewise renews "their holy Covenant with God" (44) on July 31 and is immediately rewarded with a victory. Having found the appropriate method of achieving reform—communal renewal of the church covenants—New England becomes an unstoppable force in Mather's narrative of the war.

The reversal, from faithlessness and social disruption, through despair, to the restoration of faith and social unity, is completed on August 12, 1676. Philip is in flight, "but as he was coming out of the Swamp, an English-man missed of his aime, but the Indian [who was part of the English contingent] shot [Philip] through the heart, so as that he fell down dead" (47). Indians had fought alongside the colonists throughout the war, but only here does Mather emphasize their role as allies. In Mather's account they have at this point entirely returned to their "uncivilized" ways, turning their weapons against each other just as the colonists had done one year earlier. "Thus when *Philip* had made an end to deal treacherously, his own Subjects dealt treacherously with him" (47). The victory, and with it the symbolic reversal of Indians and colonists, is clearly tied to the idea of covenant renewal: "*since they renewed their Covenant with* [God], and that so they might have their hearts raised and enlarged in ascribing praises to God, he delivered *Philip* into their hands" (42). Having turned away from God, and from any sense of communal agreement on basic issues, New England turns to itself again through covenant renewal "*with God and one another*" (42; Slotkin and Folsom 69).

In the preface to *Brief History,* Mather discusses the role of the historian (to endeavor "to relate things truly and impartially"), and the way the historian achieves that goal in a specific narrative (by resolving "to methodize such scattered observations" as are available to him). In historiographic terms, his explanation of the historian's purpose and method is vague, even rudimentary. But when he published the *Brief History* in 1676, he had it bound with a sermon, *An Earnest Exhortation to the Inhabitants of New England,* that elaborates the method and purpose of the history in terms his contemporary audience could understand. Why were we subjected to a terrible war? he asks. Certainly not because of church matters (read: the Halfway Covenant): our "fathers" asserted the same principles of Congregational polity as we, and "God did wonderfully own this People [then], and suffered no Weapon that was formed against them to prosper" (9). As he declared in *The First Principles of New-England,* there has been no doctrinal apostasy in New England. In fact, he insists, "*Religion is our Interest* [in New England] and that which our Fathers came into this Land for" (10). Implicitly in the *Brief History* and explicitly in this sermon, Mather refashions the early years of the colony's settlement along the lines of Edward Johnson's history, erasing the doubt, confusion, and greed that Winthrop recorded, and sketching in their

place a picture of the founders as men driven by a humble and holy urge to worship God in the way they thought best. But whereas Johnson was content to incorporate doctrinal and political controversy into a larger providential plan in which the New England orthodoxy was soon to play a victorious role, Mather removes all controversy from the past. There are no grays, no forms of dissent, in his picture of the founding generation.[13]

Early in the sermon, he presents this simplified picture of the past. But then he moves forward in time to the point at which King Philip's War began, when that pure past could be contrasted with the impure present. The "*first generation* which was in this Land, had much of the power of Godliness, but the present *Generation* hath . . . but little of the power of Religion" (14); or, again, "the Interest of *New-England* [has] indeed changed from a Religious to a Worldly Interest" (15). This series of neatly dichotomized statements is meant to be the logical explanation of the condition of the colonists that Mather described metaphorically at the beginning of the history. The sons have turned away from the fathers' concerns. This is declension, but it is declension of a specific sort: not of principles, but of adherence to those principles.

The colonists' "re-turning" to those principles is also put into familiar typological terms. Mather equates the generation of Israelites that escaped from Egypt with the first generation of settlers in New England. Doing so allows him to compare the sons of each group of settlers:

> we finde that the second Generation, of them who came out of Egypt, whilst yet in the Wilderness having also a difficult undertaking before them, being to engage with their Heathen Enemies, and in other respects their state and case to be parallel with ours, they did most solemnly renew their Covenant with God. (17)

Like Bradford (in "Some observations"), Wigglesworth, and Norton, Mather typologizes history into a "first" and "second" times; but whereas Wigglesworth's and Norton's types suggest that the "disciples" are passive (they must wait for Christ or His Spirit to reinvigorate them), Mather's types suggest that the people can effect their own "re-turn" to spiritual harmony. This sermonic strategy points finally to the same conclusion as did the historical one: "Let there then be no more Plantations erected in New England," Mather says, "where people professing Christianity shall live like

Indians" (23). Through covenant renewal—that is, a communal renewal of social purpose—the colonists can restore the "natural" order of things.

Narrative history and hortatory sermon complement each other, working almost as strophe and antistrophe to delineate New England's problems, and the only solution to them.[14] Casting his audience into the role of savages, Mather argues that the only sure method of reform—the only sure method of becoming themselves once again—is covenant renewal. "Some people" may disagree; but it is precisely their intransigence that provokes the "correcting" hand of the Lord (*Earnest Exhortation* 7). Social and spiritual harmony will be delayed until that correcting hand, via the narrative of Mather's history or the logic of his sermon, forges a consensus.

The rhetoric Mather employs concerning the so-called first generation in *Brief History* and in the accompanying sermon is prominent in the writings of his contemporaries. And in another history and sermon, written and published together in 1677 after King Philip's War had drawn to a close, Mather showed how the rhetoric could be adapted to different circumstances. *A Relation of the Troubles which have hapned in New England by Reason of the Indians there* describes New England's battles with the Indians in the sixty years prior to King Philip's War. Flashes of the familiar rhetoric are here: "for the most part," the historian says at one point, the settlers of Massachusetts Bay came "not so much on account of the Trade, or to prosecute any worldly interest, as on account of Religion" (22). But there are only flashes, and even these are tempered: "for the most part."

The strategy and tone change because Mather broadens his canvas to the whole history of Indian-white relations in seventeenth-century New England. The boundaries of his subject here are not so much temporal, as they were in the *Brief History*, as they are social: he limits his narrative to Indian troubles that have threatened the public peace, isolating specific moments when the more "normal" peaceful course of Indian-white relations was diverted toward battle or war. So, for example, in one incident in 1614, "an unworthy Ship-master whose name was Hunt" enticed twenty-seven Indians onto his boat and took them to Gibraltar, where they were sold as slaves. "Yea," Mather concludes from the incident, "that inhumane and barbarous Feat was the unhappy occasion of the loss of many a mans estate and life, which the Barbarians in those beginning times did from thence seek to destroy" (2). The narrative focuses on incidents like these and others in which the Indians are the antagonists. The narrative recounts a history of tensions that are kept in precarious balance until the explosion of war in 1675.

There are good and bad Indians in *A Relation of the Troubles.* Indians like Samoset and Squantum treated the English very kindly, serving as mediators between the Plymouth settlers and the neighboring Indian tribes, in the early 1620s. In another instance, Mather quotes an angry sachem who, after suffering several indignities, asked the English to remember their once-amicable relations: "When you came into this land, I was your friend, we gave gifts to one another. I let you have land as much as we agreed for, and now I would know of you if I or my men have done you any wrong" (19). The colonists admitted that he had never done them any wrong and they punished the colonist who had antagonized the Indian chief. But then there were Indians like Philip who, despite being bound by a covenant not to make war, conspired throughout the 1660s "against the Colony, under whose protection and Jurisdiction he had submitted himself" (72). In 1671, the English bound him to another series of covenants, but he broke those, too, falling at last "to open Rebellion and bloodshedding amongst the English" (75). Mather insists in *A Relation* that Indians such as Philip give little regard to the covenants by which men relate to each other within a harmonious community. Here, Philip is figured not so much as an uncivilized "other" as he is a member of the community who refuses to respect the community's laws.

Appropriately, there are also two types of colonists. "It is easy to observe," Mather says at the end of *A Relation of the Troubles,*

> from the *History* of these *Troubles,* that whereas there have been two sorts of men designing settlement in this part of *America,* some that came hither on the account of Trade, and worldly Interests, by whom the Indians have been scandalized, others that came hither on a Religious and conscientious account, having in their Eye, the Conversion of the *Heathen* unto Christ. (75)

Mather's goal is not simply to tap into contemporary rhetoric about the early settlers of New England. It is to show that white men and Indians alike have their correct "place," and that the rejection of the covenanted order by "bad" white men or "bad"

Indians leads to "troubles," at any point in New England's history. The narrative does not record all such troubles, of course. Mather declares that his historiographic method here involves recording only those troubles that "endanger" the "publick peace" (75). What he isolates, then, are those Indians who have forsaken their covenants with the colonists and those colonists who have forsaken their covenants with God and with the community. Whenever people step away from their socially accepted roles, the public peace is endangered.

Unlike the *Brief History*, this history has—and needs—little shape. Mather is concerned only with establishing the general historical pattern of cause and effect, of which King Philip's War is one example. The lesser instances of the pattern come at the reader with a staccato-like effect, establishing proof by sheer repetition. The accompanying sermon, *An Historical Discourse Concerning the Prevalency of Prayer*, performs the same role for this history as *Earnest Exhortation* performed for *Brief History*, providing the terms by which the audience can understand that pattern and can avert, by acting rightly, yet another repetition of the troubles they have just read. Ranging through biblical, ecclesiastical, and secular history, Mather simply lists (again the staccato-like effect) instances when prayer diverted the normal course of events.

In *Brief History* and *A Relation of the Troubles*, the rhetoric of a golden age of piety in the first years of settlement cuts ambivalent swatches. On the one hand, the rhetoric shapes the goal for which the rising generation is to strive. The point is not so much that the present generation is bad, the point is to try to make it see that it can be better. The rhetoric becomes a rallying cry, a way of uniting a people who, because of their disagreements, do not yet understand that only by conforming to the advice of the historian and establishing consensus through covenant renewal can they persuade God to stay His correcting hand and to restore peace. On the other hand, because it emphasizes the negative, the strategy is capable of backfiring at any time. No group wants to hear for too long how degenerated, apostasizing, and evil they are. That is why some ministers, as Mather himself would later do, began to soften their rhetoric in the mid to late 1670s.

Because some ministers did so, and because Mather did not immediately follow their lead, some critics have argued that Mather was an anomaly in his own time. "Mather's efforts at writing history," Michael Hall has written concerning the *Brief History* and *A*

Relation, "were obsolete even in his own day" (*Last* 126). However, a close look at the most popular history of King Philip's War, William Hubbard's *A Narrative of the Troubles with the Indians in New England* (1677), shows that Hall overstates the case. True, Hubbard and Mather were rivals. Hubbard had been chosen by the assistants to give the 1676 election-day sermon, which Mather had apparently wished to give. Disagreeing with Hubbard's observations in that sermon, Mather began to compose the *Brief History* and the accompanying sermon soon after election day in early May 1676. He hurried the two works into print in August because he knew Hubbard was also working on a history of the war, and he wanted his to be the first and authoritative version.

Indeed, several comments in Hubbard's *Narrative* and Mather's *A Relation* reveal the animosity that existed between the two men in 1676–1677. In the "Advertisement to the Reader," for example, Hubbard defends the subject matter of his history by arguing that "The matters of fact [herein] related (being rather Massacres, barbarous inhumane outrages, then acts of Hostility, or valiant atchievements) no more deserve the name of a Warre, then the report of them the title of an History" ("Advertisement to the Reader" n.p.). He takes two swipes at Mather here: the recent "troubles" are not worthy of being called a "Warr" and the recording of those events cannot be called "History," or even "Brief History" (as in *A Brief History of the Warr With the Indians in New England*). It must be referred to simply as a "narrative." To Hubbard, these two asumptions were linked because, while all histories were narratives, not all narratives were histories; narratives were less formal than histories, their subject matter often restricted to a personal account of one's experiences (though not in Hubbard's narrative), their narration restricted to a chronological record of "facts." Statistics and facts, not the sort of heroism associated with the epic, supposedly guide the account. Each event is in its appropriate place, and no conception of the meaning of the whole warps the event's meaning. According to Hubbard's preface, then, Mather is simply making too much of King Philip's War and of his own relation to it as interpreter. Mather, in turn, indicated in the preface to *A Relation of the Troubles* (published the next year) that he had outdone Hubbard. Hubbard's history deserves notice, he admits, but "most of the things here insisted on, are not so much as once taken notice of in that *Narrative.*"[15]

A close reading of Hubbard's *Narrative* does reveal a number of differences between Mather's and Hubbard's histories of King Philip's War. One senses, first, the lack of an organizing principle in Hubbard's narrative. The colonists' victories and losses are each simply attributed to "providence." The Indians are neither simply "Devills" nor simply innocent: they are conniving and conspiratorial (9, 13–17, 48), but they also have legitimate complaints against the United Colonies.[16] And the *Narrative* ends with many loose ends left untied, as if Hubbard were insisting that, because it is not a formal history, his narrative needs no formal closure. Structurally, the narrative describes a simple curve, inconsistently set forth in metaphors such as the "tide" (67), which turns completely when God so wills it, or the "height" (80) of sufferings, reached when troubles are seemingly overwhelming. Each of these ambivalences about the form of the book is tied to Hubbard's point in the narrative: "God grant," he concludes, "that by the Fire of all these Judgements [during King Philip's War], we may be purged from our Dross, and become a more refined People, as Vessels fitted for our Masters Use" (115). The recent troubles have not been punishments for wrongs committed so much as they are trials that God has imposed to make the colonists more useful and more fit vessels.

To Hubbard, the war is less a "correction" (as Mather would have it) than a "purgation," the difference being that corrections are applied to thinking, responding beings whereas purgations are applied to objects (metals, bowels).[17] Mather insists that the colonists can be held responsible for the war; Hubbard is not so sure. His colonists, for example, have not become savages, and they do not shoot each other. Thus, Mather treats the strange death of Lieutenant Adams's wife as a sign of the "unnatural" state of affairs in New England, while Hubbard treats it differently: "The Lieutenant of the Town, Adams by name, was shot down by his own Door, and his Wife mortally wounded by a Gun fired afterwards accidently in the House" (63), he says simply. Hubbard does not "improve" the incident; his is a world in which accidents happen. Mather's is not. When Hubbard does adopt Mather's method of turning minor incidents into tropes, he does so without blaming the war on the colonists' sins:

> As Captain *Mosely* came upon the *Indians* in the Morning, he found them stripping the Slain, amongst whom was one *Robert Dutch*, having been sorely wounded by a Bullet that rased to his Skull, and

then mauled by the Indian Hatchets, was left for dead by the *Salvages*, and stript by them of all but his Skin; yet when Capt. *Mosely* came near, he almost miraculously, as one raised from the Dead, came toward the *English*, to their no small Amazement; by whom being received and cloathed, he was carried off to the next Garrison, and is living and in perfect Health at this Day. May he be to the Friends and Relations of the Rest of the Slain an Emblem of their more perfect Resurrection at the last Day . . . as a Testimony to the Truth of their Religion, as well as Love to their Country. (39–40)

Robert Dutch is simply a "souldier"—and the seventeenth-century spelling is appropriate in this context—who has not "caused" the war by his actions, and who cannot end it through covenant renewal or prayer. But he, and the community, can be made more perfect by his miraculous survival. His case represents the difference between Mather's understanding of the history of the war and Hubbard's: Mather's colonists can save themselves, but Hubbard's cannot. Hubbard's colonists must suffer and pray and wait for God's anger to abate.[18]

However, despite these differences in methodology and argument, Hubbard elsewhere phrases the problems facing New England in a way that clarifies his essential similarity to Mather. Commenting on the physical damage done to the colony during the troubles, Hubbard argues that "It is not . . . outward force and violence that ruines a commonwealth, so much as a spirit of division, and contention arising from jealousies, prejudices, and animosities from within themselves, which doth most dangerously threaten, and most certainly foretell its destruction" (*Happiness of a People* 17). New England's problem is division from within, just as Mather had been insisting for several years. The sermon and the *Narrative* merely recommend a different method for restoring New England to wholeness. What has made Hubbard appear so modern to some readers is that he counsels religious toleration as part of that method—designating it an "errour to suppress" dissenters from the orthodoxy—and thereby seemingly severs himself from the Puritan founders (Murdock, "William Hubbard"). But this difference merely means that the causes of God's controversy with New England are different (and more generalized) in Hubbard's history than in Mather's, not the world view that generates the notion that God can be angry with a community. Hubbard's contemporary appeal was no doubt that he harped less on people's responsibility for events in the external world. But this alone does not make Mather's history obsolete, or even retrograde. Mather and Hubbard are simply different types of providential historians, figuring King Philip's War in different terms.

A NEW CRISIS

After finishing *A Relation of the Troubles,* Mather did not write another history for six years. In those years he gave some of his most powerful sermons, *Renewal of Covenant the great Duty incumbent on decaying or distressed Churches* (1677), *A Call from Heaven To the Present and Succeeding Generations* (1679), and *A Discourse Concerning the Danger of Apostasy* (1679), all of which had the same purpose: to exhort New England to adopt covenant renewal as a way of reversing apostasy, declension, and dissension. In 1679–1680 he achieved a victory when a synod of New England's ministers—the "Reforming Synod," led by him as his father had led the Synod of 1662—agreed that New England was and had been backsliding and recommended individual and communal reformation, through covenant renewal, to appease God's anger. This Synod affirmed at last the method of achieving consensus that had been the main argument of Mather's histories in the mid 1670s. Temporarily, Mather's historical arguments had become successful.

In Mather's mind, covenant renewal could accomplish two purposes. First, it was a way of forging unity, consensus, on the present state of New England and its future needs. Second, it reaffirmed each person's place within those covenants that defined him; by renewing his covenant periodically, each church member would call himself, and his neighbors, back from the kind of behavior that—as Mather's histories of the Indian wars had shown—led to "troubles." It was an internal solution to an internal crisis. Not long after the Synod of 1679–1680, however, it became clear to many New Englanders, Mather among them, that the colony faced an external threat—revocation of the colony's charter. In June 1683, the Committee for Trade and Plantations in England issued a *quo warranto* against the Massachusetts Bay charter and demanded that New England send agents to London to defend itself. The colony's delicate independent-but-dependent status as a covenanted commonwealth, which John Winthrop had puzzled out in the later sections of his *History of New England,* was being called into question.

This external threat was the product of New England's intransigence on the issue of independence from England, and of England's growing awareness of the colony's economic and military significance. Within the colony, some voices were heard arguing not only that Massachusetts should submit the charter to Whitehall, in the hope that the amendments made to it would be less drastic than its complete loss, but that Massachusetts should willingly give up its sovereignty in order to establish a better working relationship with the mother country. Mather's *Essay for the Recording of Illustrious Providences,* written in 1683 but not published until the next year, attacks both of those groups and argues that neither course of action, neither submission nor revocation, was suitable for New England.

Illustrious Providences is a strange work. By his own account, Mather conceived of the project when he found, amid the papers of John Davenport, a manuscript setting forth a *Design for the Recording of Illustrious Providences.* At a meeting of ministers in 1681, he suggested that a similar work be written to set forth a record of God's "Illustrious Providences" toward New England. The ministers agreed, and they offered to send him authentic accounts of such providences as they could find. He was to give shape to the material and write whatever other sections were necessary. The product of this collaboration reflects two important ironies.

First, although *Illustrious Providences* seems scientific, it is not. Mather's interest in the natural sciences had been piqued by the comet of 1680, and he had written at least three works on comets and "natural signs" by the summer of 1683; but he had little interest in performing empirical research himself (Hall, *Last* 166–67) and his reading, although it included Boyle and Kepler, was hopelessly limited not only by his geographic isolation but also by his intellectual isolation from European thought. Mather drew back "appalled," Robert Middlekauff has noted, at some of the conclusions drawn from empirical evidence by English scientists. Read as science, *Illustrious Providences* is nothing more than unsubstantiated curiosa marked by what, even in 1683, is an extreme "lack of sophistication." Middlekauff goes on to say that the "book carried the same purposes as Increase's studies of comets did—to undermine the authority of scientific explanation of natural phenomena and to substitute the ancient sense of the divine mystery in life." These providences are, by the late seventeenth century's own notion of science, unscientific: they prove that the illustrious providences of God cannot be measured or anticipated, much less fully comprehended (Middlekauff 142–45).

The second irony is that, while it seems to have little to do with history, *Illustrious Providences* is a genuine historical work. It is not, as we might expect, a chronological history. Instead, Mather records God's providences thematically, under twelve headings that include "Sea-deliverances," "Remarkables about Thunder and Lightning," "Apparitions," and "Remarkable Judgements." These "are *Magnalia Dei*"—as Mather says in a series of sermons given on the same subject—"things wherein the glorious finger of God is eminently to be seen" (*Doctrine* 12). The incidents recorded in *Illustrious Providences* are reminiscent of those in Winthrop's *History* (Mary Dyer's "monstrous birth," for example) and Johnson's *Wonder-Working Providence*—all three writers are "providential" historians. But there is an important difference in Mather's history of providences. Until now, New England's historians had used "magnalia" solely in the service of the history of New England or, even more narrowly, of their own community. Mather includes long sections that have little, if anything, to do with New England: remarkables that occur everywhere in nature, for example, or those that have specifically taken place in England or in Germany. In part, this broadened focus can be attributed to a breakdown in Mather's method of obtaining information: not every minister in the colony, he complains near the end of the work, has been "diligent in observing the works of God" (*Essay* 260). But, even more, it is an indication of broader cultural changes facing New England in the 1680s.

After all, if ministers were lackadaisical about such a project as this, one could only wonder about the faith of the converted (lukewarm) and of those in both Englands who favored revocation of the charter (ice cold). *Illustrious Providences* was constructed as a long proof against the skeptics of New England's covenanted status.

The first axiom of that proof is that God can indeed intervene in the normal affairs of man and nature. Perry Miller has suggested that the sheer quantity of individual, "atomistic" providences recorded in *Illustrious Providences* represents a fragmentation of the "coherent sweep of history" offered by Bradford or Johnson (*From Colony to Province* 145).[19] Instead, the overwhelming quantity of "magnalia" is meant to be irrefutable evidence, through repetitive and cumulative examples, of the doctrine of divine providence. The tremendous storm, complete with "artillery of Heaven" (hail), that buffets Springfield, Massachusetts, in 1682 is not so remarkable for its ferocity, as for the "Divine Providence" that no one was "killed in [its] fearful desolation" (225–26). A small child has her cranium pierced by an iron rod and not only survives but goes on to live a normal life (23–24). Two distressed ships meet in the middle of the Atlantic—one has only water, the other only bread and meat, both crews survive (21–22). Aware that any one of these stories could be construed as happenstance, Mather seeks to overwhelm his audience, whose faith in divine providence—and New England's mission—seemed to be wavering.

The second axiom is that God's interventions take place in the present era, not simply in some dim and misty past. Within each thematic grouping, Mather moves carefully from providences that occurred decades, even centuries, earlier to those that occurred very recently. In the opening chapter, "Of Remarkable Sea Deliverances," he records and narrates "sea" providences from, respectively, the years 1635, 1668, 1669, 1681 (twice), and 1683.[20] Each chapter of *Illustrious Providences* presents a similar pattern. History itself, Mather argues within each type of providence, continues to disclose God's active intervention in the contemporary affairs of the world.

The third and final axiom is that God favors some people more than others. Quakers, Catholics, heretics, and dissenters from the orthodoxy are singled out for negative providences, fearful signs that God does not support them. Puritans, however, not only receive positive treatment in a number of narratives here, but they understand better how these providences work. Mather tells the story of one "prophane man, who was also a persecutor of [Puritans], . . . riding abroad" in a thunderstorm with his wife, "who was eminent for godliness." She asks him "why he was so much afraid?"

> To whom he replied: Are you not afraid to hear these dreadful thunder claps? No (saith she), not at all, for I know it is the voice of my Heavenly Father: and should a child be afraid to hear his fathers voice? At which the man was amazed, concluding with himself, these Puritans have a divine principle in them, which the world seeth not, that they should have peace and serenity in their Souls when others are filled with dismal fears and horrors. He thereupon went to [a Puritan he had persecuted], bewailing the wrong he had done him, begging his pardon and prayers, and that he would tell him what he must do that so his soul might be saved: and he became a very godly man ever after. (94–95)

The divine providence here is that such a man could and would be saved; but Mather also makes the point that godly Puritans, because of who they are, need never fear divine retribution.

The only possible conclusion, of course, is that in this time (1683) and in this place (New England) "the glorious finger of God is eminently to be seen" (*Doctrine* 12). In the penultimate chapter of *Illustrious Providences,* Mather sets forth the conclusion himself: "That remarkable judgement hath first or last fallen upon those who have sought the hurt of the people of God in New-England, is so notorious as that it is become the observation of every man" (253). Obviously, all men did not observe that—otherwise Mather would have had no need to write the history itself—but his goal is to make them see it. He follows that statement with a coda, of sorts, a brief narrative concerning two Indians who thought "to swallow us up quick when their wrath was kindled against us." The first, "bloody Simon," boasted of the mischiefs he had done and the English he had killed, until he himself was shot by another Indian—as in *Brief History,* a sign of the "unnatural" state of Indian society. Later, when the English asked how Simon did, the Indians answer, " 'Worse than dead.' . . . Thus was the wickedness of that murtherer at last returned upon his own head" (254). The second Indian, Squando, was a "principal actor" in King Philip's War. One day, after the war, a specter appeared to him, "requiring him to kill himself, and promising him that if he did obey, he should live again the next day, and never die more." Squando's wife and friends urge him not to follow the advice, but "Nevertheless, he since hath hanged himself, and so is gone to his own place. This was the end of the man that disturbed the peace of New England" (255).

Those who attack New England, the coda reads, will themselves be attacked, will be brought low by their own machinations. Behind those secondary causes lay the real one: God's decision to intervene on behalf of New England, "this Israel in the wilderness" (253). This is what Perry Miller meant when he said that *Illustrious Providences* "is a concerted counter-attack upon enemies, or at least skeptics, of the covenant theology" (*From Colony to Province* 143). But Miller neglected an equally important purpose of the work. The history is—like the histories Mather wrote in the 1670s—an attempt to create consensus among a divided and quarreling people. As a civic leader, Mather had sided with the popular faction and argued that New England should challenge the revocation of the charter in court, not submit it for revisions. As a historian, he defended that decision by attacking New England's perceived enemies, warning them that to assault New England was to assault God. At the same time, *Illustrious Providences* asked its audience to believe again in the myth of New England's special role in history. Mather does not, as Miller concludes, "surrender . . . the idea of national covenant" (*From Colony to Province* 145) in *Illustrious Providences*. One senses that, by this time, Mather knew all too well the direction events in New England would take. But, in his mind (at least as we see it refracted through this history of providential intervention), New England's status as a chosen community remained intact. What had changed was the enemy, and accordingly the historian's audience. His strategies as the self-appointed historian of his culture therefore changed, too.

RETREATING FROM HISTORY

From 1684—when the old charter was finally revoked by a writ of *scire facias*—to 1686, the government of Massachusetts was in legal limbo. In that year Edmund Andros arrived to govern what was now the Dominion of New England. Andros regarded New England as merely a province of the British empire, to be governed with no regard for the traditions that had developed in the nearly seventy years of settlement. New England felt the effects immediately. In 1688, in an attempt to lobby King James directly for the reinstatement of the original charter, Increase Mather sailed for England.

In his four years there, Mather wrote and published seven works that defended either his own actions as an unofficial agent of New England, or New England itself. Three of the seven works were broadsides posted in Boston or London, and a fourth was a list of "Reasons for the Confirmation of the Charter Belonging to the Massachusetts Colony" that Mather apparently circulated among the members of King William's Privy Council in 1689–1690.[21] In these highly polemical works Mather does not, for the most part, concern himself with history or historiography. But the other three titles are histories, really, the last ones Mather would ever write. Together they project a vision of New England's history that is different from the one he had espoused for twenty years. By looking closely at them—one written in 1688, one in 1689, and the third in 1691—we can see a crisis in Mather's historical imagination.

Mather wrote *A Narrative of the Miseries of New-England, By Reason of an Arbitrary Government Erected there* in the autumn of 1688, sometime after William's invasion had been announced but before James had fled the country. Early in the narrative, Mather informs us that he had recently told James II, during a private audience, "that if a Foreign Prince or State should, during the present troubles, send a Frigate to *New-England,* and promise to protect them, as under their former Government, it would be an unconquerable temptation" (8). This temptation to shift loyalties to another prince and state was treasonous no doubt, since at the time Mather wrote this narrative James was still king of England and William's eventual triumph no sure thing. It was a measure of the erosion of James's political support, and hence his desperate need to curry the support of nonconformists and Whigs, that he ever tolerated such a statement, if indeed Mather ever uttered it.[22]

Whether he actually did utter it, Mather's inclusion of the statement in the *Narrative* dramatizes just how far, rhetorically, he was willing to go to retrieve Massachusetts Bay's 1629 charter. Threatening James was merely one way of trying to achieve that goal. Here and elsewhere in the late 1680s, Mather also adopted the political rhetoric of the Whigs, attempting to ground his arguments for the restoration of the charter in a language that Parliament, and later William, would understand. "The language of his Puritan's providential world view virtually disappeared," Michael Hall has written concerning these pamphlets, "to be replaced by the language of Whig politics" (*Last* 223–24). On behalf of the colonies, Mather continuously rehearses such pat phrases as "the Ancient Rights and Priviledges" of Englishmen, and the preservation of the people's "Rights, Priviledges, and Properties."[23] Although in theory the 1629 charter had guaranteed the rights and liberties of Englishmen to the Bay colony's settlers, this sort of rhetoric was new to Increase Mather. It had no place in his narrative histories of New England, built as they were on the covenant not on the common law, on New England's history not England's.

Mather's threat that New England might shift loyalties to anyone who would restore its charter government reveals, in essence, a problem of authority. To argue, as he does there and as the Whigs do later in defense of the Revolution, that it is "an illegal and unjust thing to deprive good subjects . . . of their *Ancient Rights and Liberties*" (*Narrative of the Miseries* 7–8) is to locate authority primarily in the common law, which supposedly guaranteed the rights of Englishmen against just the sort of "arbitrary" and absolute government that Andros, no less than his "master" James, tried to enforce (*Narrative of the Miseries* 1–2). Perhaps it is not surprising, then, that Mather seems ambivalent in his use of Whig rhetoric. In the next pamphlet, *A Brief Relation of the State of New England*, published in the summer of 1689 before William's thoughts on the colonies were known, Mather seems of two minds; juggling different rhetorical strategies (covenant theology versus Whig politics), he seems unsure which best supports his demand for the charter's restoration. He begins by announcing the "myth" of New England's special status, as if he had never heard of the loss of the charter and all that its loss implied:

> *New England* differs from other Foreign Plantations, in respect of the Grounds and Motives inducing the First Planters to remove into that *American* Desert; other Plantations were built upon Worldly Interests, *New England* upon that which is purely Religious. . . . [Its colonists] were, and are *Non-conformists* [to the Liturgy, Ceremonies, and Church-Government by Bishops]: It was grievous to them to think of living in continual difference with their Protestant Brethren in *England*; upon which account they resolved on a peaceable SECESSION into a corner of the World; and being desirous to be under the Protection of *England*, about twenty worthy Gentlemen obtained a Charter from King *Charles* the First . . . which giveth them Right to the Soil . . . which, notwithstanding, they purchased their Lands of the Indians, who were Native Proprietors. (3–4)

"Different" from other planters, nonseparating, meek, fair to the Indians: these settlers resemble those whom Mather described in the 1670s, when he urged New Englanders to reform themselves in his image of their fathers. Echoing Johnson's history, Mather then goes on to describe New England after the Pequot War: "the Plantation increased, and prospered wonderfully; yea, so as cannot be paralleled in any History: never was place brought to such a Considerableness in so short a time; that which was, not long since, a howling Wilderness, in few years time, became a pleasant Land" (5).

Yet, in the same pamphlet, that rhetoric of the covenanted community is juxtaposed to the rhetoric of the revolutionaries, to the litany of complaints about rights abrogated, privileges denied, and property confiscated. "It is certainly for the Interest of *England*, that *New England* be incouraged; and preserved in all their Rights,

Priviledges, and Properties" (8). No doubt, Mather admits, the Bay colonists "have been more rigid and severe [in the affairs of the church] than the Primitive Christians or the Gospel doth allow of"—a surprising admission—but this in itself is no reason for their charter to have been "Ravished" (7). After all, he concludes, those Englishmen born in New England "have the true inherent Spirit of the Old," are in essence no different from other Englishmen living in, say, London. New Englanders, Mather blithely asserts, are "but Men, [and] have had their failings as well as other Men in all places of the World" (7). Hence, they deserve the same liberties as all Englishmen. Is New England different from England? or the same? It is not clear. The historian pits the rhetoric of the New England Way against the rhetoric of an emerging Whig ideology.

There is an almost schizophrenic quality to *A Brief Relation*, a sense that two types of rhetoric—representing two visions of history, one religious and one secular—are competing with each other. Mather was not being duplicitous; he had despaired. Once again, as in the 1660s, he found himself in a predicament in which one part of his mind or heart told him to hold on to the past he knew, while another part of him—experience perhaps—told him that compromise was necessary, that a stand that was too idealistic was dangerous. At some level, he must have understood that the rhetoric of declension would not make sense to anyone outside New England (if, as we can infer from his argument in *Illustrious Providences,* New England itself could even make sense of it). He had already shown that he could put the language of Whigs to good use. His despair at ever regaining the old charter, coupled with an uncertainty about New England's future, produced an uneasy and confusing mix. That confusion is reflected in the argument and style of this short history. *A Brief Relation* is the one history Mather wrote in which my argument—that his histories always urge consensus upon a divided people—does not hold true. Mather was himself divided when he wrote it.

Increase Mather was, in many ways, a practical man. His ambivalent use of Whig rhetoric in 1688–1689 was one element in a strategy ultimately designed to convince James, Parliament, William—anyone and everyone who would listen—to restore the Bay colony's original charter. The third of these works, *A Brief Account Concerning Several of the Agents of New England,* written in October 1691 after the new charter had passed the Great Seal, turns the

Whig rhetoric in the direction of New England. In large part, Massachusetts Bay's new charter was a product of Mather's efforts at court (Hall, *Last* 240–53; Murdock, *Increase Mather* 211–62). Although the political basis of the old colony's government was wiped out (and with it the vision of a Puritan commonwealth that had sustained Edward Johnson's and Increase Mather's historiographic efforts), Mather was yet proud of the special accommodations New England had received. While lobbying for the colony in London he had resolved, he says, "to get as much Good, and prevent as much Hurt to the Country as possibly might be," and he insisted for the rest of his life that he had done just that (*Brief Account* 11; *Autobiography* 338–39).

But he understood all too well that, under the new charter, the "saints" would no longer retain political power in the Bay colony. The practical effect of the Glorious Revolution, in Massachusetts, would be to redistribute communal authority: the king, through his hand-picked governor, would appoint judges, sheriffs, and justices of the peace, and could veto the election of members of the council; the people—now defined by property, not church membership—would elect the assembly; the ministers would function only in the affairs of the church. The General Court would call no more synods. Although this sort of charter was not what he had come to London for, it was still better than the charters most provinces of the Crown had received. But he was perfectly aware of the way uninformed New Englanders might react when they saw it. *A Brief Account* tries to anticipate their anger and defuse it by explaining the positive aspects of the new charter.

The narrative itself indicates that Mather had learned the new charter's meaning well. In the opening sentence we can even sense a change in the way he addresses his countrymen: "I may rationally suppose that an Account of my Negotiation in *England,* where I have been attending the great Affair of *New-England* for more than Three Years, will be expected from me" (3). The measured cadence of his phrasing and the calm and eminently rational tone are clues to Mather's style, which is dramatically different from the tone and style of his writings in the 1670s. The language here sounds more like that of a later ambassador to London, Benjamin Franklin, than it sounds like Mather's. The argument of the narrative is this:

> That by this New Charter great Priviledges are granted to the People in *New-England,* and, in some Particulars, greater than they formerly

enjoyed: For all *English Liberties* are restored to them. . . . [And those liberties] are as a Wall of Defense about the Lord's Vineyard in that part of the World. (15–16)

The language of the Whigs now applies to New England. Aside from the realities of the charter (which did grant New England religious freedom, a franchise based on property, the right to elect representatives to the General Court), one can see in this how much Mather has changed. New England is no longer "special"; it is "English." So much so that he concludes this pamphlet by referring to the new charter as a "MAGNA CHARTA, whereby Religion, and English Liberties, and some peculiar Priviledges, Liberties, and all Men's Properties, are Confirmed and Secured . . . to Them and their Posterity for evermore" (22). In 1662, Mather had been concerned that the transmission of full membership in the church be only to children of visible saints; in 1691 he was concerned that the transmission of liberty and personal property be to the children of all true-born Englishmen. The world had changed, and for the good of New England he had tried to change with it.

A Brief Account Concerning Several of the Agents of New England is not a history in the sense that Mather's other histories are "history": it is not a history of New England. It is a history of his own negotiations in London, and a statement expressing, in fact, the end of New England's history as he and other New Englanders had known it. These English liberties, he points out calmly, "are as a Wall of Defence about the Lord's Vineyard in that part of the World" (16). The wall that Edward Johnson imagined, which surrounded the primitive purity of God's "Temple" in New England, was comprised of godly, civil magistrates who enforced conformity. Mather's wall indicates the nature of his compromise: the relative autonomy of New England, both in the church and in the state, could be preserved only by insisting that Anglicanism or Presbyterianism in the church and liberalism in politics had as much right to exist as did the old New England Way. He had learned the lesson of the 1660s well. Compromise was better than dissension.

Unfortunately for Mather, compromise did not guarantee consensus, as he soon discovered. He returned to New England on May 14, 1692, and found himself—as he had upon his return in 1661—a stranger in a strange land. Already, several "witches" had been jailed in Salem; in less than a month the first of twenty victims, Bridget Bishop, would be killed. The parallels between Mather's two four-year sojourns to England run deep. In 1692, New England seemed to have once again lost its sense of identity, not simply because of the witchcraft episode (though it was perhaps symptomatic), but because the old way of doing things was proving unworkable in the contemporary world. Mather experienced once again a sense of exile both from England and from the Puritan commonwealth that had been New England. After his first return, he had after much resistance come to accept the changes his fathers had made in the structure of New England's church and society. He had turned to history as a way of understanding and explaining those changes, and as a way of creating consensus among colonists who seemed even less willing than he was to conform to those changes.

After 1692, however, having accepted the changes in government and society imposed by England, Mather turned away from history: the province he had known personally had little relevance, in his mind, to the province he now inhabited. The rhetoric he had championed in the 1670s was not completely dead. On occasion, as in *Ichabod* (1702), one of his greatest sermons, he could even marshal it in support of the "Civil Charter Government [with] which God has favoured" New England (80). But none of his works written after 1692 deal with the historical status of New England, except in an oblique way; most deal with church doctrine and polity. For ten years or so, his debates with Solomon Stoddard over church membership, with the Brattles over the Brattle Street Church, and with the rectors of Harvard College over his presidency involved his conception of the type of society New England was and would be; but his conception remained merely implicit in those debates. It was as if he were retreating—as he had done in *The Mystery of Israel's Salvation*—from history, both real and written, retreating into questions that did not demand an explanation of New England's past. Only this time he did not formally work out a vision of history that incorporated the recent changes New England had undergone.

I have emphasized that Mather did not write histories of any sort after 1692. It is instructive to note, however, that he tried to finish writing his own memoirs in the 1690s, and beyond, and could not. The first part of the *Autobiography* was written in 1685, and it comprises the first forty-two pages of the published text. In the second section, apparently written in 1694 soon after his return from London, he begins to approach his own lived past in a sustained way. This second part is more overtly public and political than the first, as if he had suddenly become aware of his own role in colonial history. But its twenty-eight pages of published text slides gradually into excerpts from the diary he kept while in London, as if it were impossible for him to write history, possible for him only to transcribe his own words. Sometime after 1715 Mather resumed the autobiography, but he did not proceed very far, falling into self-pity, abortive beginnings, and finally, resignation to his own death (346–50, 352–53, 355–58, 360). He could not, in the end, even finish writing his own life. The memoir is surely a metaphor for his own attempts at writing New England's history.

Robert Middlekauff makes a similar point about Increase Mather's career: "The father," he says, comparing Increase to Cotton, "gave up on New England; the son did not" (196; see also 161, 164, and 174). Middlekauff bases his argument on a shift in Mather's sermon rhetoric, in his use of typology, and in his conception of New England. I would add that we can base it, too, on his retreat from history. As a historian, Mather wrote for twenty years in the belief that the past could somehow be reauthorized to achieve social harmony in the present: for example, the "first principles of New England" could without a doubt be rediscovered, first by the historian and then by people, who would then quit their squabbling when they understood the "true" purpose of New England. Out of what he perceived as a fragmented and fragmenting culture, Mather attempted to forge a more tightly knit society; history was in pieces, and Mather tried in various historical narratives to sew it back together again. But the loss of the charter by which New England could still proclaim itself a Puritan commonwealth changed all that for him. Although Increase Mather continued to work publicly for what he saw as the good of the colony, he quit writing New England's history. For him, the past could no longer have relevance to the colony's future. He left the task of reseeing the past, and rethinking the authority through which one could narrate it, to another historian.

Back to the Future

Cotton Mather's
Magnalia Christi Americana

4

After 1660, while Increase Mather wrote historical narratives to address specific crises, there were insistent and repeated calls for a comprehensive history of New England. "It is much to be desired there might be extant *A Compleat History of the United Colonies of New-England,*" John Higginson and Thomas Thacher wrote in the preface to Nathaniel Morton's *New Englands Memoriall,* "that God may have the praise of his goodness to his People here, and that the present and future Generations may have the benefit thereof" ("To the Reader" A2). Daniel Gookin began to write such a comprehensive history, though he finally called on someone else to finish the task; Gookin claimed he composed his more narrowly focused *Historical Collections of the Indians in New England* (ca. 1674) precisely because he had not heard of anyone else writing about God's providences to New England: "Being unwilling that a matter of so great a concernment for the honour of God and the good of man, should be buried in oblivion, [he] adventured in his old age . . . to draw some rude delineaments of God's beautiful work in this land" (86).[1] "It's a great pitty," Joshua Scottow wrote as late as 1694, "before the present Generation pass off the Stage of Action, that there should not be a compleat History laid up in our

Archivis" (286). These calls reflect the anxious attitude toward the past expressed by Wigglesworth and Morton and Mather in the middle decades of the century: the sense that the connections to the beginning of the enterprise had been lost and could only be reconnected—"re-membered"—through an act of narration. In 1680 William Hubbard was officially commissioned and subsidized by the General Court to write a comprehensive history of New England; he finished it in 1682, but it was not published by the government. Perry Miller suggests that it was repressed by Increase Mather and others who were "displeased" with it (*From Colony to Province* 136). He is probably correct, although Hubbard's moderate stance on London's attempt to revoke the Bay colony's charter in 1683 might have displeased more New Englanders than were simply in Mather's circle.

More generally, however, Hubbard's *A General History of New-England, from the Discovery to MDCLXXX* seems to have failed by not clearly demonstrating the purpose of New England's past. For, on any number of specific issues, Hubbard's narrative takes positions that Increase Mather and other traditionalists would have found proper: New England is a "literal" Canaan (22; see also 51, 58, 60, 63, 96–97, etc.); the people are conceived as unruly, greedy, unable to control their selfish desires (159, 587); church polity manifests a "middle way" (182–84, 332–33); the early years of settlement are conceived as "the golden age of New England, when vice was crushed, as well by the civil, as sacred sword" (248); Anne Hutchinson is quite correctly "purged" from the colonies in 1637 (297); and so on. More often than not, Hubbard's narrative appears to be as orthodox as any of Increase Mather's.

His narrative lacks, however, an organizing principle that makes sense of New England's decline after mid century. "The affairs of the world are carried in a movable wheel," Hubbard says at one point, "wherein it is oft found that what is highest in one season is laid quite underneath soon after" (379). Here, as in his history of King Philip's War, Hubbard attributes change not to the community's failings but to the normal course of events. Perhaps for this reason, the narrative is structured by "lustres," a word derived from the Latin *lustrum,* which was the ceremonial purification of the entire Roman population after the census every five years. These five-year cycles are repetitive and predictable, and metaphorically they do indeed "purify" New England's past, in part by denying cultural conflict (the early years are a "golden age"

[248]) and in part by refusing to grind contemporary axes—the Halfway Covenant, the failings in the people, the lists of sins, the meaning of King Philip's War—that might give rise to conflict. In the narrative, history is driven by nothing other than those five-year periods, by time itself, as it were: a historiographic method that makes Hubbard's narrative appear quite modern. Events in Hubbard's *General History* are certainly not driven by the express will of God, nor by the perversity of dissenters, nor by doctrinal controversy, moral laxity, or the passing of generations. For all of this, Hubbard is still a providential historian: for example, several chapters in the middle of the history discuss "memorable accidents in New England" in a way that is quite reminiscent of Increase Mather's method in *Illustrious Providences*. As I have argued earlier, Hubbard is really no more modern than Increase Mather or Joshua Scottow. Grounded as those historians were in what Richard De Prospo calls "theistic discourse," Hubbard in the *General History* was simply a rather ineffective storyteller. There does not seem to be any point to New England's history. It was those politics, not anything that the orthodox would have found particularly displeasing, that eventually made Hubbard's history, by the decision of the General Court not to publish it, literally unreadable for most of his contemporaries.

CRISES

On the night of Friday, March 30, 1688, Increase Mather put on a disguise, walked past the agent of the Dominion of New England who was waiting to arrest him, and slipped out of Boston. A week later he sailed for England to lobby King James for the reinstatement of Massachusetts Bay's original charter. Four years later, having successfully negotiated a compromise with King William's advisors, Mather was to return to New England—a much-changed New England after the Glorious Revolution—with a new charter in hand and a royally appointed governor, Sir William Phips, at his side.

William entered London in December 1688 and assumed power in February of the next year. One of his first acts was to confirm, for the time being at least, colonial governors and charters. However, New England was exempted from the order, largely through the efforts of Mather, who managed to convince William to recall Edmund Andros and to grant Massachusetts a new charter. Thus,

while the other colonial governors were notified of James's abdica-
tion and William's acceptance of the crown, and of their own status
in light of those events, Andros knew no more than anyone else in
New England. Perhaps less. Incoming ships brought rumors of the
events to Boston throughout February and March, but Andros was
in Maine, fighting Indians, and did not catch wind of these events
until early April. When he did, he hurried back to Boston. At about
the same time, John Winslow arrived from the West Indies bearing
a copy of William's Declaration, which had announced his invasion
to deliver England from the clutches of popery. Andros tried to
suppress the news, but it was too late. He had—according to his
accusers—trampled on the rights and liberties of individuals. He
had abolished the colonial legislature, challenged the validity of
long-standing titles to real estate, and forbidden regular town
meetings. He had struck down the very laws that had identified
Massachusetts as a Puritan commonwealth. He had allied himself
to a Catholic king who himself ruled arbitrarily, and he was (it was
rumored) allied with the French. The iron was hot, and Massachusetts struck it, probably after receiving verification in the next few
days of William's success.[2]

On April 18, 1689, a crowd began to gather in the streets of
Boston. Members of Andros's party were jailed, and at noon the
Declaration of Gentlemen, Merchants and Inhabitants of Boston, a defense of the revolution then in progress, was read to cheering Bos-
tonians. Andros surrendered Fort Hill later in the day, and in less
than two days the Glorious Revolution in Massachusetts was complete. Several months later Andros was sent to England, and until
William settled a new government on the colony, the old colonial
legislature and its governor Simon Bradstreet were returned to
power. By the middle of May, Connecticut, Plymouth, and Rhode
Island had followed Massachusetts' lead, ousting Andros's regime
and replacing it with their former charter governments.

Although the *Declaration* rehearsed familiar grievances against
the Dominion government, it was still so carefully written that it
suggests the Glorious Revolution had been planned in advance.
The orchestration of Andros's overthrow suggests the same, for it
was accomplished without bloodshed, without a single identifiable
leader, and without the usual confusion attendant upon a change
of regimes. It was an orderly transfer of power. The "gentlemen,
merchants, and inhabitants of Boston"—note that ministers have
given way to gentlemen and merchants—had apparently planned

Andros's overthrow for a week or more, fearing two possibilities as William's success became apparent: Andros might oppose the revolution in England and declare New England for James, or he might declare openly for William, be confirmed as governor, and so continue to wield his arbitrary power. Had Cotton Mather and the other leaders known already that Andros was to be recalled, their revolution would not have been necessary. As it was, the events of April 18 proved effective propaganda for New England's agents in London. See, they were able to say, New England is a loyal, Protestant colony wholly devoted to the same attitudes and principles as William and his new subjects.

Propaganda became an important tool as the New England colonies waited for William to turn his attention to them. It was one reason that Massachusetts, which had successfully conquered the French colony at Port Royal in May 1690, organized an assault upon Canada in August of the same year. The assault, led by William Phips, was botched from the very beginning. Scores of men lost their lives in the ill-conceived scheme, and Massachusetts lost so much money on the enterprise that bills of credit had to be printed to pay its soldiers, although a number of taxes had already been levied to pay for the expedition. The bills rapidly depreciated.

At first, the Glorious Revolution and the planning of the Quebec expedition seemed to put New England back in control of its own destiny. Resuming the old charter government and taking the initiative in Canada were attempts to reassert their own sense of identity. But the collapse of the assault and the uncertain news from the agents in London combined to reveal deep social discord. The government, and especially Phips, was criticized for the failure of the expedition; worn-out troops and a wary public were suspicious of the bills of credit; in London the agents could not agree on a strategy, for Mather was now asserting it was best to pursue a new charter, and Elisha Cooke was convinced that only the old charter would do. Their disagreement mirrored a similar split in New England opinion.

Then, in February and March 1692, a conspiracy of witches was discovered in and near Salem village. The devil, Cotton Mather later wrote, pushed New England "into a *blindman's buffet*" in which people mauled one another in the dark (qtd. in Levin, *Cotton Mather* 216). Without agreeing that the devil was the perpetrator, I believe Mather's metaphor is an accurate interpretation of the events at Salem in 1692. Not until Increase Mather emphatically stated in *Cases of Conscience Concerning Evil Spirits* (1693; delivered as a lecture on October 3, 1692) what his son had said more equivocally all summer—that spectral evidence, or indeed any inferences drawn from the behavior of afflicted persons, was not credible—did the community begin to see that its fear and misguided zeal had blinded it to the absurdity of spectral evidence.[3]

Increase Mather and the new governor, Sir William Phips, had brought with them the new charter for Massachusetts. Although the colony had not regained the old charter and the freedom that went with it, it did gain a very favorable settlement, one that would eventually help to shape the events of the 1770s and the "charter" of another new government in the 1780s. But not everyone in Massachusetts was pleased with the settlement in the 1690s. Elisha Cooke, representing a conservative faction that favored isolation, continued to complain that Increase Mather had betrayed the colony when he accepted the new charter. Others were not happy with Mather's choice of Phips as governor or with the composition of the first legislature. The 1693 elections returned only half of Mather's appointees and added several of his staunchest opponents, including Cooke. The new government was split by factions. By 1694 Phips, who was surely more comfortable as a ship captain or militia commander than as governor, had to face a growing number of complaints about his administration, most of which were lodged in London by Tories who wanted William to appoint a governor less sympathetic to a traditional conception of New England. Phips returned to London to answer the charges against him, but he died early the next year before his case could be heard. In 1697 Richard Coote, Earl of Bellomont, was appointed governor of Massachusetts, New York, and New Hampshire, with additional power to command the militias of Connecticut, Rhode Island, and the Jerseys.[4]

Bellomont was a military man. He was given the three governorships and military powers in other New England colonies because of the threat posed by the French and the Indians to all of New England. King William's War (1689–1697), the American phase of the War of the League of Augsburg, pitted the colonists against the French and their Indian allies. Most of Massachusetts remained relatively well protected in the war, but the northern frontiers—including Maine, New Hampshire, and the Massachusetts and New York borders—were at the mercy of guerrilla attacks that were difficult for the isolated villages on the frontier to answer effectively.

Andros had, in fact, been trying to secure the fort at Pemaquid, Maine, in 1689 when news of William's accession to the throne reached him; and later, Phips was forced to spend much of his time on the northern frontier, skirmishing with Indians, securing defense lines, and constructing Fort William Henry at Pemaquid. In the minds of New Englanders in the 1690s, New France was a nightmare that would not go away. Ironically, Bellomont's governorship—he died in office in March 1701—coincided with the peaceful interval between King William's War and Queen Anne's War (1701–1714; known in Europe as the War of the Spanish Succession).

The witches, the battles with the Indians and French, a government in transition, the defeat in Canada: New England in 1692 was distressed. No area of society was spared. The religious controversies of these years do appear to be muted, in part because there was no dramatic controversy like the Halfway Covenant, but even more because as the century wore on religious controversies had a less wrenching effect on society as a whole. The Halfway Covenant had affected every church, and therefore every churchgoer, and had forced New England to revise its sense of itself. But by the end of the century, more and more, religious controversies had a wrenching effect only within the ranks of the ministers. When, for example, Solomon Stoddard went beyond the Halfway Covenant in the 1670s and admitted his whole congregation to the Lord's Supper, Increase Mather vigorously complained. The two men debated the issue at the Reforming Synod in 1679. The contest ended without a clear winner, although Stoddard did manage to have the Synod reword one of its tenets, so that only a public profession of faith—not a conversion narrative, as New England churches had demanded ever since Anne Hutchinson broached her errors—was demanded of applicants. That was another innovation, one that (if Stoddard's reports about his "harvests" could be believed) worked effectively to enlarge his church. Eventually, Stoddard took his doctrine to its logical conclusion, admitting to the Lord's Supper—to the church, in a sense—anyone who wished to receive the sacrament. "The great design of this ordinance," he wrote, "is for the strengthening of faith; therein is offered to us special communion with a crucified Saviour" (337). In his hands the sacraments became converting ordinances, ways to bring as many people as possible into the flock, not winnow them into the elect and nonelect. Those New Englanders who still considered themselves orthodox were outraged. The English government had subverted the foundation of the godly commonwealth from without, and now Stoddard was doing so from within.⑤

Stoddard's assertions were paralleled by the founding of the Brattle Street Church. John Leverett and the Brattle brothers, Thomas and William, decided in 1699 to build a new church in Boston. All three men were liberals willing, like Stoddard, to turn their backs on what they felt were the outdated and ineffective notions of the founders of the New England Way. They recruited Benjamin Colman (Harvard, '92) to minister to the Brattle Street congregation. Colman had been preaching in England for several years under the auspices of the Presbyterian Board, and in his sermons, his prose style, and his tolerance for new ideas, he clearly represented the new catholicity of taste and refinement then fashionable in England. In the *Manifesto* (1699) that he and his brethren published to explain the new church's principles, Colman discarded several major tenets of the New England Way. All children would be baptized in the new church (*that* resolved the problem of halfway membership!); visible sanctity, not a conversion narrative, would be necessary for admission; ministers were to be chosen not by the few "saints" but by anyone who contributed to the maintenance of the church. According to the new charter, one's position in the state was now determined by property; the Brattle Street Church bid to have one's position in the church determined by financial contribution. In addition, Colman had himself ordained in London, shunning the traditional laying on of hands by local ministers. It was, on the whole, a stunning rejection of certain New England traditions.

In addition to their principles, Leverett and the Brattles had ulterior motives—they wanted Increase Mather out of the Harvard presidency. They achieved that goal in 1700 when the General Assembly voted to require the president of Harvard to reside in Cambridge. Mather tried living there but finally told the Court that he would have to be replaced if he could not live in Boston. The Court then offered the position to Samuel Willard, who was more liberal than Mather on religious and educational issues and so for Leverett and the Brattles an acceptable alternative to Mather, but he declined the position for the same reason, whereupon the Court offered him the vice-presidency of the college. Willard accepted, since the residency statute did not apply to the vice-presidency; no president was appointed until after his death in 1707.

So, in effect, Willard became the president of Harvard though he did not live in Cambridge. The incident was a slight to the Mathers and what for some people they represented—stodgy, narrow ideas that had no place in New England's future (Hall, *Last* 280–89; Murdock, *Increase Mather* 348–60).

Protestant sects that dissented from the orthodoxy had been making advances in New England ever since the Restoration. Baptists built a meetinghouse in Boston in 1678, Anglicans in 1690. Quakers lived unmolested in the colonies as early as the 1670s. But Stoddard and Colman represented radical and dissenting change from within the traditions of the New England Way. Earlier in the century, the orthodoxy had not permitted such overt dissent to flourish, though it had allowed certain types of covert dissent (the Presbyterianism of Parker and Noyes, for example) to exist.

Without a doubt, New England society had changed dramatically under the 1691 charter in at least two important aspects. First, church and state went their own ways. Perry Miller notes, "the last time that a ruler of Massachusetts . . . formally and officially asked advice of the churches" was during the Salem witch trials (Miller, *From Colony to Province* 195). The authority of ministers in the state was greatly reduced (Hall, *Faithful* 176–278). And conversely, the state no longer acted as the protective arm of the churches. Officially, no Hutchinsons would be banished after 1691, no Quakers hanged.

Second, the idiom with which the community defined itself— already strained by events like the revocation of the original charter and the decisions of the Reforming Synod—shifted in the 1690s. Stoddard's disavowal of the type of congregationalism practiced by the founders is symptomatic. Even his staunchest opponents, Increase and Cotton Mather, moved toward more accommodating positions in these years, endorsing the *Heads of Agreement* uniting the Congregational and Presbyterian wings of the church in 1691 (a point that Cotton emphasizes in *Magnalia Christi Americana*) and gradually redefining man's sanctity in terms of visible piety rather than the evidence of sanctification demanded by the founders. Most New Englanders were still Calvinists, but a new sensibility began to infiltrate their submission to an inscrutable sovereign God: covenant theology began to lose its power to explain adequately, man's abilities were spoken of more highly, the rights of true-born Englishmen became the working "model" of one's place in society. New ideas were introduced, and old words like *piety* began to take on new meanings.[6]

New Englanders were very aware in the 1690s that the new charter they had received from William represented a dramatic new beginning to their history. Joshua Scottow, in *A Narrative of the Planting of the Massachusetts Colony* (1694), saw the period from 1684 to 1692 as a "Junctor of time" connecting the founders' world to the "Halcyon Dayes" promised by the new charter (318). His historical narrative is in fact designed to locate the cause of that junction in time, which explains why the first half of the narrative is taken up with exonerating the first generation of settlers, while the latter half details the causes—witchcraft, various lusts, pride, refusal to implement the church polity of the Cambridge Platform—"of these dismal dayes" between charters (306). New England has brought upon itself the loss of the original charter, wars with the Indians, God's departing glory.

Anthony Kemp has studied Scottow's concept of history in the *Narrative,* and he notes how the prose often seems "to have no syntactical direction or movement at all" (136), how the narrator seems unable to read the signs strewn in the past, how Scottow's use of the trope of the wheels within the wheels (from Ezekiel) to describe New England's history "is a strange typological identification, because, even in its original biblical context, it is uninterpretable, representing God self-revealed as unfathomable enigma, enigma within enigma" (137–38).[7] Scottow seems quite lost inside history, not simply in the ways already described, but also in his skepticism that "Halcyon dayes" really will return under the new charter. His New England seems stuck within that gap in history, not capable of progressing beyond it. "Oh that we might experience these things [God's Spirit, mercy, grace, and so on]," he laments at the end of the history (330). He is not convinced his people can. Clearly he is not (as Sacvan Bercovitch has claimed) insistent that New England stands outside time, as a perfect human undertaking that is resistant to secular history.[8] He is only too aware that New England, like all other human communities, is subject to the vicissitudes of time. Not surprisingly, his narrative overtly takes the jeremiadic line on the specific causes of New England's recent changes: "The Lord took delight in our Fathers, and they in him; we have left the Lord, he hath forsaken us; they Walkt with him, we contrary to him . . . we are sold and scattered among the Heathen" (306). He asks his audience to repent. But in any number of ways, Scottow reveals a fundamental uncertainty about the meaning of New England's history. He has no good answer to those skeptics who ask, "What is become of the *New-Heaven,* and the *New-Earth,* of your Non parralleld Reformation you boasted of? . . . what is become of your resolved Revolution, which God is now Plagueing you for? and the Complication of Lies, made to encourage and further it?" (317). He isn't sure what has happened to it, and he senses that under the new charter the right kind of repairs cannot be made: "the Churches of old, and late, have Degenerated into Anarchy or Confusion, or else given themselves up, unto the dominion of some prelatical Teachers to rule at pleasure . . . and they will do the same for the future" (326).

Cotton Mather was more sure. And his massive history, *Magnalia Christi Americana,* was designed to provide an answer, one way or another. He begins with the same assumption as does Scottow: that New England's history has been neatly dichotomized. The earliest readers of the history perceived this. One purpose of *Magnalia,* wrote John Higginson in his "Attestation," is "That the *Names* of such Eminent Persons as the Lord made use of [in New England] . . . may be embalmed, and preserved, for the Knowledge and Imitation of Posterity" (vii). Grindal Rawson agreed, adding in a prefatory poem that "the Dead in [Mather's] rare Pages Rise." Benjamin Thompson took the imagery of death and resurrection even further:

> Is the Bles'd MATHER *Necromancer* turn'd,
> To raise his Countries Father's Ashes Urn'd?
> *Elisha*'s Dust, Life to the Dead imparts;
> This Prophet, by his more *Familiar Arts,*
> *Unseals* our *Hero*'s Tombs, and gives them Air;
> They Rise, they Walk, they Talk, Look wond'rous Fair.

The imagery in these encomiums was drawn from *Magnalia* itself, which abounds in references to interment, burial, graves, gravestones, epitaphs, sepulchers, ashes, urns, memorials, funerals, decay, and embalming. Death is everywhere in Cotton Mather's history of New England.

Providential historians held that the past did not really exist. Events that human beings perceived as having happened or that they anticipated happening in the future were all one in God's mind. Standing outside time, He could see the whole pattern in the fabric of history, while mankind could make out only a "web," here and there, on the "loom of time." "Judge not this Web while in the Loom," Edward Taylor pleads, "but stay / From judging it untill the judgment day" (325). (Of course, a historian's limited perspective did not preclude him from writing history *as if* it were seen through God's eyes: Edward Johnson proved that in his *Wonder-Working Providence*.) Human beings, writing from limited perspectives, were forced to fix meaning by declaring the past dead and its meaning intelligible, evident, and stable, even though their interpretation of events often retained a measure of uncertainty about the meaning of the past (Levin, "Forms").

As I have suggested, though, the past is "dead" in *Magnalia* for an even more specific reason than this. Mather provides a clue in "A General Introduction":

> 'Tis possible, that our Lord Jesus Christ carried some Thousands of *Reformers* into the Retirements of an *American Desart*, on purpose, that, with an opportunity to enjoy the precious *Liberty* of their *Ministry*, tho' in the midst of many *Temptations* all their days, He might there, *To* them at first, and then *By* them, give a *Specimen* of many Good Things, which he would have his Churches elsewhere aspire and arise unto: And *This* being done, He knows not whether there be an *All done*, that *New-England* was planted for; and whether the Plantation may not, soon after this, *Come to nothing*. (xx)

Here Mather is echoing John Winthrop who, more than sixty years earlier in "A Model of Christian Charity," had said that the colony shall be "a praise and glory, that men shall say of succeeding plantations: the Lord make it like that of New England" ("Model" 295). Mather indicates that the model was indeed intended for "Churches elsewhere"—England, Europe, Virginia, wherever—and that New England is now caught between the "all done" world of the first planters of the colony and some other world, some other purpose, that cannot yet be discerned. Mather's *Magnalia* was written within what he, like Scottow, perceived as a gap or "junctor" in history, within a particular period of time radically unlike other, "normal" periods. Hence, he can assert that "whether *New England* may *Live* any where else or no, it must *Live* in our *History*" (xxi). New England as it once was is dead, and Mather's own hope in the narrative is either to revive it or embalm it: either to make it live in reality once again or to make it reside in the pages of *Magnalia Christi Americana*.

For Cotton Mather, the event that "killed" New England was the imposition of the new royal charter in 1691. The circumstances surrounding the imposition of the charter—particularly Increase

153
/
sense of
purpose

key
issue

[handwritten margin notes: Cotton Mather's attribute toward; new to chapter 1691; OK]

Mather's role as a lobbyist for the colony and Cotton Mather's meditations on it in *Magnalia*—have led at least one scholar to read the history as "a sustained propaganda offensive to make the charter . . . the standard of a new conservatism."[9] Certainly Cotton Mather defended the charter throughout the 1690s; but, as the references to "raising" or "embalming" the dead indicate, *Magnalia* is not so much a defense of the new charter as an attempt to restore the spirit or life of the old charter in the days of the new. New England, Mather admits many times, has been dramatically altered. The question now is how, exactly, to read the seventy years of settlement that came to an end in 1691 and, then, how to go forward when the future has been severed from the past that New England had often used as a measure of its potential. The "*Judgments* of God," Mather tells us later in the history, "are a sort of a *Book* put into our Hands. . . . But can every Man read this Terrible *Book?*" No, he goes on to say, only a minister of God writing as a historian can "help [us] as well as we can to *Spell* the *Divine Lessons* contained in it" (VII: 106).

Standing in the gap between two worlds—one dead, the other seemingly powerless to be born—Mather reads the terrible book of New England's past for us. He does so, I shall argue in this chapter, by revising New England's past, and by revising it in such a way as to invite his audience to participate directly in the creation of the future, warning them in the process that they can do so only with the aid of the historian, the public man of letters who can see farther and more clearly than can they.

[handwritten: (seems least "intertextual"]

PROGRESS VERSUS CONTINUITY

The 1702 publication date of *Magnalia* is deceptive in a sense, for Mather composed most of the history in the years from 1694 to 1698, and he even incorporated into the massive framework previously published material he had written as early as 1689.[10] As he notes in "A General Introduction," *Magnalia* is "a sort of Rapsody made up (like the paper whereon 'tis written!) with many little Rags" (xxv). The framework for those rags is a seven-part division of the history of seventeenth-century New England: colonization (Book I), the lives of the governors (II), the lives of ministers trained in Europe (III), Harvard College and the lives of those ministers trained there (IV), the faith of New England as it was agreed on by synods (V), illustrious providences (VI), and "disturbances" of social peace and religious harmony (VII). *Magnalia* is actually seven separate histories: in each chapter Mather reaches back to events early in the century and then traces his theme forward in time to the decade (1688–1698) he refers to in Book VII as "Decennium Luctuosum." (The method is reminiscent of his father's in *Illustrious Providences*.) The whole is much more than simply "The Ecclesiastical History of New England" (as Mather's subtitle has it); it is a comprehensive history of the region, just the sort of "compleat history" community leaders had been calling for throughout the previous thirty years.

As Mather reaches back in time in each of these books, we can see him revising New England's past, just as Puritan historians had done before him. In Book I, for example, he revises the purpose of New England's mission. Winthrop had first defined that purpose to be the institution of a model that would guide other New World plantations and perhaps even Europe; Johnson had declared it to be a mass "removal"—a tactical "errand"—out of which Christ would draw soldiers for the impending war against the Antichrist; Increase Mather had emphasized personal and communal covenant renewal, defining New England's special and separate status as it derived from the piety of the first-generation settlers. Cotton Mather sees the past differently. Why was the city upon a hill founded in the first place? "It was PERSECUTION," he says. "Flocks" of nonconformists were "*driven into the Wilderness*" by a party within the Church of England led by Archbishop Laud, a party that "misemploy[ed] their heavy *Church-keys*" (I: 15, 21). The dissenters' "*Errand into the Wilderness*" (Mather retains the phrase even as he alters its meaning) was to preserve the "*Primitive* Principles, *and the Primitive* Practises" until such time as the Church of England came to its senses and ousted that false party.[11] In Mather's version of events, the settlers did not leave England willingly; their removal "was indeed a *Banishment*, rather than a Removal." The "*English* Hierarchy" of the church "banished them into this Plantation" of Massachusetts Bay (I: 17, 21).

However terrible banishment was to those settlers (and Book III presents a series of vivid pictures of their struggles in the wilderness), Mather now perceives it to have been a fortunate mistake. The colonists "were *Truer Sons* to the Church of *England,* than that part of the *Church*" that had banished them (I: 21); and their success as "a Receptacle of Protestant Churches on the *American*

Strand" proved in time to be a boost to the Reformation (I: 1). Rejected by the Church of England, its mother, New England proved in the course of time to be a most faithful and correct son, preserving intact the "family's" identity, and (Mather shrewdly hints) adding to its parents' material prosperity: "[I have described] the *Foundations* of those *Colonies*," he says at one point, "which have . . . enlarged the *English Empire* in some Regards more than any other Outgoings of our Nation" (I: 27).

Within Book I, Mather's revision of the mission affects his narration of the history of New England in two important ways. First, in a move designed to define New England's new identity, he informs us that the New World belongs to England. "If this *New World* were not found out first by the English," he says, "yet in those regards that are of all the *greatest*, it seems to be found out more *for* them than any other" (I: 3). Accordingly, he begins the book with the story of Gasper Coligni, a devout French Protestant whose attempt in the sixteenth century to begin a plantation in Brazil fails miserably. Mather quickly informs us "*that in* our Age *there has been another Essay, made not by* French, *but by* English PROTESTANTS, *to fill the certain Country in* America *with Reform'd Churches*" (I: 1). This essay was New England, of course. This tie to English origins, as we might suspect, is central to the reconfiguration of identity that Increase Mather had begun to suggest in his 1689–1691 pamphlets: the "ancient rights and liberties" (*Narrative* 8) of Whig politics and history apply as much to New England as they do to England.

Second, Mather backs away from the millennial optimism of Winthrop and Johnson: "I am going to give the *Christian Reader* an *History* of *some feeble Attempts* made in the *American Hemisphere* to anticipate the State of the *New-Jerusalem*, as far as the unavoidable *Vanity* of *Humane Affairs*, and *Influence* of *Satan* upon them would allow of it" (I: 4–5). The key word here is "anticipate." Mather subdues the rhetoric of New England's "chosen" status, instead defining the colony as an all-too-human effort to institute the most perfect "*Church-Government*" possible. All-too-human because, as Mather quotes John Robinson (minister to Bradford's band of Pilgrims when they were in Holland), "the Lord hath *more* Truth yet to break forth out of his Holy Word" (I: 14).

The progressive unfolding of truth is a key theme in *Magnalia*. Many times Mather assures us that change is continuous, that at no time in the past did "all Men . . . *see all Things*" (IV: 176), and that New England itself has steadily progressed toward a more enlightened understanding of humanity. Book V, the history of New England's synods, is the clearest example of this declaration. Commenting on the necessity, earlier in the century, of a public confession of faith for full admission to individual churches, Mather remarks "That [the] *unscriptural Severities* urged in this matter by several of our Churches, in the beginning of the Plantation, are now generally laid aside" (V: 44). What seemed to be a "primitive principle" then was gradually revealed to be unnecessary.

A similar sort of change occurs in the years following the Synod of 1662: the same ministers who had publicly opposed the Halfway Covenant "came to see that the Rigidity of their former Principles, had been a failing in them" (V: 82).[12] The three synodical decisions that Mather transcribes in Book V, in addition to the 1691 *Heads of Agreement* that united the Congregational and Presbyterian wings of the Church of England, represent the gradual reduction of the "FAITH and the ORDER in the Churches of New-England" (V: title page) to their essential elements.[13]

What remains at the end of the century (and here Mather again tries to locate the essentials of his country's character) is the short "Confession of Faith" owned and asserted by the Reforming Synod in 1680. This document is thoroughly Calvinist, as were the documents upon which it was modeled.[14] Surprisingly, however, the Confession is restricted solely to matters of faith, leaving a wide latitude of opinion on church discipline, government, and order, so wide (at least as Mather construes the document here) that Anglicans, Presbyterians, and Anabaptists could find common ground with the New England orthodoxy even though their church government was quite different from that of Congregationalism. Mather's bid in this is to reduce factionalism and sectarianism by making irrelevant many of the questions, such as the use of vestments or the rejection of infant baptism, that had divided England since the Elizabethan Settlement. Here, as elsewhere in the 1690s, then, words like *piety* came to have new meaning: the definition of piety now includes the toleration of a variety of Christian sects. Within Mather's narrative itself, one local and obvious effect of this revision is that many seventeenth-century dissenters from the New England Way are rehabilitated. Some churches, for example, had dissented from the Reforming Synod's 1680 confession of faith and had drawn up their own confessions in the following years: "Nevertheless," Mather insists, "all [that] *Variety* has been the exactest *Unity,* all those *Confessions* have been but so many *Derivations* from, and *Explications* and *Confirmations* of, that *Confession* which the *Synods* had voted for them all" (V: 4). The "exactest Unity" lay in the core of faith.

More obviously, dissenters like Roger Williams are rehabilitated. Early in Book VII, Mather charts Williams's progress in the 1630s from Salem to Plymouth to Salem again and finally, after his *"Banishment"* (an ironic choice of words in light of Mather's reconstruction of New England's own history) from the Bay colony, to Rhode Island. Aside from his annoying tendency toward "Giddiness" and "Confusion," Williams's real error was not his criticism of the Bay colony government in the 1630s, his rigid separatism, or his quarrel with John Cotton over church doctrine and polity in the 1640s; it was his tendency to cause divisions among the people. Mather reports that Williams organized the Salem church behind his "Aberrations"; he "Preached against the *Patent,* as an *Instrument of Injustice"* to the Indians (VII: 8); and he encouraged John Endicott to cut the cross out of the flag because it was a "Popish *Idol"* (VII: 9). In short, he undermined unity. When we put aside the "non-essential" differences that made him do so, however, Williams proves "to have had the *Root of the Matter* in him, during the *long Winter* of [his] Retirement" to Rhode Island (VII: 9). He wrote books against the Quakers (who were still outside the pale of the "exactest Unity"), and he "extinguished" various *"Disturbances* of the Country"* (VII: 11).[15] Thus, in the end, Williams is assimilated into the main line of New England history; his disagreements with orthodox theologians of the discipline and order of the New England Way—in particular, John Cotton—are elided.[16] They were, in Mather's version of the past, nonessential.

Mather condemns the seventeenth-century orthodoxy for its intolerance of dissenters from the New England Way, just as he rehabilitates individuals who in hindsight appear to have the "root of the matter" in them. (He uses this phrase also to describe John Wheelwright, after his banishment was revoked in 1643 [VII: 15].) In his account of Quakerism in New England, for example, Mather does not fail to report that four Quakers were executed in Boston between 1659 and 1661. We should remember that intolerance was an integral part of New England's identity at mid century. "I dare take upon me," Nathaniel Ward had written in 1647, "to proclaime to the world . . . that all Familists, Antinomians, Anabaptists, and other Enthusiasts shall have free Liberty to keepe away from us, and such as will come to be gone as fast as they can, the sooner the better" (6–7, 12). Fifty years later, Mather seems at first to agree with Ward: "I appeal to all the reasonable part of Mankind, whether the Infant Colonies of *New-England* had not cause to guard themselves against these [Quakers]" (VII: 24). They were insane, he points out; two of them went so far as to appear stark naked in church one day. But, he admits, it was wrong to put them to death, and "I will inform the World of a better *Vindication* for my Country than ["guarding" themselves from the Quakers by restrictive laws]: namely, that they did by a Solemn Act afterwards Renounce whatever *Laws* are against a Just *Liberty of Conscience*" (VII: 24). It is not clear what solemn act Mather has in mind here. Not until the Act of Toleration was passed in England in 1689 and subsequently imposed on New England did the Puritan orthodoxy, however unwillingly, accept the notion of limited toleration. Mather implicitly acknowledges this fact when several pages later he transcribes part of his own 1690 election-day sermon in which he is still making public appeals for toleration: "A Man has a *Right* unto his Life, his Estate, his Liberty, and his Family, although he should not come up unto these and those Blessed *Institutions* of our Lord" (VII: 29). But, despite this vagueness as to particulars, he does insist that New England had come to see the error of its attempts to keep people's consciences for them. Liberty of conscience was exactly Roger Williams's point in the 1640s; Mather recognizes it as an "orthodox" view in *Magnalia*.

The issues of the purpose of New England's mission, of faith (rather than discipline) as a basis for religious practice, and of religious toleration are just several examples of Mather's attempt to accommodate the legal, political, and cultural changes created by the new charter. However, at other times, particularly in the middle books of *Magnalia* (II–IV), both Mather's interpretation of history and his method of presenting it appear quite different.[17] The method here is biographical:

> I . . . introduce the *Actors* [Mather says concerning these books] that have, in a more exemplary manner served those *Colonies*; and give *Remarkable Occurrences*, in the exemplary LIVES of many *Magistrates*, and of more *Ministers*, who so *Lived*, as to leave unto Posterity, *Examples* worthy of *Everlasting Remembrance*. ("General Introduction" xix)

Whereas, on one hand, progress toward essential ideas and liberties is often a key theme in the narratives in Books I, V, VI, and VII (perhaps reassuring England that the colonists were not quite as provincial as might be imagined), on the other hand, the continuity of New England's history is a key theme in these biographies.[18]

In the introduction to Book III, Mather asks his audience to admire the figures in the biographies that follow, for "*They are of- fered unto the Publick, with the Intention sometimes mentioned by Gregory . . .: That* Patterns *may have upon us the force which Precepts have not*" (III: 1). Readers have noted the similarity of the many biographies in *Magnalia*, even going so far as to catalogue their essential elements (Gay 64–65).[19] But, as David Levin has shown, Mather's theme in the middle books is precisely one of "variation within essential uniformity" (IV: 4); Mather's heroes "are unique versions of an essential type," whose uniformity we are meant to see (*Cotton Mather* 261–65).[20] In Book II the pattern of each governor's life is that of a "shield" to the churches of New England. In Book III the pattern of each minister's life is that of strong, faithful, and intelligent leadership in the primitive churches of America; Mather uses the phrase "*De Viris Illustribus*" as a subtitle to the book because Jerome's book of that title attempted to free early Christians from the unjust reproach of being poor, weak, and ignorant men. Like Norton, Morton, and Scottow, Mather consciously directs this pattern to the cultural sons of those fathers, "the *Generation* which are now rising up, *after the Death of* Cotton, *and of the Elders that out-lived him.*" Doing so, he hopes, will stem the "fearful *Degeneracy* . . . rushing in upon those Churches" of New England" (III: 11). In Book IV the pattern of each Harvard-trained minister's life is that of learning and virtue combined (IV: 140). These lives are patterned to show that the "fearful *Degeneracy*" mentioned in Book III is not complete: usually the "Tree withers when its Top is lopt off," Mather points out, but "*Harvard-Colledge* had . . . prevented it" by nurturing fit replacements for the English-trained generation (IV: 140).

Through a series of biographies, each of these books attempts to present a specific "type" of Christian in his "essential" nature. These types, civil and religious, represent qualities that, Mather insists, must remain constant over time if a Christian commonwealth is to succeed. From Winthrop to Phips, the magistrates are the "walls of New England" ("*Novanglorum* MOENIA" [II: 15]), guarding God's "People from all Disasters, which threatned [*sic*] them either by Sea or Land" (II: 59). The same holds true in Book III, where the virtues of doing good, guarding against spiritual declension, and preaching the Word faithfully (III: 18, 24, 25–26) are as evident in the life of John Cotton (III: 14–32) at the beginning of the book as they are in the life of John Baily at the end (III: 224–38); and the same holds true in Book IV, where the lives of Harvard graduates from John Brock ('46) to his brother Nathaniel Mather ('85) represent "Instance[s] of unusual *Industry,* and no Common *Piety*" (IV: 211).

There is an argument here in the middle books of *Magnalia* that critics, their senses dulled by boredom or mistaken assumptions, have missed. Within each of the three books, Mather presents "epitomes" of a single type. Those three types are roughly equivalent to the three motifs of "purity, peace, and plenty" announced by Edward Johnson in *Wonder-Working Providence:* the civil magistrates represent the peaceful "walls" of protection from enemies of pure reformation, the English-trained ministers the "purity" of the churches, and the Harvard-trained ministers the continued "plenty" of God's people in America. These elements as they are established in the middle books become the identifying characteristics of a New England already familiar to us from Johnson's *Wonder-Working Providence:* the New Jerusalem.[21]

Mather's argument and narrative method in *Magnalia* are ambivalent: is New England more English than it is New? or more New than English? is progress or is continuity the key to New England's past? This ambivalence is in part a function of his own uncertainty about the future of the country: even Jesus Christ "knows not whether there be not *All done,* that *New-England* was planted for; and whether the Plantation may not, soon . . . *Come to nothing*" ("General Introduction" xx). Mather imagines two possibilities: New England may be absorbed into the English nation, in which case a Whig outlook and methodology is entirely appropriate to the country's history; or New England may yet succeed as the vanguard of the Reformation, as a city upon a hill, in which case an outlook and methodology designed for a Christian commonwealth is most appropriate. The future is contingent.

An ambivalence, as Mather himself first pointed out, also distinguishes the prose in *Magnalia.* To some readers, he says in the "General Introduction," he will "seem to have used . . . a Simple, Submiss, Humble *Style.* . . . Whereas *others,* it may be, will reckon the *Style* Embellished with too much of *Ornament,* by the multiplied References to other and former Concerns, closely couch'd, for the Observation of the *Attentive,* in almost every Paragraph." Many critics have observed the ornamentation and allusiveness of *Magnalia*'s prose, but only a few have perceived that the "prose of the

Magnalia is both baroque and plain" (Levin, *Cotton Mather* 266). Indeed, in the course of the narrative Mather adopts numerous styles, more in fact than can be simply classified as either baroque or plain: graceful, economical, and straightforward narration, witty puns, rococo opening paragraphs in the biographies, lurid and violent captivity narratives in Book VII, providential language in Book VI, transcribed documents of the New England Way in Book V. In this respect *Magnalia*, like *Moby-Dick*, reflects the omnivorous reading and many talents of its author.[22]

However, Mather's statement concerning his prose indicates much more than an awareness of his own diverse prose styles; it is a recognition that his reader's interpretation of *Magnalia* depends on his or her perspective. The prose will seem different to different readers. He makes a similar point later in "Pietas in Patriam": "the *Eye* sees not those Objects which are applied close unto it, and even lye upon it; but when the Objects are to some distance removed, it clearly discerns them" (II: 70). If truth is the object to be discerned in and by the history—"*Historia est . . . Lux veritatis*" ("General Introduction" xxi)—then what Mather's readers need is not just light but also the proper perspective from which they can bring truth into focus.

Mather in the "General Introduction" is fascinated by the prospect of how many readers will be unable to perceive the truth in the narrative that follows—how many lack the correct perspective from which the truth can be discerned. In New England alone, he says, there are "a considerable number of loose and vain Inhabitants," who of course will find the history useless; "a number of eminently Godly Persons, who are for a Larger [Church] way, and unto these my Church-History will give distast"; and "some among us, who very strictly profess the *Congregational Church-Discipline,* but [who] at the same time . . . have an unhappy Narrowness of Soul, by which they confine their . . . Kindness too much unto their own Party; and unto those my *Church History* will [also] be offensive." And, he adds, "If it be thus in my own Country, it cannot be otherwise in That whereto I send this account of my own" (xxvii). Some critics ascribe this kind of statement in Cotton Mather's work to his "pedantry" (Gay 60). But Mather perceived that in the "English," or "catholick" (Hall, *Faithful* 273), atmosphere of New England in the 1690s many people—even some "Good Men," he admits—were unable to discern the truth. His society had fragmented into contending factions that could not understand one another; a common language and vision had been lost/Men could not see clearly. "If a *Book* of some Consequence be laid open before one that cannot *Read,* he may Look and Gaze upon it; but unto what purpose, as long as he cannot understand it?" (VII: 106).

In those times, with New England's status as a holy commonwealth apparently negated by the new charter and with a number of competing perspectives available to his audience, Mather self-consciously casts himself in the privileged role of a "*Sacer Vates*" (II: 72), or sacred seer, able to correct the audience's vision. Mather is the historian who can see the past, understand the present, and foretell the future. I have argued from the beginning of this book that New England never experienced what one critic (voicing a common misunderstanding of Puritan culture) called a "golden age" when "all the cultural norms of the community were fused . . . with extraordinary success"; from the first days of the settlement, competing voices ("perspectives") attacked the "remarkable hegemony" of the orthodoxy, forcing it to listen to them, to respond to them and, often, to modify its current vision of New England.[23]

It is worth remembering that Winthrop in his own *History* had been unable to locate a perspective from which he could satisfactorily accommodate (or silence) competing voices and comprehend New England's history. Johnson reconstructed history from God's point of view, placing his version of the past within a divine vision of New England's history and thereby subordinating (and in effect silencing) competing perspectives. Increase Mather tried many times to locate points of consensus from which a pattern of meaning, and hence a renewed purpose for the colony, could be maintained. Each historian, in other words, constructed narratives and adopted specific narrative strategies that could defuse dissent and create consensus, and that could center New England's mission within a carefully circumscribed set of boundaries. To do so, to effect a future different from the present, each historian had to revise the community's history.

In response to a different cultural crisis (some of the elements of which I detailed earlier in this chapter), Cotton Mather's narrative strategy is to insist, first, that his particular reconstruction of New England's history is his and his alone:

> had not my Heart been Trebly Oak'd and Brass'd for such Encounters as this our History may meet withal, I would have . . . tried,

whether I could not have Anagrammatized my Name into some Concealment. . . . Whereas now I freely confess, 'tis COTTON MATHER that has written all these things; *Me, me, adsum qui scripsi; in me convertite ferrum.* [It was I, I myself who wrote this! Hurl your spears at me!] ("General Introduction" xxv)

He makes the same point less emphatically when he defends his prose style by telling the story of the sculptor Polycletus, who made two statues, one "according to the Rules that best pleased himself, and the other according to the Fancy of every one that look'd upon his Work." His critics loved the first and derided the second. Just so, Mather indicates, has he composed *Magnalia* according to his own rules, not someone else's ("General Introduction" xxiii). Second, Mather attempts to convince his audience of the rectitude of his privileged vision, not through rules but through the force of examples: "Patterns," he indicates more than once in the history, "*may have upon us the force which* Precepts *have not*" (III: 1). Through the story he tells, he wants his audience to reconsider their "perspective" and, hopefully, to readjust it.

Having looked generally at Mather's strategy, I now want to look more closely at the narrative itself, to see how these notions of continuity and change and perspective are played out in what seems to me to be the best colonial history written in New England. Let me interject, however, a word about my method in this analysis of *Magnalia*. In perhaps the most influential work that has been done on Cotton Mather's history, Sacvan Bercovitch has argued in *The Puritan Origins of the American Self* that Mather's style—his rhetoric, more inclusively—is representative of "early New England rhetoric" (114). Using Mather's "Nehemias Americanus" as an example, Bercovitch claims that Mather fuses history and allegory, "autobiography and sacred history," "fact and promise" (127)—a whole series of opposing terms that English and European writers supposedly kept separate—in a successful effort to establish American identity as "a rhetorical (rather than a historical) issue" (132). *Magnalia Christi Americana*, Bercovitch says, is "the supreme colonial expression of what we have come to term the myth of America" (132); the Puritans' legacy to the United States was precisely the belief that here "secularism and orthodoxy [were] entwined" (163).

Bercovitch's assumptions, and conclusions, differ from mine: to him, the history of seventeenth-century New England is the history of the unchanging and "remarkable hegemony" of the orthodoxy (97–98); Cotton Mather wrote history only to "obviate" it (134);[24] and *Magnalia* is a supremely self-assured document that manifests "no . . . tension" about New England's role in either secular or sacred history (134). I mention his interpretation not so much to attack it, for the model he derives from "Nehemias Americanus" and from Puritan rhetoric more generally has proved to be quite suggestive and quite useful; I mention it so that I might juxtapose his method of examining *Magnalia* with mine. Bercovitch focuses on an eight-page slice of Mather's eight-hundred-page history, an approach that to me seems slightly suspect given the range of styles, strategies, and methods employed by Mather in that history. He tried to work around that problem by treating "Nehemias Americanus" as representative of larger wholes such as *Magnalia*, Mather's thought, early American Puritan rhetoric, American exclusivism.

I want instead to examine *Magnalia* by looking fairly closely at Book II and Book VII, examples of the two basic types of history Mather employs, biography (continuity) and communal history (progress). In doing so, I do not want to isolate one section of *Magnalia* as representative of the whole; I want to study the development of Mather's rhetoric both through time (since each of these two books ends with an appendix that was clearly written late in the history's composition) and also through the imaginative space, the narrative, of each book. By doing so I hope to establish, among other things, that Mather does not try to "obviate" history in *Magnalia;* like the other Puritan historians I have examined in *Authorizing the Past,* he simply tries to revive its relevance for a contemporary audience, to use the particular narrative he has constructed in order to forge a future different from the one he saw impending. In *Magnalia Christi Americana,* Mather formalizes and thematizes that very point.

REAUTHORIZING GOVERNMENT

"Nehemias Americanus. The Life of John Winthrop, Esq.," is the second biography in Book II; it follows the biography of William Bradford and precedes those of Edward Hopkins, Theophilus Eaton, John Winthrop, Jr., and—in an appendix that was first published separately in 1697—William Phips. One of the most striking patterns in "Nehemias Americanus" is Winthrop's tendency to give speeches; indeed, Cotton Mather's Winthrop is primarily a voice. When, for example, Winthrop is informed during a particularly harsh winter that a poor man in Boston had been stealing from his woodpile, he calls the man before him and tells him to "*supply* [him] *self at my Wood-Pile till this cold Season be over.*" (The italics indicate that Mather is allowing Winthrop to speak in his own words.) He then asks his friends, "*Whether he had not effectually cured this Man of Stealing his Wood?*" (II: 10). His "speech" cures the man.

Later in the narrative after the Antinomian Controversy has drawn to a close, Winthrop is accused by members of his church of pushing too hard to have Hutchinson, Wheelwright, and the others banished. Against the advice of the elders, he speaks to the congregation, and in that speech on the powers and fallibility of magistrates he "marvellously convinced, satisfied, and mollified the *uneasie Brethren* of [his] Church," so that after a little while all the former "differences" between Winthrop and the church "wore away" (II: 12). During the Hingham Affair, his little speech on liberty "dissolves" the "Spell" that was upon the "Eyes of the People," so that "their *distorted* and *enraged* notions of things all vanished" (II: 13). Visiting Plymouth in 1632, his speech on the origins of the word *goodman* "put a lasting stop to the Little, Idle, Whimsical *Conceits,* then beginning to grow Obstreperous" in that town (II: 14). These speeches reveal Mather's purpose in the biography. He does not conflate self and corporate enterprise, as Sacvan Bercovitch has so eloquently argued. Rather, he first "erases" Winthrop's self through his repeated insistence that Winthrop "overcame" his self, that he is "chiefly to be considered as a *Governour*" and not as a private person in the narrative (II: 9), that his purse (II: 10), his estate (II: 14), his time, even his woodpile were not his own. There is no "self" in the narrative.

Then, Mather insists that Winthrop's speeches, not his self, form the walls of New England to which he refers at the end of the biography (II: 15). Of course, the words in those speeches are not Winthrop's own: they come from God, who called Winthrop to office through the vote of the "saints" (a point that Mather emphasizes) and who directs Winthrop's actions in his capacity as magistrate. Like his Old Testament type, Nehemiah, Winthrop does not literally build the walls of the new commonwealth himself; instead, he speaks to the people and they, then, must perform or make visible his words. "Then I told them of the hand of my

God which was good upon me, . . . And they said, Let us rise up and build" (Nehemiah 2.18). But Winthrop's words, unlike Nehemias's, do not eventuate in a literal wall; they give rise to a people that, in Mather's narrative, are "edified": "their *distorted* and *enraged* notions of things all vanished" (II: 13), the historian remarks after one typical incident. The people are made to see more clearly. The etymology of the word _edification_ is instructive in this context, as it was in *Wonder-Working Providence;* it means both to build and to instruct. In the narrative, Winthrop's words perform both those tasks. They instruct the people, and they "build": not a literal wall, but a figurative wall that contains or defines New England, that indeed is New England, in a sense. The protagonist of "Nehemias Americanus" gives voice to authority and to truth; the theocracy's divinely appointed governor "speaks" the community into being.

Although Mather does quote Winthrop liberally, he is not simply an amanuensis:

> And know, that as the *Picture* of this their *Governour,* was, after his *Death,* hung up with Honour in the *State-House* of his Country, so the *Wisdom, Courage,* and Holy *Zeal* of his *Life,* were an Example well-worthy to be Copied by all that shall succeed in *Government.* (II: 9)

What we get in the biography is a "portrait," though Mather elides this fact by suggesting that the "Example" presented here is equivalent to the governor, while the act of "copying" will be done by Winthrop's successors in the government. Indeed, Mather insists, it is necessary that Winthrop be imitated, precisely because there is no longer any assurance that, appointed by the king or elected by propertied men (not saints who belong to one of New England's churches), a New England magistrate in 1700 will be wise, courageous, or zealous, much less speak for God. In other words, Mather argues, better a lifeless copy of Winthrop hanging in the statehouse than a living creature of the king inhabiting it.

One irony of the Glorious Revolution is that, while it restricted the king's power in England, it reasserted his power in the colonies (Lovejoy, *Glorious Revolution* 377–78). In this sense, Mather addresses the crisis of authority that was brought on by the Glorious Revolution in New England by rhetorically shifting authority away from the king and toward the colonial historian-artist who creates

rhetorician
authority

authoritative examples or models for the community. Note, for example, how the analogy just referred to is skewed: Winthrop's pictorial representation was, after his death, hung on the walls of the statehouse by his contemporaries, signifying the general regard in which Winthrop as governor was held; "similarly," his wisdom, courage, and zeal are to be "Copied" by magistrates in the 1690s and also "hung" (or manifested) in the "State-House." Yet where are Winthrop's "Wisdom, Courage, and Holy Zeal"? In the grave, as is the face from which the portrait was painted? Obviously not. They exist only in the narrative entitled "Nehemias Americanus." Rhetorically, Mather suggests that the act of hanging Winthrop's portrait in the statehouse is equivalent to the act of imitating his virtues. However, those virtues must be isolated and recorded by the historian, who thus assumes a privileged role in the formation and execution of public policy. In the absence of Winthrop, or of any leader sanctioned as he was by God, the historian assumes at least in part the role of communal spokesman.

Mather's epigraph to "Nehemias Americanus" plays with this idea: "*Quicunq; Venti erunt, Ars nostra certe non aberit* [But whatever winds blow, our art will surely never pass away]" (II: 8), he wrote, quoting Cicero. Mather explicitly valorizes the storyteller. He recognized no doubt that with the passing of the theocracy, the ministry as well as the governorship underwent diminution. Hence, he assumes the role of historian and privileges that role, because he understands that the traditional sources of authority have been undermined by the loss of the original charter and the community's (or at least his own) concomitant loss of faith in its avowed purpose. By writing the historical John Winthrop out of what purports to be his biography, Mather attempts to ground his own vision of the future in the disembodied words—the vocal presence—of the dead governor.[25]

In this sense, the words are really no longer Winthrop's; for Mather, in choosing his narrative materials, has authorized them in his own particular ways. By "de-composing" Winthrop's self—and I do not think the metaphor and pun are too farfetched, given that the narrative ends with an "epitaph," indicating that something is buried in the narrative—Mather attempts in "Nehemias Americanus" to ground the reconstruction of his community following the Glorious Revolution in the values of the past, as Winthrop had verbalized them, but he does so through a changed source of authority. What we begin to see in this narrative is the belief that the "man of letters"—the historian, in particular—can "see" farther than magistrates and ministers, the traditional figures of authority in seventeenth-century New England. This is not the "origin of an American self," to refer to Bercovitch's book again, though it is perhaps one origin of the idea of the "man of letters" that develops in the eighteenth century in both England and the American colonies. Along these lines, then, Mather's "Nehemias Americanus" epitomizes and, in its narrative structure, thematizes the value of narrative in times of ideological crisis such as the colonies experienced after the Glorious Revolution: its capacity to criticize perceived cultural reality (the unsuitability of the Crown's appointing governors in the colony), and then to reconceive that reality and to envision an alternative reality, which it is up to the author's readers—as it was for Nehemias's auditors—to "build." In response to a perceived sociocultural need, Mather has reauthorized the past in a quite different way from the way Johnson or Increase Mather did.

It might help to point out that this question of colonial authority was much debated in the 1690s; Mather was writing at a time when many other intellectuals were debating the question of cultural authority. For example, in his history of the Glorious Revolution in Connecticut, *Will and Doom* (1692), Gershom Bulkeley steadily lambastes Connecticut's leaders because in deposing Andros, the king's rightful viceroy, they usurped the authority of the king. "Unlawful, usurped, or tyranical authority is truly no authority," Bulkeley states, "and is call'd authority but by a catachreses" (94). He in effect turns the language of the revolutionaries in Connecticut against the revolutionaries themselves, arguing that it was they who imposed arbitrary power, not Andros and certainly not the king. Throughout the diatribe, with incantatory regularity, Bulkeley raises the issue of authority: Who are the "authors" of revolution? what right do they have to assume power? to authorize a government? (for example, 85, 92, 93, 95, 101, 107, 112). Bulkeley is confident that he is not a revolutionary, either in his actions toward established, traditional authorities—the king of England and, more broadly, the "law of nature and right reason" (94)—or in his writing of history itself. "We therefore take ourselves to be indispensibly oblig'd to make these things known," he says concerning his purpose in *Will and Doom*, "so as . . . they may come to their majesties knowledge without false glosses, lest otherwise we be involved in the same guilt and our blood be upon our own

heads" (255). Bulkeley insists that he is not "painting" or embel-
lishing in *Will and Doom;* he is simply telling things as they are. For
to "falsely gloss" the events of the past would, in his historiographic terms, be a kind of revolt, would be to continue the revolution, to continue to undermine traditional sources of authority,
not just of the king or of reason or of nature, but of the past itself,
the authority of history. Unlike Cotton Mather, Bulkeley is not interested in reauthorizing power in a postrevolutionary world. He
was content with the old order of things and now wants that order
restored. Bulkeley's rhetoric of history was as conservative as his
politics.

In "Nehemias Americanus," however, the historian artist uses
his talent to write about the magistrate, to paint him in such a way
that "*the Sons of* New-England" can "Copy" (II: 1) him in their own
lives. The historian's power is circumscribed only by the fact that
the people tend already to see his subject as he sees him. For
Mather insists that the people, though blind at times, are truly able
to "see" Winthrop in the end: after the Hingham affair, they
"would not . . . entrust the Helm of the *Weather-beaten* Bark [that
is, the government] in any other Hands" (II: 13); after his death,
they hang his "*Picture*" with "Honour in the *State-House*" (II: 9).
Mather is able to elide his own role as "painter" precisely because
it seemed to his audience that he wasn't painting or re-creating
Winthrop, that he was merely presenting him as he really was.

However, at the end of Book II, in an appendix, Mather's reconstruction of his biographical subject is more obvious. He begins
"Pietas in Patriam: The Life of His Excellency Sir William Phips"
with what is perhaps his most famous metaphor, that of himself as
"chemist."[26]

> If . . . *Quercetanus,* with a whole Tribe of *Labourers in the Fire* . . . find
> it no easie thing to make the common part of Mankind believe,
> That they can take a *Plant* in its more vigorous Consistence, and
> after a due *Maceration, Fermentation* and *Separation,* extract the *Salt*
> of that *Plant,* which, as it were, in a *Chaos,* invisibly reserves the *Form*
> of the whole, with its vital Principle; and, that keeping the *Salt* in a
> *Glass* Hermetically sealed, they can, by applying a *Soft Fire* to the
> *Glass,* make the *Vegetable* rise by little and little out of its *Ashes,* to
> surprize the Spectators. . . . 'Tis likely, that all the Observations of
> [many famous] Writers . . . will find it hard enough to produce our
> Belief . . . that by the like Method from the *Essential Salts of Humane
> Dust,* a Philosopher may, without any Criminal Necromancy, call up

the *Shape* of any *Dead* Ancestor from the Dust whereinto his Body has been Incinerated. . . . When we . . . in a *Book*, as in a *Glass*, reserve the History of our Departed *Friends*; and by bringing our *Warm Affections* unto such an History, we revive, as it were out of their *Ashes*, the true *Shape* of those Friends, and bring to a Fresh View, what was *Memorable* and *Imitable* in them. Now, in as much as *Mortality* has done its part upon a Considerable Person, with whom I had the Honour to be well acquainted, and a Person as *Memorable* for the Wonderful *Changes* which befel him, as *Imitable* for the *Virtues* and *Actions* under those *Changes*; I shall endeavour, with the Chymistry of an Impartial *Historian*, to *raise* my Friend so far out of his *Ashes*, as to shew him again unto the World. (II: 37)

Two points in this metaphor are pertinent. First, someone (presumably the author) must provide the fire, the "warm affections," by which Phips can be revived. He cannot be revived without sympathy, without bias. Second, Mather subtly changes the metaphor as he pursues the analogy: the plant reconstituted rises as itself, as a vegetable; however, a friend reconstituted rises both in its "true *Shape*" and in a "Fresh View." That is, the alchemical process somehow condenses the essence of the biographical subject, making his picture "true" but nonetheless "new."

Both points are relevant for a consideration of "Pietas in Patriam," for both suggest the problem of perspective. The picture of Phips in the narrative depends upon the author's particular sympathy for Phips. Without it, the picture will not come to life; with it, the picture will be lifelike, "true," and "Fresh." In other words, Mather inverts the modern notion of successful biography, which claims that detachment is necessary for an accurate picture of another self. Only by applying his sympathy to Phips's elements can Mather produce a view of him that is new, and yet true, which others apparently do not share.

play between biography

The audience needs a fresh view of Phips in 1697 because Phips's governorship had ended badly in 1694, with the "irascible and controversial" Phips (Levin, *Cotton Mather* 249) dying in London while trying to answer the charges brought against him by Joseph Dudley. Phips "had the Disadvantage," Mather states, "of being set at *Helm* in a time so full of *Storm* as ever [New England] had seen," and he goes on to detail Phips's troubles with "the People" and, more particularly, with Elisha Cooke's "little Party" (II: 70). Winthrop had guided a similarly "*Weather-beaten* Bark" and somehow retained his popularity throughout each of the controversies he faced; Phips is attacked from all sides and does not retain his popularity (if indeed he ever had any). Hence, Mather warns his audience—the people of New England—that from their perspective they cannot see Phips correctly: "the *Eye* sees not those Objects which are applied close unto it" (II: 70). His job as historian is to provide those readers with a more correct way of seeing Phips, a perspective from which they can bring him into focus. His authority for doing so is simply that he can "see" Phips more clearly.

It is not surprising that Phips has been misperceived by the people of New England since, as the subtitle of the biography indicates, he underwent many "Memorable *Changes*" in his life (II: 35). Born to a father who was "obscure," he becomes self-fathering, "*A Son to his own Labours*"; once a shepherd "in the wilderness," he becomes a rich man; raised in "the furthest Village of the Eastern Settlement of *New-England*" (II: 38), he becomes a knight well known on the streets of London; not having even seen Boston until he was eighteen, he becomes royal governor of Massachusetts. Phips's most famous statement—"*Thanks be to God! We are made*" (II: 41)—is uttered when he discovers that his crew has located the sunken treasure of a Spanish wreck in the Bahamas, but it also applies to Phips throughout the narrative, since he is continually being made and remade. And if he were not remade this one last time, by the historian as "alchemist," he would either "be Buried in Eternal Oblivion" or remembered like "Judas in the Gospel, or *Pilate* in the Creed, with Eternal Infamy" (II: 72). Mather admits, in other words, that his version of Phips is a refiguring of the historical person, constructed through his own "sympathy" for the man and with an awareness of the "people's" dislike for him. But why, then, this particular figuring? Given the biased authoring and biased reading (that Mather anticipates, at least), what is the point of the narrative?

The structure of the work provides a clue. "Pietas in Patriam" is loosely divided into three symmetrical parts of seven sections each: the rise of William Phips (sections 1–7), his progress (sections 8–14), and his fall (sections 15–21). The first part traces his ascent from obscure beginnings to knighthood. Mather uses the trope of "scaffolding" to show how Phips raised himself to the "*Quality*" (II: 42) of a gentlemen, to a level of eminence necessary for one, even in the changed political circumstances of the 1690s, to be considered for knighthood and governorship. Part of this raising includes the discovery of the Spanish wreck, which makes him wealthy and his name known. This first part ends with Phips vowing to dedicate himself to the interests of New England, turning the "old *Heathen* Virtue of PIETAS IN PATRIAM, or, LOVE TO ONES COUNTRY . . . into Christian" (II: 42). That is, the first part ends with a "conversion," but not of the sort usually delineated by the typical seventeenth-century conversion narrative.

The second part of the narrative shifts the focus toward New England and the role of the risen Phips within its history, a shift signaled by the opening lines of section 8, which tell of "the Miseries which were come, and coming in upon poor *New-England,* by reason of the *Arbitrary Government* . . . imposed on them" in the late 1680s. The rest of that section details the events leading up to and surrounding the Glorious Revolution in Massachusetts in 1688–1689. Phips undergoes more changes, meanwhile, including a religious conversion in section 9. Mather records Phips's conversion narrative in its entirety—Levin suggests that Cotton Mather had even helped Phips to write it (*Cotton Mather* 180)—including Phips's telling comment, "I knew, *That if God had a People any where, it was here.* And I *Resolved to rise and fall with them."* Phips's conversion, in other words, is as much a conversion to New England as it is to religiosity. "*I will now expose my self,*" Phips states, "*while I am able, and so far as I am able, for the Service of my Country: I was born for others, as well as my self"* (II: 47). Instead of submitting to Christ's will, Phips submits to New England's.

Even after section 8, this second part of the narrative continues to blur the distinction between Phips and New England. Both, for example, have undergone "memorable changes" in recent years. The Glorious Revolution, like Phips's discovery of the Spanish wreck, is an act of self-assertion, especially since Mather goes to great pains to emphasize the careful and conscious orchestration of events on April 18, 1689, the day of the "*Revolution* which delivered New-England from grievous Oppressions" (II: 46). New England's "conversion" on that day and Phips's conversion a year later are companion events in "Pietas in Patriam," indicative of the way Phips has hitched his wagon to New England's star. Hence, much of this second part of the narrative seems to have little to do with Phips's biography; instead, it details the story of a group of shipwrecked sailors (section 12), the devaluation of the bills of credit following the failure in Canada (section 12), and Increase Mather's lobbying for a new charter in London (section 14).

The third part of the biography begins with more changes, specifically the passage of the new charter for Massachusetts in 1692, which delivered "them from the Oppressions on their *Christian* and *English* Liberties, or on their Ancient Possessions," (II: 58) and which made Phips the governor. Mather's defensiveness about the new charter and his father's role in procuring it is well known (Levin, *Cotton Mather* 203), and he begins this third part of the narrative by insisting that Phips was the perfect choice for governor "under the Changes in some things unacceptable" imposed by the charter. Why perfect? Because Phips has given up his self as regards New England, and he conforms to its will. He is a servant of New England, not of Whitehall and not of himself. And indeed, throughout the Salem witch trials (section 16) and the war with the Indians in the Eastern Plantations (section 17), Phips remains submissive to the requests of the country. At one point he tells the General Assembly:

> *You may be sure, that whatever Bills you offer to me . . . I'll pass them readily; I do but seek Opportunities to serve you; . . . and whenever you have settled such a Body of good laws, that no Person coming after me may make you uneasie, I shall desire not one Day longer to continue in the Government.* (II: 58)

As the official civil and military commander of New England in this third part of the biography, Phips tries to protect the country, to serve as a shield, but Mather's narrative indicates not only that Phips is unsuccessful, but that Phips himself merely conforms to the popular will. For example, it seems significant that Mather does not mention in the biography itself the fact that Phips built a fort at Pemaquid, "the finest [fort] that had been seen in these parts of *America*" (VII: 81). Phips literally did engage in building a "wall" or a "shield" around New England.[27] In "Pietas in Patriam" Phips does not shape or "edify" New England; it shapes him. Rhetorically speaking, he has been "made" by the country. There is no "self" in this narrative—as there was not in "Nehemias Americanus," though for different reasons.

Mather's rhetorical strategy in "Pietas in Patriam" is precisely to implicate Phips's life in the life of New England and, by extension, the life of every New Englander. Having seen the qualifications for governor reduced to merely his being selected by the Crown—surely one of the "unacceptable" aspects of the new charter—Mather strives to "convert" and isolate patriotism into the defining characteristic of successful governorship (and citizenship). Mather chooses not to portray Phips as a forceful and visionary governor—as he had portrayed John Winthrop, for example—because he is bidding to redefine the governor as the servant of the people and not, as the king would have it, the leader of the people. In this role, Mather insists, Phips was "perfect": he had no will of his own. "*I do but seek Opportunities to serve you,*" Phips says. Unfortunately, from Mather's point of view, the "people"—misled by factions, arguments, and prejudices—had not yet seen Phips in this way. Mather's view is indeed the "Fresh View" that they need, not just of Phips but of themselves and of their own power, should they choose to exert it. Mather has turned Phips into a metaphor for a new political relationship between rulers and people.[28]

The middle part of *Pietas,* which ignores Phips completely at times, speaks to the people in figurative language that extends and amplifies Mather's portrait of Phips in the first part of the narrative. For example, Mather tells the story of a group of soldiers shipwrecked on an island in Canada during the retreat from Quebec. With winter coming on, the soldiers build rude "*Chimney-less things* that they called *Houses,*" set apart one day of the week for fasting, and place their few provisions in a public storehouse. Their careful organization suggests a particular sort of community: "This little Handful of Men were now a sort of *Commonwealth,* extraordinarily and miserably separated from all the rest of Mankind." This language suggests two stories familiar to any of Mather's New England readers: Plymouth Plantation during the winter of 1620–1621 and New England during the late 1680s. The second is more pertinent here, since the narrative elsewhere directly concerns itself with the Glorious Revolution. The makeshift community—small, isolated, seemingly unimportant—faces severe trouble when from among their ranks "a wicked *Irishman*" (Governor Andros was Irish) begins to steal food from the public storehouse. The times being extraordinary, the punishment of stealing from one's own brethren is severe: "This . . . *Stealing,* if it had not been stopp'd by some *exemplary Severity,* they must in a little while, by *Lot* or *Force,* have come to have *Canibally* devoured one another" (II: 53). Dissension, in other words, might lead to the community's devouring of itself through a sort of self-consumption. So when the Irishman continues to steal, the little society is forced to rise up and put the wretch "past *Stealing* . . . [and] past *Eating* too" (II: 54). He, like Andros during the Glorious Revolution, is excised from the body

politic because he did not or could not see the good of the community; he put his own good ahead of his community's. Like Edward Johnson's "epitomes" in *Wonder-Working Providence,* this little
commonwealth serves as a synecdoche for New England, itself
"shipwrecked" by the loss of the 1629 charter, imposed upon by
"foreigners," and saved by the concerted action of "the people"
in a moment of crisis.

When Phips does appear in the middle part of "Pietas in Patriam," he does so as a failed guardian of New England. The Quebec expedition, the Salem witch trials, and the war in the eastern
plantations are marred by poor planning, bad decisions, and misdirected zeal. Throughout, Phips moves with his patriotism intact
but with a befuddled understanding of events that only serves to
emphasize Mather's conception of him as a trope for New England, which itself wanders bewildered through the sorrowful decade of the 1690s in *Magnalia.* Phips remarks, for example, that
the meaning of the Quebec expedition was "*too deep to be Dived
into!*" (II: 51)—unlike, obviously, the shipwreck upon which he
made his fortune. He brings the Salem witch trials to a halt not
because he understands the crisis, but because he does not: he
"beheld . . . Exasperations which the Minds of Men were on these
things rising unto," the cause of "which perhaps might have puzzled the wisdom of the wisest Men on Earth to have managed" (II:
64). The narrator knows what the trials were about—"a *War* from
the *Invisible World*" (II: 64)—but Phips does not.

Phips's confusion about the witch trials helps to explain how
Mather means for us to read Phips's death in the third part of
"Pietas in Patriam." After all, if Phips rises and falls with New England, as he said in his conversion narrative and as Mather has
given us to believe, then must we not read his fall and death as the
fall and death of New England? We do, but with two provisos. First,
we must note that Phips "falls" because of that "little Party of Men,
who thought they must not *sleep till they had caused him to fall*" (II:
70). Because of them, Phips returns to London, significantly, to
restore his "Integrity" (II: 70). That is, dissension in New England
is reflected in Phips's own apparent disintegration. The problem
with New England during Phips's governorship, in other words, is
internal, is caused by the community's own factionalism and fragmentation. Should that party, and others like it, retreat from persecution and rejoin the larger community, Phips's character would
necessarily return to its unified, integrated condition. Or—and

this seems to be Mather's rhetorical ploy—should it suddenly be able to "see" Phips as having integrity, it would then desire to rejoin the community.

Second, though Phips died in London in February 1694/95, he is here being "raised" or "resurrected"—Mather's metaphors from the first section of the biography—in this narrative itself. Similarly, New England has "died": neither Phips nor Increase Mather could save it from the Crown's assertion that it was now merely a province to be governed by an appointee of the king. But its "vital Principle," its "true *Shape*," can indeed be revitalized, raised, resurrected, as Mather is attempting to do (II: 37). Out of the lost past, Mather suggests that the virtue of patriotism can be brought into the present and used to unify a bewildered community; if so, New England might indeed live again, not in the pages of *Magnalia*, but in reality. After all, when Mather wrote "Pietas in Patriam," he knew that the next governor of New England would be another "foreigner": the preface written by his brother Nathaniel Mather is even dedicated to that governor, the Earl of Bellomont. In a sense, the biography is a plea to the Crown's appointee that, whatever his other loyalties, he first "serve the [New England] Publick in all it's [*sic*] Interests" (II: 70). It is a plea that he manifest "love" for the country and the people. More broadly, "Pietas in Patriam" is a plea to New Englanders to imitate William Phips: to carry into an uncertain future the one indispensable quality that will resurrect, in the 1690s and beyond, the essence of New England under the 1629 charter. Phips's regeneration will be New England's if the people can learn to "see" and to "sympathize" with the protagonist. "Pietas in Patriam" will be both impetus for and synecdoche of social revivification.

In a sense, then, "Pietas in Patriam" logically extends the patriotism so haphazardly evinced by Edward Johnson: threatened and intimidated by English doubts about the colony's special status, both historians retreat to an emotional defense of the country. In addition, Mather's self-conscious stance as the holy seer whose perspective prevents Phips from sinking into "Eternal Oblivion" (II: 72) is the logical extension of Increase Mather's many attempts to forge consensus in the 1670s and 1680s. Cotton Mather's bid for consensus here in Book II of *Magnalia* is that of "love to one's country." Whatever else is salvaged from the wreck created by the loss of the old charter, patriotism is necessary if New England is to retain any measure of independence from England.

In another sense, however, Mather has broken with his predecessors. "But whether *New England* may *Live* any where else or no, It must *Live* in our *History!*" Mather wrote in "A General Introduction" to *Magnalia*. He seems there to suggest that the revivification of New England exists only on the page or in the epic-making imagination of the author.[29] Another extended metaphor clarifies Mather's meaning, however. It comes from the middle sections of "Pietas in Patriam," where Phips is seldom discussed in any straightforward way. Describing the effects of the disastrous assault on Canada, Mather discusses at length the debt into which the country was plunged. "In this *Extremity* they presently found out an *Expedient*" (II: 51): paper money, funded on a special tax, to be collected over the next two years. Bills are printed (they were, Mather insists, impossible to counterfeit), the government and wealthy citizens back them to raise "Credit" among the people, "and they *Circulated* through all Hands in the colony pretty comfortably." Although some people, Mather admits, did not have faith in the bills, believing them "*Wast Paper*" not bills of credit, this "expedient" did "no less then save the Publick from a perfect Ruin" (II: 52).

Note what has happened here. The public faces a financial crisis; money, which can only work if the community has faith and trust in it, is printed; it is accepted; the crisis is solved. *Magnalia*, remember, is also paper currency: "a sort of Rapsody made up (like the Paper whereon 'tis written!) with many little Rags" ("A General Introduction" xxv). And amid the cultural and social crises of the 1690s—new charter, witchcraft hysteria, Indian wars, party politics—Mather prints his own paper currency, funded once again by what his audience can give in future years (that is, patriotism) and workable only if they have faith in its possibilities. Phips, before his and New England's conversions, could dive into a shipwreck and draw gold and silver from it; that option is not available either to Mather or New England after 1689. New England has no specie or bullion of its own in the new circumstances of the 1690s; everything will be directed, apparently, from London. Yet the "expedient" of "Pietas in Patriam" (and, by extension, of *Magnalia Christi Americana*) can, if the people are willing, save the public from ruin, by circulating among them and creating public faith and credit, creating the belief in itself by which the community can, paradoxically, save itself. New England "must" live in this history, and Phips "must" live in his biography, because Mather had the "warm affections" to bring both back to life. In that sense, both exist only in the author's imagination and in the words on the page. But, finally, Mather's strategy is to make both live elsewhere too: in the people of New England. And the "vital principle" of Phips, as well as New England, can live in the people only if they, temporarily, have faith in an "expedient," the text, designed to serve as paper currency, which will in time be no longer necessary. The essence of the things themselves—of New England as it once was—can be reclaimed ("resurrected") only through the audience's faith in Mather's narrative.

Thus, in spite of the historian's insistence on their essential similarity, the biographies in Book II move from the publicly accepted vision of Winthrop to the privately held (though publicly urged) vision of Mather; from the notion of the governor as the forger (he who constructs walls) of communal identity to the notion of the historian as the forger (he who makes fictions) of that identity; from a past in which the hegemony of the orthodoxy was complete to a present conceived as a battleground of opposing forces unable to "see" the good of the whole. Here in Book II (as well as in Books III and IV), where Mather most wanted to urge a connection to the past, he finally grounds his narrative in the discontinuity of New England's recent history. The differences between Winthrop as governor and Phips as governor could not be ignored. The old New England had been killed: "*Write now* [Phips's] *epitaph,*" the elegy at the end of the narrative tells us, "'*twill be* Thine own . . . *more needs not be exprest,* / *Both* Englands, *and next* Ages, *tell the Rest*" (II: 75). But the future might tell a different story. With the historian's help, the community could yet be revived and the past be reconnected to the present. Only if the historian's vision were ignored would the past remain dead.

EFFECTING THE FUTURE

The structure of Book VII of *Magnalia* mirrors that of Book II. Relatively short chapters, here relating the "afflictive disturbances" suffered by the churches of New England, are arranged thematically and chronologically. They are followed by a long appendix, "Decennium Luctuosum," written later in the decade than the chapters and bringing the narrative down to a moment upon which the future of New England hinges.[30] The explicit theme of this book, remember, is that New England has evolved and is still evolving toward higher and greater truths. But the shift from the chapters to the appendix indicates that, as with "Pietas in Patriam," Mather perceives a gap in New England's history in the 1690s, and that the audience is responsible for effecting their own future beyond that gap.

The sixth and final chapter in Book VII brings New England's history down to 1689 with a jeremiadic response to the colony's afflictions: "since . . . *Degeneracy* has obtained so much among us, the Wrath of Heaven has raised up against us a Succession of other *Adversaries* and *Calamities* . . . to Rescue us from which the Jealous Kindness of Heaven has not made such *Quick Descents* as in *former Times*" (VII: 56). In the narratives in Book VII, these adversaries and calamities do not, for the most part, attack the body; they attack the soul. Mather describes hypocrites in the church (chapter I), Separatists and Familists (chapter II), Antinomians (chapter III), Quakers and Anabaptists (chapter IV), and impostors posing as ministers (chapter V). These opponents of the Puritans attack the soul by "enchanting" the mind and the eye. "*Evil Spirits,*" Mather states, "have . . . much operation on the *Minds* of many People" (VII: 40): Roger Williams "Enchant[ed]" the church at Plymouth to join with him; John Wheelwright "was under such *Enchantment* that he could be brought by no means to see his Evil"; the Quakers issued "*Prophecies* which *Enchanted* all the World into a Veneration of them"; and the most successful of the impostors, Samuel May, "was all over pure *Enchantment*" (VII: 8, 15, 22, 35).[31] New England defeats these adversaries by banishing them from the colony; the civil government simply prevents them from working their enchantments on the people. Mather records none of the efforts to disenchant adversaries (like Anne Hutchinson and Samuel Gorton) that Winthrop claims to have made in the *History of New England*. All are tossed quickly into the wilderness (including four Quakers who would later be hanged for returning). Neither does Mather cast these attacks into a symbolic pattern, as Johnson did in *Wonder-Working Providence*. The "molestations" of the people occur throughout the century at sporadic intervals. The connection between Samuel Gorton (chapter II) and the impostor Samuel May (chapter V) is simply that each adopted a method of spiritual enchantment best calculated to do damage in a given situation. Comparing New England to Christ in the wilderness, Mather points out that the colonists were destined to meet "with a continual *Temptation* of the *Devil*" (VII: 4). And as long as the

government continued to see rightly, to recognize, dispel, and
expel enchanters, New England remained strong.

Chapter VI, a record of "*The Troubles . . . with the* Indian *Salvages*," breaks this pattern of spiritual affliction in that the wars it
describes are physical and are linked to the "Sins of the Land"
(VII: 44) just as Increase Mather and Joshua Scottow had said they
were. But Mather's jeremiadic stance here is only half-hearted.
Many times, incidents interpreted by Increase Mather as "judgements" are recorded by Cotton Mather simply as normal incidents
of war. For example, Increase Mather interpreted the colonists' act
of mistakenly shooting each other as a sign of discord, a reversion
to "uncivilized" ways (*Brief History* 5); Cotton Mather sees no such
significance in the incident:

> Our Forces kept a strict Eye upon the Motions of the *Enswamped*
> Enemy; but finding if once we squeezed Our selves into those Inac-
> cessible Woods, we merely Sacrificed one another to our own Mis-
> takes, by firing into every Bush that we saw to stir, as expecting *a
> Thief in every Bush*; we were willing rather to *Starve* the Beast in his
> den, than go in to *Fight* him there. (VII: 47)

Similarly, Cotton Mather takes the example of old man Wakely,
whose family was destroyed and who was himself killed by the Indians, and uses it to describe not New England (as Increase Mather
had done) but those "Provinces . . . where they made it so little of
their own Concern to gather any *Churches*" (VII: 55). The lesson
of Wakely's death is only for those colonists in the provinces who
ignore the church, not for the typical New Englander.

Having stripped such incidents of their synecdochic quality,
Mather narrates the history of King Philip's War in chapter VI without insisting on the meaning of the war that Increase Mather had
advanced in the 1670s. Indeed, in Book VII of *Magnalia*, victory
against King Philip is achieved because the Indians, not the colonists, become "enchanted": "Finally, a *Visible Smile of Heaven* was
upon almost all the Enterprizes of the *English* against [the Indi-
ans]: And an unaccountable Terror at the same time so Disspirited
them, that they were like Men under a *Fascination*" (VII: 52). New
England's fortunes having turned—"The *time limited* by Heaven for
the Success of the *Indian Treacheries* was . . . expired" (VII: 52)—the
colonists pursue the victory, killing or subjugating the opposing
forces. Mather sees King Philip's War as a physical attack by Satan,

who was usually a bit more subtle than that. But "King *Philip* is not the only *Python* that has been giving [New England] Obstruction in their Passage and Progress" to the New Jerusalem, he says (VII: 56). Throughout the six chapters of Book VII, the success of that "Progress" is never called into doubt: "I have," Mather says, "by a True and Plain History secured the Story of our Successes against all the [enemies] in this *Woody* Country" (VII: 56). The Indians, just like familists and separatists, are overcome and cast out. (The colony, Mather reports in "Decennium Luctuosum," "extinguished whole *Nations* of the *Salvages* at such a Rate, that there can hardly any of them now be found under any Distinction upon the Face of the Earth" [VII: 61].) "Reader," Mather concludes, "'Twas not unto a *Delphos,* but unto a *Shiloh,* that the Planters of *New-England* have been making their Progress" (VII: 56), despite these spiritual and physical attacks. "And the whole congregation of the children of Israel assembled together at Shiloh, and set up the tabernacle of the congregation there. And the land was subdued before them" (Joshua 18.1). As in "Nehemias Americanus," the history of New England as Mather narrates it here reveals the success of God's chosen people through their just governing of their affairs.

But "Decennium Luctuosum," the long appendix to Book VII, calls into question New England's supposed attainment of that Shiloh—the subjugation of the land. It is, Mather says, the history of a "War that has for *Ten Years* together been multiplying *Changes* and *Sorrows* upon us." As his use of the present tense indicates, Mather wrote "Decennium Luctuosum" before the end of the war; but, he claims, the war is "so far in prospect, as to render its *History* seasonable" (VII: 57). We have, again, the idea of perspective: Mather has the war "in prospect," and his view of it "Aims at the *doing* of *Good,* as well as the *telling* of *Truth*" (VII: 59). His perspective includes a word, "Changes," that was very important in "Pietas in Patriam." The first half of Book VII may have featured *progress* toward a more enlightened city upon a hill, but the second half traces mere *changes* that leave the future open to the same uncertainty that we saw in "Pietas in Patriam."

At first glance, Mather's narrative of the sorrowful decade seems utterly confusing. The thirty "articles" he uses to structure the events of the war are broken up by "mantissas," "digressions," "relations," "accounts" transcribed from other narratives, and two dialogues in which Mather tries to "disenchant" an Indian and a

Quaker. The narrative is disconnected, almost disjointed; and the narrator seems to be playing a game with us concerning his identity:

> I Pray, Sirs, ask no further [who wrote this]; let this Writing be like that on the Wall to *Belshazzar,* where the Hand only was to be seen, and not whose it was. . . . [In] the mean time, as a far greater Man once was called, *Ludovicus Nihili,* which you may make *Lewis* of *Nothingham;* so the Author will count himself not a little favoured, if he may pass for one of no more Account than a *No-body;* which would certainly make a very *blameless* Person of him. (VII: 58–59)

Yet as Kenneth Silverman points out, referring to the anonymous early editions of "Decennium Luctuosum," the narrative itself reveals at every turn the "hand" of Cotton Mather (Silverman 200): the allusions are more learned and the prose style more ornate than most New English writings of the period; the dialogue with the Quaker not surprisingly involves "a Minister of *Boston*"; a sermon appended to the history had been given by Cotton Mather at a public lecture in 1698. This particular version of the narrative is also printed within *Magnalia,* which was issued with Cotton Mather's name in capital letters on the title page. Although supposedly anonymous, "Decennium Luctuosum" insists that more than just the hand of the author be recognized.

In addition, the narrative in "Decennium Luctuosum" is disturbed by moments of extreme violence.

> [The Indians] fell to Torturing their Captive *John Diamond* after a manner very Diabolical. They *stripped* him, they *Scalped* him Alive, and after a *Castration,* they slit him . . . with *Knives* between his *Fingers* and his *Toes;* they made cruel *Gashes* in the most fleshy Parts of his Body, and stuck the Gashes with *Firebrands* which were afterwards found sticking in the Wounds. (VII: 80)

Set against Mather's typically learned and carefully styled prose, these passages fairly leap out at the reader, reinforcing the sense of disruption caused by the narrative breaks and the persona's reticence. Silverman attributes Mather's reticence and these other narrative disturbances to Mather's "conflict over his writing," describing them as "unconscious strategies for resolving [that conflict], stammerlike devices that at once express and cancel" (200). If so, then it is difficult to understand why the rest of Book VII, which is a relatively fluid narrative, should not manifest the same conflict, the same "stammering." Or, indeed, why all of Mather's writing would not "at once express and cancel." Mather here is writing, as he did in the appendix to Book II, from what he perceives as a period of great cultural uncertainty; he describes confusing changes in self and society, and he adopts a highly self-conscious stance toward his materials. These ambiguities suggest an argument concerning *Magnalia* that is different from Silverman's argument, as well as a larger argument about the intellectual climate in New England in the 1690s.

Throughout "Decennium Luctuosum," the historian calls attention to himself and to the reader: "Before we pass to another Year, stand Still, *Reader,* and *Behold* some *Wonderful Events* proper *here* to be Introduced" (VII: 67); "All that I will say is, That if thou canst read these Passages [relating captivity narratives] without Relenting Bowels, thou thy self art . . . *Petrified*" (VII: 71); "And now, Reader," he says at the end, "I will conclude our History of the *Indian War*" (VII: 95). These moments seem designed to remind the reader that this war is being narrated, that the historian's view presented here is but one perspective on events. It is, the historian says, "a rare thing for any Two men concern'd in the same Action, to give the Story of it without some *Circumstantial Difference*" (VII: 60). Accordingly, when he arrives at "a *Difficult Point*" (say, the origins of this war), his method is to "Transcribe Two or Three Reports of the Matter now in my Hands, and leave it unto thy own Determination" (VII: 61). Later, recounting the appearance of "*Demons* in the shape of Armed *Indians* and *Frenchmen*" at Gloucester, Mather transcribes someone else's account of the incident— "because the Relation will be Extraordinary," he remarks, "I will not be my self the Author of any one Clause in it"—and leaves the question of whether or not Satan was behind it "unto thy [that is, the reader's] Judgment, (without the least offer of my own)" (VII: 84). The reader is not asked to accept the narrator's judgment, as in "Pietas in Patriam," but is asked to bring his or her reasoning abilities to the narrative. Earlier, I quoted Mather's statement that only the historian can read the book of history; he goes on to say, however, that "every serious *Christian*" can "take [that] *Book*" and, with the historian's help, "*Spell* the *Divine Lessons* contained in it" (VII: 106). In other words, the reader's role in "Decennium Luctuosum" is not as a spectator of history, but as a participant in the understanding of it.

The historian acts as a guide through this sorrowful decade, presenting evidence (hence, "articles," a legal term appropriate to a people under covenant obligations), variant opinions, firsthand accounts, even voices (Quakers' and Indians') that dissent from the religious orthodoxy. Throughout the narrative, he asks his readers to form their own opinions of the events he describes. His insistence on narrative disruption is part of this effort to keep his readers engaged in the task of "spelling" the lessons of the war. Taking all this into account, we should not be surprised to find that "Decennium Luctuosum," unlike the "Life of Phips," has no identifiable shape. At times, the historian hints that the dilation and contraction of a heart might be an appropriate metaphor for the events of the decade (VII: 93), but the narrative itself does not clearly sustain such a regular alternating pattern. An identifiable shape, after all, implies a specific end to a history: Johnson's technique of describing successive purifications through purity-peace-plenty (and the concomitant metaphors of lukewarm-hot-cold) implies the end-time triumph of New England's "souldiers"; Increase Mather's view in *A Brief History of the Warr With the Indians* that New England is circling forward through time implies future failures (downward turns) but ultimately the perfect reformation of New England. "Decennium Luctuosum" has neither shape nor end: Article XXVII is subtitled "*The End of the* Year; *and, we hope, of the* War" (VII: 92). But we soon find that though this "*present History*" draws to a close, "the end of this *Year* did not altogether prove the end of the *War*" (VII: 93). The written text (the paper document) ends, but "the long WAR [that] is the [history's] Text" does not.

By imposing an identifiable shape on history, a historian coordinates available data into a pattern, which once established acts as a filter for our understanding of the relevance of individual events. Although it insists on the significance of certain events that might, under another interpretation and narrative structure, be ignored or forgotten, any one particular narrative structure tends to restrict meaning, since only those events that fit the pattern are interpreted as significant. In "Decennium Luctuosum," because of his desire to resist the imposition of closure, the historian tries in a sense to work against this fact of narration, tries to expand the significance of the war to include all aspects of New England culture in the 1690s. Hence, although the title page promises the "History of . . . the Long War . . . with the *Indian Salvages*" (VII: 57), Mather intimates that the Salem witch trials might be part of the same history.

> The Story of the Prodigious *War*, made by the *Spirits* of the *Invisible World* upon the People of *New-England*, in the Year 1692. hath Entertain'd a great Part of the English World with a just Astonishment: And I have met with some strange things . . . which have made me often think, that this inexplicable *War* might have some of its Original among the *Indians*, whose chief Sagamores are well known unto some of our Captives to have been horrid *Sorcerers*, and hellish *Conjurers*, and such as Conversed with *Demons*. (VII: 81–82)

He then transcribes a narrative that recounts the assault of a town near Boston in 1692 by the specters of "*Frenchmen* and *Indians*." Similarly, late in the history, Mather notes that "while the *Indians* have been thus molesting us, we have suffered Molestations of another sort, from another sort of Enemies [that is, the Quakers], which may with very good Reason be cast into the same *History* with them." The Quakers, like the specters in the previous example, are "enchanters" determined to "Poison the *Souls* of poor People, in the very Places where the *Bodies* and *Estates* of the People have presently after been devoured by the Salvages" (VII: 96). Mather resists the restriction of subject matter in the narrative, just as he resists the closure of form, hoping to force his reading audience to take responsibility for interpreting the events he describes. He tries to engage his reader at a very high level of interaction.

Attacked on the physical frontiers by Indians, on the spiritual frontiers by Quakers (VII: 96), and internally by "*Spirits* of the *Invisible World*" (VII: 81), New England stumbles through the narrative, through the 1690s, unable to resolve the many wars in which it is engaged. At the end of "Decennium Luctuosum," it is a country poised between two futures: it may be "a *Dark Land* . . . fill'd with these [Quakers]" (VII: 101) or it may be a land that resists "the unaccountable *Enchantment*" of that "Poor Deluded People" (VII: 100); it may be a land free from Indian warfare or it may be a land scourged even further by Indian "Salvages" (VII: 60). We "have sometimes been told," the historian reminds us, "that even in the Beating of a *Pulse*, the dilating of the Heart, by a *Diastole* of Delight, may be turned into a contracting of it, with a *Systole* of Sorrow" (VII: 93). However, Mather writes "Decennium Luctuosum" from what he perceives as that gap in history when the question is not simply whether the next movement of the heart is diastole or systole, but even whether there will indeed be another heartbeat. The future is contingent. It depends upon his audience's behavior in the future.

Mather ends the history, as he ended "Pietas in Patriam," by
trying to look into the future. "If every *Wise Man* be a *Prophet*," he
says, "there are some yet in [New England] that can *Prophesie*"
(VII: 103). He offers us a number of "Prognostications," none of
which assures New England of a hopeful future. Like Scottow, he
does not have confidence in New England's future. Expect judgments, he advises, "for the Quarrel of the Covenant must be
avenged"; and "consider what fearful Cause there may be for thee
to expect sad THINGS TO COME" (VII: 101, 103). His refusal to
predict the sort of triumph that Johnson did or to level the sort of
warning that Increase Mather did (in, say, *Illustrious Providences*)
indicates that the reader's role here is the same as it was in "Pietas
in Patriam." He or she is a participant, not a spectator, in the formation of New England's history. Mather tells the story of a town
called Amyclae,

> which was Ruined by *Silence*. The Rulers, because there had been
> some false Alarums, forbad all People under Pain of Death to speak
> of any *Enemies* approaching them: So, when the *Enemies* came in-
> deed, no Man durst speak of it, and the Town was lost. *Corruptions*
> will grow upon the Land, and they will gain by *Silence*. 'Twill be so
> Invidious to it, no Man will dare to speak of the *Corruptions*; and the
> Fate of Amyclae will come upon the Land. (VII: 104)

The future is in the hands of the readers if, having with the historian's aid "spelled" the history contained in "Decennium Luctuosum," they are not silent and submissive. Of course, the implied
reader in the narrative is still one who learns to see the past from
the perspective of the historian; "*Observe wisely*," Mather says in the
sermon "Observable Things" that ends *Magnalia*, "and you cannot but *Observe* the Language of Heaven in the Circumstances thro'
which we have passed for a whole *Decad* of Years together" (VII:
118).

His insistence that his readers make their own decisions—in the
course of reading the narrative, in the course of coming to see the
past as a referendum on the future—should obviously not be taken
for a freedom to read any meaning we wish into the text. Cotton
Mather was neither a democrat nor a practitioner of deconstruc-
tion. We should take it as his insistence that, if "Decennium Luctuosum" was to effect a future in which "New England lives," his
readers must understand their role in that city upon a hill and

actively participate in its creation. Together with the patriotism they were asked to drag across the historical gap of the 1690s in "Pietas in Patriam," Mather's readers are now asked to bring their reason, their "Judgment" (VII: 84), their ability as individuals to fight the enchantments that afflict not only religious faith but national faith. Otherwise, the only New England that survived the loss of the charter would indeed be the one the historian has "read" for us in these pages, the "Rags" of paper.

Authorizing the Past

Cotton Mather's greatest public and political success came, like William Phips's, in the three years following the Glorious Revolution. Not yet thirty years old, he directed the affairs of the influential North Church; he had been chosen to write *The Declaration of Gentlemen and Merchants,* which was read aloud on the morning of Andros's overthrow in Boston[32]; and his works had begun to appear in print at the feverish rate that would, in time, make him the most famous colonial writer of his day. In England, his father lobbied on New England's behalf in the court of William and Mary, and Cotton Mather's reputation was enhanced by that connection. But "Cotton Mather's brief career as a powerful force in Massachusetts politics virtually ended in the autumn of 1692" (Levin, *Cotton Mather* 232). The public's perception that his defense of the Salem witch trials, *The Wonders of the Invisible World* (1692), did not (as promised) "vindicate the country, as well as the judges and juries" involved in the trials (qtd. in Levin, *Cotton Mather* 219); Robert Calef's stinging attacks on Cotton Mather; the downfall of Phips's government in 1694; the belief held by many people that Increase Mather had settled for too little in the new charter—all these factors played a part in Cotton Mather's political decline in the mid 1690s.

His conception of *Magnalia Christi Americana* in 1693 (see Mather, *Diary* I: 166) and his execution of the project over the next five years coincides with the waning of his and his family's political power. We should not be surprised to find, then, that in writing the history Mather gradually began to privilege the historian, elevating him to the role of the "man of letters" who "sees" the past—and potential future—of the community more clearly than others. In both "Pietas in Patriam" and "Decennium Luctuosum" the historian comes to see himself as a "disenchanter," enacting

cultural revitalization

the role that in previous colonial histories, even in sections of *Magnalia* written earlier in the decade, ministers or the governor or the civil government had presumably played. The shift indicates not simply Mather's perception that political developments in New England in the 1690s had left the future of the colony uncertain, but also his perception that direct political power had passed him by.

In this sense, we should read not only *Magnalia* but also Mather's feverish rate of textual production throughout his life (which most commentators regard as an oddity) as a method of managing reality, of influencing public policy on issues that range from social reform to religion to politics. Benjamin Franklin's connection to Cotton Mather is not just through one of Mather's books (Franklin, *Autobiography* 1317); it is through Mather's example as America's first public man of letters. We should also note, in regard to *Magnalia*, that Mather is acutely and perceptively aware in the 1690s of the issues that would shape the eighteenth-century Anglo-American world: the way the Glorious Revolution had redefined both the Crown's authority and the people's relationship to their rulers (including the redefinition of "the terms by which future magistrates [in New England] would be judged" [Gura, "*Life of Phips*" 441]); the role of "representation" (of gold, of the people, of the self) in creating and re-creating reality; the problematics of a self cut loose from its moorings in classical and Christian notions of selfhood; the problem of narrative authority in a culture that would no longer rely on familial or cultural prestige to sanction its speakers. His writing, like that of so many of his contemporaries (Swift and Dryden come to mind) and like that of Franklin later in the century, was designed not as a retreat into the private imagination, but as an intervention in history.

In the 1690s, the past was indeed "dead." New England as Increase Mather had known it as a young man, as well as the various New Englands that Cotton Mather had read about in Bradford's, Winthrop's, Johnson's, and Increase Mather's histories—those were things of the past. Every line of *Magnalia* evinces the belief, however, that the rhetoric of a reconceived and reauthorized history could help to affect, perhaps even effect, New England's future, if not as the old colony reborn, then as a new province where the ideals and attitudes of the first seventy years of settlement would be reborn. At his most hopeful, Mather attempts to "revive" New England, much as (aided by the "warm affections" of his audience) he revived Sir William Phips in "Pietas in Patriam." Such a revival might not result in a New England identical to the one that existed under the old charter, but it would still restore the community to its self-avowed status as a city upon a hill. "Yea," Mather cries near the end of the history,

> but let all *New-England* at the same time learn what the Welfare or the Ruin of all will turn upon. The whole World was made for our *Lord Messiah,* and the *Curse* of God will more or less plague the World, according to the Respects which that *Second Adam,* our *Lord Messiah* finds in it. But *New-England* is by a more Eminent Profession that *Immanuel's Land.* Let the Interests of the Christian Religion in *Reformed Churches* be . . . preserved among us, then *All will go well!* (VII: 108)

"I have proposed," he said eight hundred pages earlier, "to preserve . . . the Interest of *Religion,* in . . . that little country NEW-ENGLAND. . . . A *Reformation of the Church* is coming on" ("General Introduction" xx). New England might yet be the city that lit the way.

At the very minimum, though, and at his most persistent, Mather uses the word *preserve* to mean embalmment, not protection. Not only can America "*Produce*" great persons—even heroes, he says—but "*America can Embalm* [them]" (IV: 185) when need be. To stop degeneracy in the land, he says in "Johannes in Eremo":

> I'll show [the sons], the *Graves* of their *dead Fathers;* and if any of them do retreat unto a Contempt or Neglect of *Learning,* or unto the *Errors of another Gospel,* or unto the Superstitions of *Will-Worship,* or unto a *worldly,* a *selfish,* a *little* Conversation, they shall undergo the irresistible Rebukes of their Progenitors, here fetch'd from the dead, for their Admonition. (III: 11)

The biographies, in particular, are designed to cherish the memories of the fathers (one definition of the word *embalm*): to keep their piety, their learning, and their incipient patriotism alive within a society progressively given over to the forms of a provincial, English society.

Whatever the "national" implications, Cotton Mather's *Magnalia Christi Americana* was designed not to obviate history, but to use the reconstruction of history to hasten the millennium. Throughout the uncertainty concerning New England's political

future in the 1690s, he focused his chiliastic hopes upon 1697 as
the year of the Second Coming; much of *Magnalia* was written with
that date in mind (Levin, *Cotton Mather* 276–78). When that year
came and went without the Antichrist's downfall, he simply moved
the date forward into the future. As for the church, he says in "Decennium Luctuosum":

> I [agree with] what was asserted in the Sermon Preached at our
> Anniversary Election, in the year 1696. "The *Tidings* which I bring
> unto you are, that there is a REVOLUTION and a REFORMATION
> at the very Door, which will be vastly more wonderful than any seen
> by the Church of God from the beginning of the World. I do not
> say that the *next Year* [that is, 1697] will bring on this *Happy Period*;
> but this I do say, the bigger part of this Assembly, may . . . live to see
> it . . . : The mighty Angels of the Lord Jesus Christ will make their
> Descent . . . at the Approaches of their Almighty Lord." (VII: 101)

Typically, the sermon he quotes from was his own, the historian
reaffirming the theologian's conclusions. The separation of roles
was not accidental: the minister is (for the most part) heard, the
historian is read.[33] And it is in a quite literal sense, the historian
insists, that the document we hold in our hands as we read is
meant to bring that "happy period" closer: "Reader," he says,
"*The Book now in thy Hands, is to manage the Design of a* John *Baptist,
and convey the* Hearts *of the* Fathers *unto the* Children" (III: 1).
Again, his description of *Magnalia* in the "General Introduction"
alludes to this insistent trope: "a sort of Rapsody made up (like
the Paper whereon 'tis written!) with many little Rags." Mather
constantly keeps the paper in front of his audience, not because
of insecurity or egotism, but because, as he came to realize in the
later stages of the composition of the history, he needs more than
his audience's attention: he needs their assent. Whether New England lived or no depended on his audience's agreement with his
assessment of the past, and on its willingness to keep alive the spirit
of that past as it was refracted through the pages of the history.
Paper was the only currency through which Mather could hope,
indirectly, to govern New England.

In many ways, Cotton Mather does not break with the historiographic tradition in which he was grounded. He often claims, for
example, that he is "an *Impartial Historian*" ("General Introduction" xxii), and his narrative reveals that he could be sympathetic

to figures like Roger Williams and to the complexity of controversies like the Halfway Covenant. But William Bradford was also impartial in *Of Plymouth Plantation,* inserting documents to buttress his arguments and treating some dissenters like Williams with care and sympathy. Mather often works by examples rather than by arguments or (what in a sermon would be called) reasons. "Patterns," he says, "*may have upon* [the reader] *the force which* Precepts *have not*" (III: 1). Book VI presents a series of such patterns, each illustrating God's providence; the biographies in Books II, III, and IV are variations upon certain "patterns" of Christians; and narratives like "Decennium Luctuosum" are laced with "exploits" and events that observe "a Remembrance" (VII: 74) beyond their ordinary significance. John Winthrop and Increase Mather did the same, reading God's providence into specific incidents, and Edward Johnson made such "epitomes" a consistent part of his narrative strategy in *Wonder-Working Providence.* Mather structures the past according to an inclusive framework in which numerology (seven books, four of which are divided into seven chapters) and typology contribute to the formal argument. Edward Johnson did the same.

Yet in *Magnalia Christi Americana* Mather does break with his predecessors' histories in several important ways. One is the historian's insistence that he can "see" more clearly than other authorities or than the people. One of the farthest-reaching tenets of the Reformation was the principle of *sola fides,* which removed the center of spiritual authority from ecclesiastical institutions and relocated it in the individual soul. If, with Kenneth Burke, we then take heresy "to be the isolation of one strand in an orthodoxy, and its following-through-with-rational-efficiency to the point where 'logical conclusion' cannot be distinguished from '*reductio ad absurdum*'" (113), we can see that many of the dissenters within New England in the seventeenth century—from John Child on voting privileges for all propertied Christians to John Clarke on baptism—were stifled precisely because they challenged the orthodoxy from within its own system of logic and its own language. Political and religious leaders found many effective ways to restrain these heresies: the rhetoric of the city upon a hill, a confession of faith for church membership, restriction of voting privileges to church members, silencing, excommunication, banishment, the threat of civil punishment, even death. Despite their efforts, however, *sole fides* remained, at least in principle, part of the Puritan

ideal. But not until Increase Mather's *A Brief History of the Warr With
the Indians* did a New England historian adopt the assumption, as
part of his narrative strategy, that an individual not sanctioned by
the church or the state—the historian—is privileged over and
above other professing Christians, even above the community's traditional civil and religious leaders; again and again, remember, he
was not surprised that humiliation and thanksgiving were ineffective in reversing the colony's fortunes in the war.

The *historian* knew better. But the assumption does not consistently inform his method, even in the *Brief History;* and neither is
his own role as minister sufficiently separated from his stance as a
historian. Such an assumption and such a stance does consistently
inform Cotton Mather's method in *Magnalia.* Mather emphasizes
the role of the historian in part because, as I have indicated, he
sensed the growing ineffectiveness of traditional sources of power
in New England. By the end of the century, the power that the
governor, the General Court, and the ministry had each wielded
at one time had begun to erode.[34] Mather did not turn away from
his role as a minister; but as a historian he perceived another
angle, a more effective perspective, from which he could urge a
reluctant and confused populace forward into his vision of the future.

Mather reports in his biography of John Cotton that Cotton
"had the *Art* of *concealing his Art*" (III: 25). Mather's method in
Magnalia is just the opposite: "Pietas in Patriam" and "Decennium
Luctuosum" reveal their art at every turn. Even in the introduc-
tions to works written much earlier in the decade—in, for example, "Early Piety, Exemplified in the Life and Death of Mr. Nathaniel Mather"—Mather insists on revealing his method: my "main
scope" is "to procure *Followers*" of Nathaniel Mather's example,
and "hence I have not here made an *Oration* in his *Praise,* but given
barely a *Narrative* of his Life, and this mostly by transcribing of his
own *Memorials,* in all affecting the *plain Style* of a just *Historian*"
(IV: 210). Mather wants us always to remember that we are reading. The past has been made by the historian; the future must be
made by the readers. For if the narrative becomes, as Mather's
narratives later do for Ichabod Crane, a "most firmly and potently
believed" story, it will have lost its ability to teach us to "see" correctly, as Crane's own response to Brom Bones's trick would indicate (Irving 1063). It will be a specter that deludes and enchants
us, not a fiction that can create a better future through the hearts
and minds of its readers.

Cotton Mather in *Magnalia Christi Americana,* like all Puritan historians in colonial America, is involved in an endeavor to create the future by returning to, revising, re-"seeing" the past. Living in a time that he perceived as uncertain, as misguided, as a *decennium luctuosum,* he attempts to change the future by revising the past in such a way that a new New England might be created. His revision of the past, his trip back to the future, was a conscious, magisterial effort to control a future that, he understood only too well, was finally contingent upon the efforts of his audience. The resulting narrative history was a product of his will, and finally of his imagination, where one version of John Winthrop's city upon a hill still lit a way to the final and perfect reformation of mankind.

Epilogue

For rhetoric as such is not rooted in any past
condition of human society. It is rooted in an
essential function of language itself, a function
that is wholly realistic, and is continually born
anew; the use of language as a symbolic means of
inducing cooperation in beings that by nature
respond to symbols.

—*Kenneth Burke*

Chapter by chapter, I have tried to trace these seventeenth-century
revisions of the history, meaning, and purpose of the idea of New
England. "Each generation," Emerson wrote a little more than
two hundred years after Boston was founded, "must write its own
books; or rather, each generation for the next succeeding"
(56–57). In his own attempt at prophecy in "The American
Scholar," itself part of a literary tradition that includes Winthrop's
"Model," Emerson was in a sense simply making an observation
about literary history that applies as well to seventeenth-century
New England as to nineteenth-century America. Winthrop's *History
of New England,* Edward Johnson's *Wonder-Working Providence of Sions
Saviour in New England,* Increase Mather's *Brief History of the Warr
With the Indians in New England* and *Illustrious Providences,* and Cotton Mather's *Magnalia Christi Americana* represent successive attempts in seventeenth-century New England to respond to sociocultural crises by rewriting the past and (each writer hoped) the
future of the community. Each represents a generation's attempt
to write its own books, its own stories, its own history. As such,
these histories exist at the intersection of history and rhetoric: as
history, they claim to chart New England's past, present the truth

of providential history, and encompass confusing historical events in a comprehensible, reassuring narrative; as rhetoric, they represent "visionary compacts" of just the sort that Winthrop attempted in "A Model of Christian Charity," attempts to convince an audience of listeners or readers to accept the validity of a certain version of the past and to reform their lives so as to bring about a more positive future than the one that, according to the historian, was impending.[1] Each is an instance of the assertion that "all documents are texts that rework what they 'represent' and thus make a difference in the sociopolitical and discursive context in which they are inserted" (LaCapra, *History* 141).

Accordingly, my focus has been on the way the community's narratives of its own history, purpose, and meaning were successively altered, both to revise the meaning of past events and also to accommodate more recent, often disturbing, events. My focus has been on the way that particular narrative "strategies," in Kenneth Burke's sense, were conceived to deal with a perceived reality. These histories of New England are indeed texts that, in response to a particular sociopolitical context, reworked cultural perceptions and tried to make a difference both in the discursive context in which they were inserted and, appropriately for a culture as moralistic as the Puritan's, in the lives of the people who read them. They deserve the respect due all consequential narratives: they deserve to be understood as formal artifacts that reveal, create, and challenge the culture in which they were composed.[2]

Throughout, I have been urging us to see Puritan histories written in colonial America (and, in effect, all histories) as constructions of reality standing in peculiar need of "authorization": peculiar, it seems to me, because history purports to be truer to the "facts" than do other genres, and thus particular histories must always drape their appeals to "reality" in a convincing mantle of authority. Or, to choose a different metaphor, each history must ground its appeal to veracity on some convincing, hopefully stable foundation. Each of the histories that I have analyzed is itself, in this sense, merely a trope for the problem that all histories face: the need to locate (and relocate) the "ground" on which they can stand as a representation of what "really" happened. But also, and more particularly, these seventeenth-century Puritan histories stood in peculiar need of authorization because they were written at a time when the underpinnings of a God-centered, hierarchical, deferential society were being threatened. From the deputies' jockeying for more power in Winthrop's Boston in the 1630s, to the emergence of the Puritan commonwealth in the 1650s, to the Whig appeal to the common law as a basis for social authority after 1689, Anglo-American culture was forced to rethink itself and the bases of its authority in the seventeenth century. These histories chart, in colonial New England during the course of the seventeenth century and even among the religious orthodoxy, the subtle but growing discomfort with an older, traditional world view.[3]

Thus, I have argued, the course of seventeenth-century New English historiography is that of a series of attempts to authorize and reauthorize the past: Winthrop's assumption of the immutability, enforceability, and obviousness of truth; Johnson's appeal to the divine word of cultural creation; Increase Mather's various appeals to communal agreement (by way of the historian's mediating voice); Cotton Mather's more systematic appeal to the vision of the individual historian, raised above the mass of misperceiving citizens. Narrative authority in seventeenth-century New England was continually being refigured, from the "supernatural" (typological and verbal) appeals of Bradford and Winthrop and Johnson to the professional and "perspectival" appeal of Cotton Mather. In Mather's *Magnalia Christi Americana,* the past, for the first time in colonial America, was even professionalized, on the verge of being disciplined.

My story culminates in Mather's *Magnalia* only because I have chosen to end the story there. The mode of historical thought that I have traced through the seventeenth century does not suddenly and dramatically come to a halt in 1702, just as Puritanism itself does not "die" in 1660 or 1689 or at some other specific date. "Europe did not *decide* to accept the idiom of Romantic poetry," Richard Rorty has written concerning the contingency of language, "or of socialist politics, or of Galilean mechanics. That sort of shift was no more an act of will than it was the result of argument. Rather, Europe gradually lost the habit of using certain words and gradually acquired the habit of using others" (Rorty 6). Yet the way Rorty phrases the problem belies the certain amount of choice that is available to every individual in every culture. Many writers in colonial America—Cotton Mather and Benjamin Franklin are two who come to mind—did not simply "lose the habit" of speaking a certain way; they found new ways of speaking congenial and useful and thus cultivated a new habit because in some sense it was worth it to them to do so. My history of history writing in seventeenth-century New England insists on a certain willfulness among writers themselves, even as I agree with Rorty's assessment that change occurs through language only in gradual ways.

Indeed, I have tried to strike a balance between an individual author's creativity and his existence within a culture that limited the choices available to him. It is for this reason that, in each chapter, I felt compelled to discuss both the author's particular situation in his culture and the events that caused that culture to question itself at a specific moment in time. Edward Johnson's use of "edification" as a central trope in *Wonder-Working Providence* was both a borrowing from the culture in which he lived (which around 1650, if only temporarily, found that trope a successful means to explain its sense of itself) and also an invention of his own, in that Johnson revised and modified and expanded upon that trope to fit his perception of a particular need. The balance is a difficult one to keep, however, and I suppose that I have at times overstepped the line in both directions.

Although Cotton Mather in 1702 does speak in new ways, he still operates within what Richard De Prospo calls "theistic discourse": that is, Mather's world—despite his elevation of the historian to a preeminent level of authority—remains God centered; providence still operates in his world, even if it is the historian or the man of letters, and not the saint, who understands its workings. For Mather, history is still generated by God's providence, not by causality in any of its romantic and postromantic forms ("progress," for example).

Mather is on the verge of a fundamental shift in consciousness, however. By 1721, responding to threats by the English government to "regulate" the 1691 charter and the proprietary governments of the American colonies, Jeremiah Dummer adopts in *A Defense of the New England Charters* (1721) what Perry Miller referred to as a "secular measurement" of New England, altering "the conception of America from covenant to business" (*From Colony to Province* 388–89). Dummer's strategy is to revise New England's history so as to emphasize its "rights" to charter government, its destiny as distinct from England's, and its citizens' "privileges" as "offspring" of England. In other words, in picking up on Increase Mather's language in the 1689–1691 pamphlets and Gershom Bulkeley's in *Will and Doom*, Dummer locates cultural and historical authority in the natural "Order" of things (33). This is no longer "right reason" in aid of Scripture, as John Winthrop employed it in his *History of New England;* this is a Newtonian world where principles, determined inductively, exist in nature, in the natural order of things. For Dummer, the past exhibits clearly the fact that, when colonial charters are removed, "Oppression rushes in like a Tide, and bears down everything before it" (25). The authority for this fact is experience, the observation ("obvious" to those who have been instructed) that a like effect will follow a like cause, in New England, as has followed or will follow a like cause, elsewhere. Dummer's authority rests outside the historian himself, in the observability and immutability of the laws of nature. In the service now of New England's future as a semi-independent province during the reign of King George I, the past had been reauthorized, yet again.

It would, of course, continue to be reauthorized, to be refigured, by writers as different as Jonathan Edwards in *A Faithful Narrative* (where the appeal to the evidentiary conventions of the new science is much more overt) and Benjamin Franklin in *A Narrative of the Late Massacres,* through subject matter as different as ecclesiastical history and civil history, in narratives as different as Thomas Prince's *Chronological History of New England* and Tom Paine's *Common Sense.* Indeed, it is in this tradition that one of the eighteenth century's most famous documents, in which "We the people . . ." rhetorically and politically re-"constituted" themselves (and that document itself) as the sole sources of their own authority, can be seen to be merely one step in a long process that had no beginning and will certainly have no end.

Notes

PREFACE

1. See, for example, White, *Tropics of Discourse.*

2. See, for example, Williams, *Marxism and Literature* 21–44. In a section on "the author," Williams also comments: "Indeed any procedure which categorically excludes the specificity of all individuals and the formative relevance of all real relations, by whatever formula of assigned significance, is in the end reductive" (198). Like Leo Damrosch in his fine study of eighteenth-century nonfiction, *Fictions of Reality in the Age of Hume and Johnson,* "I am principally interested in the ways in which an individual imagination shapes its world, rather than the ways in which the world shapes all the imaginations that reside in it" (11).

3. Peter Gay's *A Loss of Mastery* is flawed. Gay is insensitive to colonial New England and misreads its historians.

4. On the varieties of history in seventeenth-century English literature, see Fussner 150–90. For a perspective from within Renaissance thought, see Bacon 182–202.

5. Of course, history tends to be written (and later saved) by the victors, and New England in the seventeenth century proved no exception to that generalization. However, I would insist that by tracing this particular strand of orthodox thought across the century I do not deny the importance or relevance of the various other strands of thought in seventeenth-century New England. Indeed, I argue quite explicitly (and not very originally by this time) that various dissenters and various kinds of dissent are necessary to our understanding of the period, precisely because the orthodoxy was forced to deal with them, forced to reject, accept, or at least accommodate their ideas. See Gura, *A Glimpse of Sion's Glory,* for example. And at various points I take into account voices like Thomas Lechford's and John Clarke's that did dissent from the more authoritative accounts of the past.

CHAPTER 1. "SCATTERED BONES"

1. See Levy, Fussner, Baker, Dean, Ferguson, and Kemp.

2. Nathaniel Morton's *New Englands Memoriall* (1669) is largely a

digest of Bradford's manuscript history; William Hubbard transcribed whole pages from Winthrop's *History of New England* into his *A General History of New England* (1684); and Cotton Mather quotes from both in *Magnalia Christi Americana* (1702). Hence, I resist using the word *unpublished* in reference to Bradford's and Winthrop's histories: they were to some extent published (made public by circulation in manuscript), but they were not printed or distributed.

    3. Rosenmeier, " 'With My Owne Eyes' "; Wenska; and Perry, "Autobiographical Structures" 100–121. White, in "Value of Narrativity," argues that chronicles such as Bradford's history intentionally lack closure, and that to read them as somehow less sophisticated or less complete than modern "histories" is to impose inappropriate aesthetic and moral standards on the past. But see Louis Mink's reply to White in "Everyman His or Her Own Annalist." Here, I go on to argue that Bradford experienced a cognitive crisis at the end of *Plymouth Plantation*. See Mink, "Narrative Form."

    4. The Mayflower Compact was made public in *Mourt's Relation,* published in London in 1622.

    5. Sargent has recently made a similar argument in "William Bradford's 'Dialogue' "; see also my own argument about Bradford and Edward Johnson in "Edifying History."

    6. A half-century ago, in their influential anthology of Puritan literature, *The Puritans: A Sourcebook of Their Writings,* Miller and Johnson claimed that the *History* "lacks the form and beauty of Bradford's history by the very necessities of the case. . . . But even as a journal his volume frequently achieves genuine literary merit" (I: 89). Their qualified praise has yet to manifest itself in scholarly journals or books. Dunn, "Seventeenth-Century English Historians," spends only two paragraphs on Winthrop's *History,* focusing on Winthrop's withdrawal into intellectual isolation at the end of his life, and briefly explaining that withdrawal as a response to England's failure to reform itself after the Civil War in the image of Massachusetts Bay. Later, Dunn published the only article that treats the *History* as a serious history ("John Winthrop Writes His Journal"). There he argues that Winthrop's historiographic vision developed as he composed the history; the later passages possess a sense of history that the early passages lack. Gay, on the other hand, finds time for only one sentence to discuss Winthrop's *History,* and even in that one sentence he means not to praise the work but to compliment William Bradford for writing "at a level of information, analysis, and style that can compete in all respects with John Winthrop's journal"—despite the fact, he goes on to say condescendingly, that "Winthrop was a gentleman who had attended Cambridge" (39). The best literary treatments of the *History* are Howard, "The Web in the Loom"; Moseley; and Schweninger 67–98.

    7. Moseley (130–47) has recently argued that Bradford's and Winthrop's histories are entirely different, that they represent two strands of

thought (Separatist and Puritan) that run throughout American cultural history. Although I would agree that there are differences in method and style in the two histories, I believe that Moseley overstates the textual case; he depends more on inadequately defined doctrinal and ideological differences between Separatists and Puritans than on a close analysis of the two histories.

8. I have modernized the spelling in Winthrop's text, but retained the exact phrasing.

9. Note that Reagan substitutes the finished product ("are") for Winthrop's and Johnson's potential ("are to be"). Reagan used Winthrop's image several times in the course of his presidency, as Moseley points out (7).

10. See Bercovitch, "Puritan Vision." Morgan notes the traditional use of shipboard rhetoric similar to Winthrop's and traces its usage in the sixteenth century, concluding that in context Winthrop's use of the rhetoric was not original, but that his application of it was creative ("John Winthrop's 'Modell' "). See also Bremer, who notes that the image of the city on a hill was used by English writers in reference to England in the late sixteenth and early seventeenth centuries. These attempts to place Winthrop's sermon in a wider context are important in understanding how and where the process of Americanization began in the seventeenth century. Hence, Michaelsen places Winthrop's sermon in the context of early seventeenth-century law and its still emerging notions of the modern contract. However, another useful approach that scholars have neglected in their zeal to discuss the supposed "errand" in the sermon is to place Winthrop's ideas more squarely in the context of English Humanism. It seems clear, for example, that here and elsewhere he is borrowing from Sir Thomas Elyot's *The Governor.* Winthrop draws his injunction to "give, lend, and forgive" (284–87), directly or indirectly, from Elyot's list of the "three principal parts of humanity": benevolence, beneficence, and liberality (120–51). This connection makes sense, given Winthrop's extraordinary self-consciousness as governor of Massachusetts throughout most of the 1630s and 1640s. I thank Douglas Peterson for bringing this connection to my attention.

11. Other scholars who note the centrality of Winthrop's sermon to seventeenth-century New England include Baritz; Bozeman, *To Live* 81–119; and Delbanco 72–74.

12. Delbanco (43) tries to bring together the "explanatory categories" of religious and economic motives for migration. On the debate itself, see Virginia DeJohn Anderson; Bozeman, "Puritan's 'Errand' "; Bremer; and Cressy 74–106.

13. See Morgan, *Puritan Dilemma* 18–44, and Moseley 31–40, for discussions of Winthrop's response to conditions in England in the 1620s.

14. At the same time, as Bozeman argues in *To Live Ancient Lives,*

Winthrop might well have been imagining a return to the "primitivism" of early Christianity.

15. Morgan's "John Winthrop's 'Model' " and Michaelsen are exceptions here. While Miller discusses the "Model" primarily in relation to England and English history, my concern is its relevance to the idea of New England—and to the future Winthrop foresaw for the colony he governed.

16. See "revolvo," *Oxford Latin Dictionary*, the first two definitions. The second definition of *revolution* I refer to here was in use at least as early as 1600 (see "revolution," *Oxford English Dictionary*, definition 7). Bozeman in "Puritan's 'Errand' " correctly argues that the trope of "errand" was not used in the first generation of settlement in New England. It was developed much later by Edward Johnson, Samuel Danforth, and others. Accordingly, I have tried to avoid the use of that trope in discussing Winthrop's sermon, even though I think it is clear that Winthrop is postulating an exclusive, chosen society in the "Model," and that he sees himself, rhetorically, as its prophet.

17. This is, of course, an important concept in both volumes of Miller's *New England Mind*.

18. Thirty years earlier, Richard Hooker had argued that the Church of England walked a "middle way." See, for example, *The Laws of Ecclesiastical Polity* I: 425–28, where Hooker describes the church as "moderate" in its reform, as opposed to the "desperate extremities" of the Puritans and the lassitude of the Church of Rome. Keeping that in mind, I must emphasize that what is most important to my argument here is not whether the Puritans actually maintained such a balance, but whether (and how) they conceived of themselves in those terms.

19. See Morgan, *Visible Saints* 82–83. The emigrants were not yet a congregation, technically, since they had not settled, formally covenanted among themselves, and chosen a pastor.

20. See Haller, especially chapter 7. But Haller's argument has been challenged; see, for example, Olsen 36–47, who argues that Foxe was much more concerned with international Protestantism than he was with the national church.

21. John Cotton's *God's Promise to His Plantations*, delivered to Winthrop's company before setting out on its journey to the New World, is relevant here. Significantly, the doctrine of Cotton's sermon is 2 Samuel 7:10: "Moreover I will appoint a place for my people Israel, and I will plant them, that they may dwell in a place of their own, and move no more" (4). See also Bercovitch's discussion of Winthrop and Cotton (*American Jeremiad* 21–22).

22. And also with William Bradford's *Of Plymouth Plantation*, begun the same year. The question of American "origins" has been hotly debated for many years. Let me insist that I do not assert either that America's literary history begins on a specific day in 1630, or that somehow New

England's literary history springs, fully formed, from Winthrop's forehead in that year. The origins of American and New English literary history depend on one's point of view, on the particular argument one wishes to make. I use the word *origins* here to mean, simply, the point at which immigrants in the New World began to conceive of themselves literarily. In chapter 2, I argue that it is not until the the late 1640s that some New English texts become "Americanized" (see Patricia Caldwell, *The Puritan Conversion Narrative*). For a critique of twentieth-century misreadings of the pre-Romantic American past, including the attempt to locate the origins of American expression, see De Prospo, "Marginalizing Early American Literature."

23. Hosmer was correct about the range of Winthrop's *History*, but not in the sense he intended. When Winthrop began the second notebook in 1636, Massachusetts Bay did indeed comprise most of New England, geographically, numerically (in terms of population), and politically. Hence, Winthrop's reference to a "History of New England" was not a misnomer in 1636, although it would have been one in 1908.

24. John Winthrop, *The History of New England from 1630 to 1649,* ed. James Savage (I: 29, 62). Here and elsewhere, I refer to Savage's first edition because his notes are, in their expansiveness, helpful for background on Winthrop and on the colony; and because Savage presents the *History* in its entirety. Hosmer's early twentieth-century edition leaves out several sections that the Victorian editor considered offensive, such as Winthrop's "scientific" analysis of the "monstrous birth" of Mary Dyer's child.

25. Bradford in *Of Plymouth Plantation* similarly relies on the authenticating evidence of documents and correspondence. Like Winthrop, Bradford was sensitive to the ways his culture and, more narrowly, his administration would be perceived by posterity.

26. On "Perfect History," see Bacon 189–91. For a poststructuralist meditation on modern notions of annals and chronicles as somehow "imperfect" histories, see White, "Value of Narrativity."

27. I am indebted to Howard, "The Web in the Loom," chapter 5, for my ideas on Winthrop's method. See also Schweninger, who argues that one theme of the *History* is the "difficulty of maintaining a spiritually unified group in and around Boston" (72); and Moseley, who argues that Winthrop sought in art and in life "a fine line of moderation" (82).

28. Twentieth-century accounts of the Antinomian Controversy include Battis; Gura, *Glimpse* 237–75; and Stoever. Documents relating to the controversy are collected in Hall, ed., *The Antinomian Controversy, 1636–1638.*

29. Winthrop begins to focus on Wheelwright as early as October 1636 (see I: 201–4, 214–17), but does not begin to focus on Hutchinson until October 1637 (see I: 246–48, 257–59, 261–63, 292–96), that is, until after he had defeated Vane in the contest for governor and consolidated the orthodoxy.

30. By then, Hutchinson was dead, and as I suggest below, Wheelwright had a political motive in repenting of his errors in this fashion, a motive that might well have influenced his account. Bush has recently suggested that Wheelwright's authorship of *Mercurius Americanus* "is much less certain than we thought" (42). His evidence, though compelling, is not convincing.

31. In 1639, Robert Keayne, a Boston merchant, was severely fined by the General Court and then admonished by the First Church for taking too much profit in the sale of nails, bridles, and sundry other items (Keayne 45–64). It is significant that Keayne's defense is that "the world or . . . any impartial man or any that hath understanding in trade" (54) would not misconstrue his actions. His carriage, he suggests, was not "contrary to rule" (Winthrop, *History* II: 162).

32. See Wall 21–92, for a discussion of this continuing struggle. For the facts of the Hingham affair as they are understood by contemporary scholars, see Schweninger 82–84, and Wall 93–120.

33. From our point of view, we can see in this statement the sort of corrupt natural liberty that Winthrop, in the "Model" and in the little speech on liberty, claimed to detest. The New England orthodoxy, as some scholars have been eager to point out in recent years, had one eye on this world all the time, despite the idealistic pronouncements of Winthrop and others. It is tempting to read Winthrop's statement and conclude that the orthodoxy's rhetoric (then as now) was merely a tool for maintaining hegemony over the powerless, and that in reality the Puritans had both eyes on this world. However, we must remember that Puritans—indeed, all Protestants—felt the injunction to be "in" this world, and that many actions might not be considered "of" it as long as they were done for the right reasons (that is, the advancement of Christ's kingdom). This view helps to explain John Cotton's supposed dissimulation during the Antinomian Controversy and, perhaps, John Davenport's act of forgery during the Third Church controversy in 1669–1670. The connection between spirit and world in Puritan thought has been a topic of interest at least since Max Weber's *The Protestant Ethic and the Spirit of Capitalism.* Even Winthrop's "Model," as I argued earlier, was very much focused on this world. All this is not meant to excuse Winthrop's apparent callousness here, but it does indicate the complexity of Puritan ideology and, perhaps, intimate just how unrealistic Winthrop's original idealism proved to be in the New World.

CHAPTER 2. Edifying History

1. See also Patricia Caldwell's discussion, in *Puritan Conversion Narrative,* of the conversion narratives given in Thomas Shepard's Cambridge congregation in the 1630s and 1640s; the applicants for church membership evince a similar sort of dejection at the realities of the New World.

Delbanco (170) argues that responses like Winthrop's, Bradford's, and Wheelwright's were paradigmatic of the first generation's experience.

2. See also, for example, Dudley, "Letter to the Countess of Lincoln"; Winslow, *Good Newes from New England;* and William Wood, *New England's Prospect.* Also, from a quite different perspective, see Smith, *A Description of New England,* in *Complete Works* I: 305–63; and *A General History of Virginia, New-England, and the Summer Isles . . .,* in *Complete Works* II: 33–474.

3. Two other commanders wrote accounts of the Pequot War: John Mason, *Brief History of the Pequot War,* apparently written in the 1670s, and Lion Gardner, *Relation of the Pequot War.* Both are reprinted in *History of the Pequot War.* See also Philip Vincent's *A True Relation of the late Battell fought in New England,* in *History of the Pequot War* 93–111.

4. Underhill seems to emphasize a similar point in his account of the two "maids" who are taken by the Pequots and eventually traded to the Dutch in exchange for seven Pequots. The eldest, though "but young," is cast as a type of David: "And though sometimes, saith she, I cried out, David-like, I shall one day perish by the hands of Saul, I shall one day die by the hands of these barbarous Indians. . . . But suddenly the poor soul [would] quarrel with itself. Why should I distrust God? . . . [He] hath said he will never leave me nor forsake me. Therefore I will not fear what man can do unto me, knowing God to be above man, and man can do nothing without God's permission" (Underhill 30). But the younger girl says nothing about her captivity. It's not clear that she understands the same lesson in it. She may not have experienced God's free grace.

5. Meserole suggests that Johnson was of a higher social standing than tradesman: Johnson's listing as a "joiner" on the registry of the ship he emigrated on in 1636 "was most likely a ruse to deceive royal officials who could have caused difficulties for the non-conformist emigrant" (147). Given the typological, numerological, and structural complexity of Johnson's history, I tend to agree with Meserole. William F. Poole's introduction to his edition of Johnson's *Wonder-Working Providence* probably still contains the best information on Johnson and the history; J. Franklin Jameson's introduction to his 1910 edition of the history is also valuable.

6. The publishing history of Johnson's book was rather strange, as Poole showed. The 1653 edition, dated 1654 to anticipate the book's appearance in London's bookstalls, is entitled *A History of New England, from the English planting in the Yeere 1628 untill the Yeere 1652,* probably to make the book's contents more readily identifiable to an English audience. Johnson's own title, and the running headline on the pages of the first edition, was *Wonder-Working Providence of Sions Saviour in New England.* Johnson's name did not appear in the first edition, although New England writers throughout the century were aware of his authorship. Sales of the history were slow, which prompted the publisher to bind his remaining copies into a work by Sir Ferdinando Gorges, *America Painted to the Life;* Gorges's son later pointed out that his father had not written those pages.

7. See also Bercovitch, *Puritan Origins* 125–32; Gallagher, "Critical Study"; Rosenmeier, " 'They Shall No Longer Grieve' "; and Seavey.

8. In chapter 1, Bradford alludes to the tripartite shape of history since Christ's death: "the ancient times," when "the gospel . . . speedily overspread . . . the then best known parts of the world" (4); the reign of the Antichrist, when "the gross darkness of popery . . . covered and overspread the Christian world" (3); and "these later times, [when] the truth began to spring and spread after the great defection made by Antichrist, that man of sin" (4). Satan, Bradford declares, has adopted the same method of subverting the Reformation in "these later times" as he did in subverting the spread of the Gospel in "the ancient times": "when as that old serpent could not prevail by those fiery flames and his other cruel tragedies . . . he then began another kind of war and went more closely to work; not only to oppugn but even to ruinate and destroy the kingdom of Christ by more secret and subtle means, by kindling the flames of contention and sowing the seeds of discord and bitter enmity amongst the professors and, seeming reformed, themselves" (5). Bradford insists that the Separatists' removal to Holland, and then to the New World, must be understood within this larger context.

9. Jameson, in a footnote in his edition of the *Wonder-Working Providence*, points out that Johnson is alluding in the first paragraph of the history "to the Declaration concerning Sports, promulgated in 1617 by James I., and repeated by Charles I. in 1633, which permitted and indeed encouraged the practice of playing games on Sundays, after church service" (23). Johnson establishes his history in the context of those years before Laud when the Puritan's resentment at being unable to purge the Anglican church of all remnants of the Catholic faith still merely simmered. On the Book of Sports and the general religious climate in England in these years, see Foster 114–51.

10. Bercovitch ("Typology") refers to Johnson's typological method as "Eusebian" or "horizontal," and he associates its use with the orthodox camp (in particular, John Cotton).

11. Bercovitch, "Typology"; Delbanco 192–93; Gura, *Glimpse* 229–33; Seavey.

12. See Sachse, for example, and Delbanco 184–214.

13. In case we did not get the point in that episode, Johnson repeats it in another short narrative, this one involving the Gortonists. Samuel Gorton, a "radical spiritist," was in trouble with the Massachusetts government from the moment he entered the colony. Johnson accuses him of stealing Indian land, begetting "damnable errors" (220), and trying to start a government according to the principles of religious and civil liberty: the Gortonists began "without any means for instructing them in the wayes of God, and without any civil Government to keep them in civility or humanity, which made them to cast off most proudly and disdainfully

any giving accompt to man of their actions, no not to the chiefest in authority" (223). Their settlement at Shawomet is, in *Wonder-Working Providence*, New England's evil twin: it lacks purity, peace, and (by implication) plenty.

14. One issue currently under debate is whether the first-generation settlers of New England conceived of an "errand" or mission that had relevance for the Old World. Virginia DeJohn Anderson, David Grayson Allen, Theodore Dwight Bozeman, Francis Bremer, and Andrew Delbanco have all researched Perry Miller's "errand" thesis and come to differing conclusions. As for my point in this paragraph, Bremer is helpful in showing how pervasive the image of New England as a "city upon a hill" was in mid-seventeenth-century England and New England (328–29). (Bremer also points out that at least one New English writer, John Allin, recognized a city in England as "a city set on a hill.") So, while Johnson probably was not referring explicitly to Winthrop's "A Model of Christian Charity," he was referring to an image that a number of writers, including John Cotton, Peter Bulkeley, John Norton, Thomas Goodwin, and Philip Nye, had used to describe New England. Earlier, I argued that Winthrop's use of the image was original in that he made certain claims on behalf of the settlers that few Protestants in 1630 were so bold as to make.

15. See 25, 30, 38, 52, 53, 155, and 275 for a few direct references. More oblique references abound. Like David, New England begins in a lowly state, is chosen by God, is given a commission, fails temporarily (primarily because of "lust"), and returns to God's favor at the end.

16. See, in Book I alone, 23, 24, 32, 33, 34, 49, 50, 52, 53, 60, 65, 77, 122, and 146.

17. Delbanco (189–93) reads the history as enervating. Critics who read it as triumphant include Tichi 46–47; Gura, *Glimpse* 229; and Perry, "Autobiographical Role-Playing."

18. Johnson makes use of similar narrative delays and reconfigurations in other places too. See, for example, 129, 151, and 170.

19. In making a similar point, Bercovitch ("Typology" 187–88) refers to such works as John Cotton's *The Bloody Tenent, Washed and Made White in the Blood of the Lamb* (1647) and Thomas Hooker's *Survey of the Sum of Church Discipline* (1648).

20. In Book III, under the heading of 1646, Johnson does adopt the more familiar New Testament image, referring to dissenters from the New England Way as "those that are so inured with the broad beaten path of liberty, that they fear to be confined in the straight and narrow path of truth" (243).

21. Delbanco reads Johnson's assertions of plenty in Book III as "a rambling catalogue of material possessions" that leaves the history "in disarray." He asserts that the catalogue is indicative of the "unreplenished expenditure of rhetorical energy" that marks the second half of the history (189).

CHAPTER 3. HISTORY IN PIECES

1. Miller, *From Colony to Province* 119–46; Ziff 128–56; and Gura, *Glimpse* 155–234.

2. Bercovitch uses some of these references to describe Norton's Cotton as a literary precursor to Cotton Mather's Winthrop in "Nehemias Americanus," that is, as a fusion of self and communal mission, of biography and communal history. It should become clear in the following discussion that I am reading *Abel Being Dead* differently: I do not see in it "the affirmation of the New England Way through the pilgrimage of its representative saint" (*Puritan Origins* 123).

3. Norton comments at one point that "Our desiderable men that remain, remove from us, and few they are who return again" (46): it is unclear whether he is speaking of those who have died, like Cotton, or those who have returned to England.

4. On dissent in mid-century New England, see Gura, *Glimpse*; and Lovejoy, *Religious Enthusiasm.* On Aspinwall's works, see Gura, *Glmpse* 138–42; and Lovejoy, *Religious Enthusiasm* 100–3.

5. It may be that we simply find those parts of Bradford's narrative more appealing to our sensibilities in a post-Romantic world (see White, "Value of Narrativity"). I am convinced, however, that Bradford really does get lost in history in Book II, and that Morton's deletion of those incidents is significant.

6. See, for example, Parrington 99–118. Generally speaking, the modern biographers of Increase Mather—Kenneth Murdock and Michael Hall—have drawn sympathetic and rounded portraits; and several critics, most notably Robert Middlekauff, have studied the whole of his work with sympathy and insight. But most scholars of New England Puritanism, particularly those interested in its literature, have simply ignored Increase Mather. In the only full-length published study of New England historians, for example, Peter Gay mentions him in passing only four times. Anthony Kemp, in his otherwise admirable study, mentions Increase Mather only once, in a footnote.

7. See Mather, *Autobiography* 280–81; and Hall, *Last American Puritan* 41–42.

8. Mather did speak on the issue of baptism in 1666, during the series of meetings that preceded John Farnum's excommunication from the Second Church, but the issue in that particular controversy was the lawfulness of infant baptism, not the question of which infants were entitled to the sacrament (Hall, *Last* 67–71).

9. There is the probability that this anonymity was also due in part to his own still-unresolved feelings toward his father (see Hall, *Last* 41, 58–60, 80–87).

10. The reasons for this delay are unclear. Hall suggests that the controversy over the gathering of the Third Church of Boston kept

Mather from publicly announcing his change of mind on the issue of the Halfway Covenant (*Last* 140). But the context surrounding Mather's reversal has never been fully explored.

11. "To the Reader," *First Principles*. Increase outlines here his reasons for putting the collection together: the Fifth Commandment, Richard Mather's "*dying Counsel*," and his own recent illness.

12. Miller, *From Colony to Province*, notes that at first the narrative locates the shift in fortunes on the day of humiliation in May: "At last, on May 9, 1676, a really immense and impressive day of humiliation was held in Boston by all magistrates, elders, and people, and a sincere repentance and reformation were sworn to. Thereupon the bottom was sounded, the crisis was over." Then, he says, Mather realized he had "miscalculated," and he relocated "the day of thanksgiving on June 29 at precisely the right moment for the upswing of action" (32). Mather "miscalculated" in real life, and perhaps even in the early drafts of the history; but in the printed version he revised those earlier miscalculations to give the impression that he had known all along that covenant renewal was necessary.

13. He does not simply "erase"; he embellishes. Purity of motives concerning the Indians, for example, becomes an important element in Mather's histories in the 1670s, and in the rhetoric of other spokesmen in the colony at that time. Hence, the *Brief History* is accompanied, midway through the narrative, by a woodcut of New England's official seal in the 1670s: a nearly naked savage stands on the fertile earth of the New World and says, "Come Over and Help Us."

14. Hall argues (wrongly, I think) that the "combination of narrative history and theoretical essay" is "awkward" (*Last* 123–26).

15. Mather, "To the Reader," *Relation* n.p. For a history of the conflict between the two writers, see Nelsen. See also Murdock, *Increase Mather* 110; Murdock, "William Hubbard"; and Hall, *Last* 112–26.

16. These complaints are recorded in Hubbard's long postscript to *Narrative*, "A Narrative of the Troubles With the Indians in New-England, From Pascatagua to Pemmaquid" 29, 77–78.

17. Gookin claims to be responding both to Mather and to Hubbard (*Historical Account* 433). He adopts both explanations—correction and purgation—to explain God's reasons for letting the war happen (438). I would suggest that the difference between correction and purgation can be exemplified in two contemporaneous works: Anne Bradstreet's "To My Dear Children" and Mary Rowlandson's *True History of the Captivity and Restoration*. Bradstreet figures herself as an "untoward child" whom God must chasten and correct with His rod to keep her on the path to salvation (Heimert and Delbanco 139); Rowlandson figures her experience as "a sweeping rain" that wipes away everything she once owned, forcing her to place her entire dependence on God (65). Bradstreet's child remains active; Rowlandson's captive is passive.

18. Hubbard's election-day sermon, *The Happiness of a People,* serves as a useful commentary on the history. His antagonism to Increase Mather's understanding of New England's history is overt. Some people, he says, have offered long lists that try to explain New England's difficulties; but he finds himself "wishing, that whatever else hath been reckoned amongst provoking evills by other hands . . . might seriously be considered and amended" (54). Instead of long lists, Hubbard locates two evils, "Spiritual Pride" and a "Spirit of Worldly-mindedness," that lie "as a worm at the root and vitals of Religion [in New England], threatning and endangering a great decay" (55). These evils are not only more abstract than the narrow and singular ones Mather locates as the cause of the war, they also do not explicitly cause the war. Hubbard does not insist that the war is the fault of the colonists, and he does not recommend "breast-beating abasement before God" to resolve it (Hall, *Last* 118).

19. If so, then we need to apply the same standard to Bradford, Winthrop, and Johnson, who also record "discrete magnalia." What Miller means is that Mather apparently fails to imbed the particular providences into a coherent, organized world view. "The scale," he says, "was no longer a coherent sweep of history, but discrete 'magnalia'; not an over-all design working steadily through a predestined course, but simply this tempest or that shipwreck, a deaf person who learned to speak, or so-and-so who was possessed" (*From Colony to Province* 145). I argue here that there is an overall design by which Mather structures *Illustrious Providences.*

20. The pattern is not hard and fast. Sometimes, Mather intersperses narratives that he does not date; on several occasions, he breaks the pattern completely. More often, as in chapter III, "Concerning Remarkables about Thunder and Lightning," he works forward in time with stories about thunder and lightning on land, then steps back in time to work forward to the present with stories about thunder and lightning at sea.

21. *The Present State of the New-English Affairs, New England Vindicated,* and *A Further Vindication of New-England.* See Mather's account of his distribution of the fourth work to the Privy Council in *A Brief Account Concerning Several of the Agents of New England* 7.

22. Obviously, Mather might have added the statement sometime after December 18, 1688, when William entered London, or December 23, when James fled England for the second time. I am not aware, however, that the manuscript of *A Narrative of the Miseries* survives, in which case we might check for later additions to the text. Hall (*Last* 220) indicates that Mather had the work printed in January 1688/89. If he did add the statement at that date, when such thoughts were safer to express, my point here would still be valid, in the sense that then it would apply to William: that is, in *A Narrative of the Miseries* Mather was already obliquely campaigning for, even threatening William with, New England's demands.

23. For example, see *Narrative of the Miseries:* the people "have been deprived of their *antient Rights and Priviledges* (1–2); "Monys have been raised by [Andros's] Government in a most Illegal and Arbitrary way, without any consent of the people" (3); the people have been "deprived" of "their *English Liberties*" (5); "it [is] an illegal and unjust thing to deprive good Subjects [in New England] of their *Ancient Rights and Liberties*" (7–8).

CHAPTER 4. BACK TO THE FUTURE

1. At the end of this work, which was not published until 1792, Gookin even gives an outline of an eight-chapter history of New England that he had projected and half-completed.

2. On Mather's efforts, see Murdock, *Increase Mather* 211–61; Hall, *Last* 212–54; and Lovejoy, *Glorious Revolution* 225–34. On Andros, see Lovejoy, *Glorious Revolution* 180–95, 233–45; Johnson, *Adjustment to Empire* 73–91; and Hall, *Last* 206–11.

3. Among many accounts of the events at Salem, see Boyer and Nissenbaum; Hansen; Miller, *From Colony to Province* 173–208; and Levin, *Cotton Mather* 195–223.

4. See Johnson, *Adjustment to Empire* 235–41, 258–63, 277–85; Hall, *Last* 264–71; Levin, *Cotton Mather* 232–33; and Cotton Mather, *Magnalia* II: 35–75.

5. See Middlekauff 124–38; Miller, "Solomon Stoddard"; Miller, *From Colony to Province* 226–47; and Hall, *Last* 147–52.

6. Among other sources, see Breen 180–239; Silverman 138–46, 227–60; and Middlekauff 191–367.

7. Kemp concludes that Scottow's narrative re-creates "the fall of the English Reformation with which Bradford's and Johnson's histories began" and thus leads to a self-conscious textualization of history ("But whether *New England* may *live* any where else or no, it must *live* in our *History!*" Cotton Mather was soon to write) that is indicative of the modern historical consciousness.

8. Bercovitch, *Puritan Origins* 104–5. Bercovitch says that Scottow quotes Herbert's lines "Religion stands on Tiptoe in our Land, / Ready to pass to the American Strand" only to recast the lines "to say just the opposite from what Herbert intended," that is, that New England is impervious to the vicissitudes of human history (105). This is true as regards Scottow's first citation of Herbert's poem (287), but Scottow goes on to quote Herbert a second time: "As gold and Grace never yet did agree / Religion alway siding with Poverty. / That as the Church shall thither *Westward* flie, / So Sin shall Trace and Dog her instantly" (328). Scottow does not solve "the problem of federal identity by raising the locale *in toto* . . . into the realm of redemptive history" (Bercovitch 105). He is well aware that the New England in which he lives is subject to historical change,

that the founders' "NEW-ENGLAND is [no longer] to be found in NEW-ENGLAND, nor BOSTON in BOSTON" (Scottow 327).

9. Miller, *From Colony to Province* 170. Middlekauff suggests, more subtly, that Mather was attempting "to work out the full significance of the new arrangements [under the 1691 charter] for New England" (215).

10. For example, his biography of his brother Nathaniel, "Early Piety Exemplified" (*Magnalia* IV: 208–22), was published in 1689.

11. Bradford had made a similar argument about primitivism in *Of Plymouth Plantation,* which Mather certainly knew of. Satan attacked the saints who led the sixteenth-century Reformation, Bradford says in the first paragraph of his history, because he was "loath his kingdom should go down, the truth prevail and the churches of God revert to their ancient purity and recover their primitive order, liberty and beauty" (3). On the primitivist element in seventeenth-century thought, see Bozeman, *To Live Ancient Lives.*

12. It is obvious that his father is included in this group of ministers. Middlekauff points out that Cotton Mather often disagreed with his father's ideas, and he had to walk a fine line between publicly disagreeing with them and adhering to his own principles (196–98).

13. This is one of Richard Lovelace's arguments in his fine study of Cotton Mather, *The American Pietism of Cotton Mather:* "there is a strong effort in [Cotton Mather's] thinking to simplify Reformed orthodoxy and reduce it to biblical essentials" (5).

14. The Confession of Faith is modeled on the Savoy Declaration of Faith and Order (1658) composed by Congregationalists in the waning years of the revolution, which in turn had been modeled on the Westminster Confession (1644).

15. Of the other seventeenth-century historians, only William Bradford treats Roger Williams with this kind of respect. See *Of Plymouth Plantation* 257, 300–301.

16. Mather is able to do this only by omitting reference to the controversy between Williams and John Cotton in the 1640s. In two important books, *The Bloody Tenent of Persecution* (1643) and *The Bloody Tenent Yet More Bloody* (1652), Williams attacked the New England orthodoxy's (and particularly John Cotton's) conception of New England as the antitype of Israel. Williams argued that the relevance of the Old Testament, its forms, ceremonies, and institutions, had been abrogated with the coming of Christ. Cotton defended himself and New England in *The Bloody Tenent, Washed and Made White in the Blood of the Lamb* (1646).

17. Levin alludes to this when he says these middle books "constitute the heart of the narrative" (*Cotton Mather* 251). Bercovitch makes the point that the biographies are set apart—or "enclosed"—"within the gargantuan federal hagiography that shapes the narrative sections (books I, V, VI, VII)" (*Puritan Origins* 129).

18. Most of the scholarship on *Magnalia* concerns these biographical sections. See, for example, Bercovitch, " 'Delightful Examples' " and " 'Nehemias Americanus' "; Eberwein, " 'In a book' " and " 'Indistinct Lustres' "; Gura, "Cotton Mather's *Life of Phips*"; and Watters.

19. In *Puritan Origins*, Bercovitch argues that "Nehemias Americanus," the biography of John Winthrop, "offers an epitome of [Mather's] biographical technique" (1). Bercovitch's argument, as any reader of *Magnalia* soon discovers, is not easily extended to most of the biographies: it is hard to see how his arguments about the fusion of self and country in "Nehemias Americanus" might be applied, for example, to the biography of Theophilus Eaton ("Humilitas Honorata"); or how his arguments about the fusion of sacred and secular could be applied to the biography of William Bradford ("Galeacius Secundus").

20. Compare Mather's statement about the confessions of faith adopted by some of the churches in New England in the 1680s and 1690s: "Nevertheless, all this *Variety* has been the exactest *Unity*" (V: 4). Mather has begun to locate unity and order amid the fragments of early New England's experience.

21. Mather subtly shifts his emphasis on the original mission of New England in these middle books: "The *Ministers* and *Christians,* by whom *New-England* was first planted, were a *chosen Company* of Men; picked out of, perhaps, all the Counties in *England,* and this by no *Human Contrivance,* but by a strange *Work* of *God* upon the *Spirits* of Men that were, no ways, acquainted with one another, inspiring them, as *one Man,* to *secede* into a Wilderness, they knew not *where,* and *suffer* in that Wilderness they knew not *what.* . . . The *Design* of these *Refugees* . . . was, that they might there, *sacrifice unto the Lord their God*: It was, that they might maintain the *Power of Godliness* and practise the *Evangelical Worship* of our Lord Jesus Christ, in all the Parts of it, without any *Human* Innovations and Impositions: Defended by *Charters,* which at once gave them so far the *Protection* of their King, and the *Election* of so many of their own Subordinate Rulers under him, as might secure them the *Undisturbed Enjoyment* of the *Church-Order* established among them" (III: 5–6; cf. III: 74). Notice that "banishment" is not mentioned. Mather combines Winthrop's sense of mission with Johnson's concept of "retreat"—although the mission was not universal (in this formulation of Cotton Mather's, though it is in others) and the purpose was not to return to England to fight the battles of the Lord. The point was to come and to worship the way they wanted. We see here the beginnings of the modern formulation that schoolchildren in the United States are blithely taught.

22. I should note here that, in this sense, my discussion of *Magnalia* is not simply the discussion of one work by Cotton Mather; it is a discussion of a crucial handful of works (some published separately) written by Mather prior to 1700.

23. The quoted phrases are from Bercovitch, *Puritan Origins* 97–98. Bercovitch's argument depends on such a reading of the early years of settlement; it allows him to establish the "hegemony" of the "myth" that Cotton Mather develops most fully in "Nehemias Americanus." On the urge to romanticize premodern communities, see Lasch 82–167. A number of critics, responding directly to Perry Miller's supposed formulation of a monolithic orthodoxy, have argued as I have that dissent was common in seventeenth-century Massachusetts (see Gura, *Glimpse;* and Lovejoy, *Religious Enthusiasm,* for example).

24. *Magnalia,* Bercovitch states elsewhere, was written "as a defense against time" ("Cotton Mather" 147).

25. Paul de Man's comments on autobiography are relevant here, perhaps. Mather presents Winthrop in the act of "speaking." Yet, de Man says, "To the extent that language is figure (or metaphor, or prosopopoeia) it is indeed not the thing itself but the representation, the picture of the thing and, as such, it is silent, mute as pictures are mute. Language, as trope, is always privative" (80). Mather establishes a tension between "voice" and "picture", precisely to obviate the distinction between the representation and the thing represented, and hence to convince his audience of the "authority" of his own text.

26. Begun in March 1696, "Pietas in Patriam" was first published in London in 1697 (see Mather, *Diary* I: 186). The version in *Magnalia* was printed from the 1697 edition.

27. The fort was destroyed in 1696. Its destruction may have seemed to Mather to parallel too closely Phips's ineffectual leadership of the province and his fall from power in 1694. Clearly, in the biography, Phips neither "edifies" nor "fortifies" New England.

28. In this sense, Mather's Phips is a "self-made man" (see Bercovitch, " 'Delightful Examples' ") only in a limited sense. For having "made" himself, Phips then "unmakes" himself in a gesture of total subordination to the public. This is a model that, dovetailing with the ideology of civic humanism, would prove attractive to the revolutionary generation, though not to nineteenth-century America. As Gura has written concerning "Pietas in Patriam": "If one accepts Mather's characterization of Phips as a new American model, he must also realize that the New England magistrate had been defined anew. Ambition could be sanctioned as long as the subject still pursued the public interest" ("Cotton Mather's *Life of Phips*" 456).

29. Bercovitch, *American Jeremiad* 89. In "Cotton Mather," Bercovitch wrote: "What [Mather's] achievement reveals is an epic work of the imagination. Built as a monument *against* realities, founded upon myth and fortified by hermeneutics-become-symbolism, the *Magnalia* survives as a testament to its author's ability to incorporate New England, the world, and time itself within the image-making imagination" (147).

30. Like "Pietas in Patriam," "Decennium Luctuosum" (1699) was also published separately prior to the publication of *Magnalia* itself.

31. In the first half of Book VII, see also 19 (Anne Hutchinson), 21 (Quakers), 26 (a specific Quaker), and 36 (an impostor).

32. Levin, *Cotton Mather* 165, argues that Cotton Mather wrote the *Declaration;* but see Silverman (436) for a contrary view.

33. The quotation is from *Things for a Distress'd People to Think Upon.* The very split between the roles of minister and historian indicates the direction in which New England was heading. By the Revolution, ministers had relatively little power to affect widespread cultural change, witness the fact that many of the Revolutionary histories were not written by ministers (see Cohen, *Revolutionary Histories* 51). On the Revolutionary ministers' attempts to cope with their loss of power and prestige, see Donald Weber's excellent *Rhetoric and History in Revolutionary New England.*

34. On the weakening of ministerial power over the course of the century, see Hall, *Faithful Shepherd.*

EPILOGUE

1. I have borrowed the phrase "visionary compact" from Pease x.

2. See J. Hillis Miller. Providential historians have often been dismissed as simplistic and naive (see Gay, for example, and Cohen 23–53).

3. For some of the ideas expresssed in this paragraph see, for example, Mink, "Narrative Form as Cognitive Instrument" 143–47; Barthes; White, *Tropics* 121–34; and Rahe 231–541.

Works Cited

Allen, David Grayson. *In English Ways: The Movement of Societies and the Transferral of English Local Law and Custom to Massachusetts Bay in the Seventeenth Century.* Chapel Hill: U of North Carolina P, 1981.

Ames, William. *The Marrow of Theology.* Trans. John Eusden Dykstra. 1968. Durham: Labyrinth, 1983.

Anderson, Virginia DeJohn. "Migrants and Motives: Religion and the Settlement of New England." *New England Quarterly* 58 (1985): 339-83.

Arch, Stephen Carl. "The Edifying History of Edward Johnson's *Wonder-Working Providence.*" *Early American Literature* 28 (1993): 42-59.

Bacon, Francis. *The Dignity and Advancement of Learning. The Works of Francis Bacon.* 15 vols. Boston: Houghton, Mifflin, 1890. VI: 77-412.

Baker, Herschel. *The Race of Time.* Toronto: U of Toronto P, 1967.

Baritz, Loren. *City on a Hill: A History of Ideas and Myths in America.* New York: Wiley, 1964.

Barthes, Roland. "The Discourse of History." *Comparative Criticism: A Yearbook.* Ed. E. S. Shaffer. Cambridge: Cambridge UP, 1981. 7-20.

Battis, Emery. *Saints and Sectaries: Anne Hutchinson and the Antinomian Controversy in the Massachusetts Bay Colony.* Chapel Hill: U of North Carolina P, 1962.

Bercovitch, Sacvan. *The American Jeremiad.* Madison: U of Wisconsin P, 1978.

———. "Cotton Mather." *Major Writers of Early American Literature.* Ed. Everett Emerson. Madison: U of Wisconsin P, 1972. 93-149.

———. " 'Delightful Examples of Surprising Prosperity': Cotton Mather and the American Success Story." *English Studies* 51: 40-43.

———. "The Historiography of Johnson's *Wonder-Working Providence.*" *Essex Institute Historical Collections* 104 (1968): 138-61.

———. " 'Nehemias Americanus': Cotton Mather and the Concept of the Representative American." *Early American Literature* 8 (1974): 220-38.

———. *The Puritan Origins of the American Self.* New Haven: Yale UP, 1975.

———. "The Puritan Vision of the New World." *Columbia Literary History of the United States.* Ed. Emory Elliot, Martha Banta, et al. New York: Columbia UP, 1988. 33-44.

————. "Typology in Puritan New England: The Williams-Cotton Controversy Reassessed." *American Literature* 19 (1967): 166–91.

Boyer, Paul, and Stephen Nissenbaum. *Salem Possessed: The Social Origins of Witchcraft.* Cambridge: Harvard UP, 1974.

Bozeman, Theodore Dwight. "The Puritan's 'Errand into the Wilderness' Reconsidered." *New England Quarterly* 59 (1986): 231–51.

————. *To Live Ancient Lives: The Primitivist Dimension in Puritanism.* Chapel Hill: U of North Carolina P, 1988.

Bradford, William. *Of Plymouth Plantation, 1620–1647.* Ed. Samuel Eliot Morison. New York: Knopf, 1953.

————. "Some observations of God's merciful dealing with us in this wilderness." *Proceedings of the Massachusetts Historical Society.* Vol. 11. Boston: 1869–1870. 465–78.

Breen, Timothy. *The Character of the Good Ruler: Puritan Political Ideas in New England.* 1970. New York: Norton, 1974.

Breitwieser, Mitchell Robert. *Cotton Mather and Benjamin Franklin: The Price of Representative Personality.* Cambridge: Cambridge UP, 1984.

Bremer, Francis J. "The English Context of New England's Seventeenth-Century History." *New England Quarterly* 60 (1987): 323–35.

Bulkeley, Gershom. *Will and Doom, or The Miseries of Connecticut by and Under an Usurped and Arbitrary Power.* Ed. and intro. Charles J. Hoadly. Hartford: Connecticut Historical Society *Collections,* 1895. 3: 69–269.

Burke, Kenneth. *The Philosophy of Literary Form: Studies in Symbolic Action.* Baton Rouge: Louisiana State UP, 1941.

Bush, Sargent. "John Wheelwright's Forgotten *Apology:* The Last Word in the Antinomian Controversy." *New England Quarterly* 64 (1991): 22–45.

Caldwell, Patricia. "The Antinomian Language Controversy." *Harvard Theological Review* 69 (1976): 345–67.

————. *The Puritan Conversion Narrative: The Beginnings of American Expression.* Cambridge: Cambridge UP, 1983.

Calvin, John. *Commentaries on the Epistles of Paul the Apostle to the Corinthians.* Trans. John Pringle. Edinburgh: Calvin Translation Society, 1848.

The Cambridge Platform. The Creeds and Platforms of Congregationalism. Ed. Williston Walker. 1893. Philadelphia: Pilgrim Press, 1960. 194–237.

Child, John. *New-England's Jonas cast up at London.* 1647. Rpt. *Collections of the Massachusetts Historical Society.* Boston, 1846. 2d ser. IV: 107–20.

Clarke, John. *Ill Newes From New England; or A Narrative of New-England's Persecution.* London, 1652.

Cohen, Lester. *The Revolutionary Histories: Contemporary Narratives of the American Revolution.* Ithaca: Cornell UP, 1980.

Colman, Benjamin. *A Manifesto or Declaration Set Forth by Undertakers of the New Church Now Erected in Boston, in New-England, November 17, 1699.* Boston, 1699.

"Copy of a Petition to Parliament in 1651." *The History of the Province of Massachusetts.* By Thomas Hutchinson. 3 vols. Ed. Lawrence Shaw Mayo. Cambridge: Harvard UP, 1936. I: 428–30.

Cotton, John. "God's Promise to His Plantations." *Old South Leaflets.* Vol. 3. New York: Burt Franklin, n.d. No. 53.

Cressy, David. *Coming Over: Migration and Communication between England and New England in the Seventeenth Century.* Cambridge: Cambridge UP, 1987.

Damrosch, Leo. *Fictions of Reality in the Age of Hume and Johnson.* Madison: U of Wisconsin P, 1989.

Danforth, Samuel. "A Brief Recognition of New England's Errand into the Wilderness." *The Wall and the Garden: Selected Massachusetts Election Sermons, 1670–1755.* Ed. A. W. Plumstead. Minneapolis: U. of Minnesota P, 1968. 53–77.

de Man, Paul. *The Rhetoric of Romanticism.* New York: Columbia UP, 1984.

De Prospo, Richard C. "Marginalizing Early American Literature." *New Literary History* 23: 233–65.

———. *Theism in the Discourse of Jonathan Edwards.* Newark: U of Delaware P, 1985.

Dean, F. L. "Tudor Theories of Historical Writing." *University of Michigan Contributions to Modern Philology.* 1 (April 1947): 1–24.

Delbanco, Andrew. *The Puritan Ordeal.* Cambridge: Harvard UP, 1989.

Dudley, Thomas. "Letter to the Countess of Lincoln." *Tracts and Other Papers.* Vol. 2. No. 4. Ed. Peter Force. 1836. Gloucester: Peter Smith, 1963.

Dummer, Jeremiah. *A Defense of the New England Charters.* Boston, 1721.

Dunn, Richard. "John Winthrop Writes His Journal." *William and Mary Quarterly* 3rd ser. 41 (1984): 185–212.

———. *Puritans and Yankees: The Winthrop Dynasty of New England.* Princeton: Princeton UP, 1962.

———. "Seventeenth-Century English Historians of America." *Seventeenth-Century America: Essays in Colonial History.* Ed. James Morton Smith. 1959. New York: Norton, 1972. 195–225.

Eberwein, Jane Donahue. " 'In a book, as in a glass': Literary Sorcery in Mather's 'Life of Phips'." *Early American Literature* 10 (1975/76): 289–300.

———. " 'Indistinct Lustres': Biographical Miniatures in the *Magnalia Christi Americana*." *Biography* 4 (1981): 195–207.

Edwards, Jonathan. "A Divine and Supernatural Light." *Jonathan Edwards: Representative Selections.* Ed. Clarence H. Faust and Thomas H. Johnson. New York: American Book Co., 1935. 102–11.

Elyot, Thomas. *The Governor.* 1531. London: Dent, 1962.

Emerson, Ralph Waldo. "The American Scholar." *Essays and Lectures.* New York: Library of America, 1983. 51–71.

Faulkner, William. *Requiem for a Nun.* New York: Random House, 1951.

Ferguson, Arthur B. *Clio Unbound: Perception of the Social and Cultural Past in Renaissance England.* Durham: Duke UP, 1979.

Foster, Stephen. *The Long Argument: English Puritanism and the Shaping of New England Culture, 1570–1700.* Chapel Hill: U of North Carolina P, 1991.

Franklin, Benjamin. *Autobiography.* New York: Library of America, 1987. 1305–1469.

Fussner, F. Smith. *The Historical Revolution: English Historical Writing and Thought, 1580–1640.* London: Routledge and Paul, 1962.

Gallagher, Edward. "The Case for the *Wonder-Working Providence.*" *Bulletin of the New York Public Library* 57 (Autumn 1983): 10–27.

———. "A Critical Study of Edward Johnson's *Wonder-Working Providence of Sion's Saviour in New England.* Diss. U of Notre Dame, 1970.

———. Introduction. *Abel Being Dead, Yet Speaketh (1658): A Biography of John Cotton.* By John Norton. Delmar: Scholar's Facsimiles and Reprints, 1978. v–xxvii.

———. "An Overview of Edward Johnson's *Wonder-Working Providence.*" *Early American Literature* 5 (1970/71): 30–49.

———. "The *Wonder-Working Providence* as Spiritual Autobiography." *Early American Literature* 10 (1975): 75–87.

Gay, Peter. *A Loss of Mastery: Puritan Historians in Colonial America.* Berkeley: U of California P, 1966.

Gookin, Daniel. *An Historical Account of the Doings and Sufferings of the Christian Indians in New England. Transactions and Collections of the American Antiquarian Society* 2 (1836): 423–525.

———. *Historical Collections of the Indians in New England.* 1674. Boston, 1792.

Gorton, Samuel. *Simplicities Defence Against Seven-Headed Policy.* 1646. Rpt. Rhode Island Historical Society *Collections.* Vol. 2. Providence, 1835.

Gura, Philip. "Cotton Mather's *Life of Phips:* 'A Vice with the Vizard of Virtue Upon It'." *New England Quarterly* 50 (1977): 440–57.

———. *A Glimpse of Sion's Glory: Puritan Radicalism in New England, 1620–1660.* Middletown: Wesleyan UP, 1984.

Hall, David D., ed. *The Antinomian Controversy, 1636–1638: A Documentary History.* Middletown: Wesleyan UP, 1968.

———. *The Faithful Shepherd: A History of the New England Ministry in the Seventeenth Century.* Chapel Hill: U of North Carolina P, 1972.

Hall, Michael G. *The Last American Puritan: The Life of Increase Mather.* Middletown: Wesleyan UP, 1988.

Haller, William. *Foxe's Book of Martyrs and the Elect Nation.* London: Cape, 1963.

Hansen, Chadwick. *Witchcraft at Salem.* New York: Braziller, 1969.

Heimert, Alan, and Andrew Delbanco. *The Puritans in America: A Narrative Anthology.* Cambridge: Harvard UP, 1985.

Higginson, Francis. *New England's Plantation. Tracts and Other Papers.* Ed. Peter Force. Vol. 1. No. 12. 1836. Gloucester: Peter Smith, 1963.

Higginson, John. "An Attestation to This Church-History of New-England." In *Magnalia Christi Americana.* By Cotton Mather. [v–x].

History of the Pequot War: The Contemporary Accounts of Mason, Underhill, Vincent and Gardner. Ed. Charles Orr. Cleveland: Helman-Taylor, 1895.

Holifield, E. Brooks. "On Toleration in Massachusetts." *Church History* 38 (1969): 188–200.

Hooker, Richard. *The Laws of Ecclesiastical Polity.* 2 vols. London: Dent, 1925.

Hosmer, James Kendall. Introduction. *Winthrop's Journal "History of New England," 1630–1649.* 2 vols. By John Winthrop. 1908. New York: Barnes and Noble, 1959. I: 3–20.

Howard, Alan B. "Art and History in Bradford's *Of Plymouth Plantation.*" *William and Mary Quarterly* 3rd ser. 28 (1971): 237–66.

———. "The Web in the Loom: Puritan Historians in Colonial America." Diss. Stanford U, 1968.

Hubbard, William. *A General History of New England, from the Discovery to MDCLXXX.* 1815. New York: Arno, 1972.

———. *The Happiness of a People in the Wisdom of Their Rulers.* Boston, 1676.

———. *A Narrative of the Troubles with the Indians in New England.* Boston, 1677.

Irving, Washington. *History, Tales, and Sketches.* New York: Library of America, 1983.

Jameson, J. Franklin. Introduction. *Johnson's Wonder-Working Providence, 1628–1651.* By Edward Johnson. 5–19.

Johnson, Edward. *Wonder-Working Providence of Sions Saviour in New England. Johnson's Wonder-Working Providence, 1628–1651.* Ed. J. Franklin Jameson. 1910. New York: Barnes and Noble, 1959.

Johnson, Richard. *Adjustment to Empire: The New England Colonies, 1675–1715.* New Brunswick: Rutgers UP, 1981.

Keayne, Robert. *The Apologia of Robert Keayne.* Ed. Bernard Bailyn. 1964. New York: Harper and Row, 1965.

Kellner, Hans. *Language and Historical Representation: Getting the Story Crooked.* Madison: U of Wisconsin P, 1989.

Kemp, Anthony. *The Estrangement of the Past: A Study in the Origins of Modern Historical Consciousness.* New York: Oxford UP, 1991.

LaCapra, Dominick. *History and Criticism.* Ithaca: Cornell UP, 1985.

Lasch, Christopher. *The True and Only Heaven: Progress and Its Critics.* New York: Norton, 1991.

Lechford, Thomas. *Plain Dealing; or, Newes from New-England.* London, 1641.

Levin, David. *Cotton Mather: The Young Life of the Lord's Remembrancer, 1663–1702.* Cambridge: Harvard UP, 1978.

―――. "Forms of Uncertainty: Representations of Doubt in American Histories." *New Literary History* 8 (1976): 59–74.

―――. *History as Romantic Art.* Stanford: Stanford UP, 1959.

―――. "William Bradford: The Value of Puritan Historiography." *Major Writers of Early American Literature.* Ed. Everett Emerson. Madison: U of Wisconsin P, 1972. 11–32.

Levy, F. J. *Tudor Historical Thought.* San Marino: Huntington Library, 1967.

Lovejoy, David S. *The Glorious Revolution in America.* 1972. Middletown: Wesleyan UP, 1987.

―――. *Religious Enthusiasm in the New World: Heresy to Revolution.* Cambridge: Harvard UP, 1985.

Lovelace, Richard F. *The American Pietism of Cotton Mather: Origins of American Evangelicalism.* Washington: Christian College Consortium, 1979.

McQuade, Donald, ed. *The Harper American Literature.* Vol. 1. New York: Harper and Row, 1987.

Mather, Cotton. *Diary.* Ed. Worthington C. Ford. 2 vols. New York: Ungar, 1911.

―――. "A General Introduction." *Magnalia Christi Americana.* 1702. [xix–xxviii].

―――. *Magnalia Christi Americana.* 1702. New York: Arno, 1972.

―――. *Things for a Distress'd People to Think Upon.* Boston, 1696.

Mather, Increase. *Autobiography.* Ed. Michael G. Hall. *Proceedings of the American Antiquarian Society* 71 (1961): 277–360.

―――. *A Brief Account Concerning Several of the Agents of New England.* London, 1691.

―――. *A Brief History of the Warr With the Indians in New England.* Boston, 1676.

―――. *A Brief Relation of the State of New England, from the Beginning of that Plantation To This Present Year, 1689.* London, 1689.

―――. *A Call from Heaven To the Present and Succeeding Generations.* Boston, 1679.

―――. *The Day of Trouble is Near.* Cambridge, 1674.

―――. *A Discourse Concerning the Danger of Apostasy.* Boston, 1679.

―――. *The Doctrine of Divine Providence Opened and Applied.* Boston, 1684.

―――. *An Earnest Exhortation To the Inhabitants of New-England, To hearken to the voice of God in his late and present dispensations.* Boston, 1676

―――. "Epistle Dedicatory." "Ecclesiastes. The Life of . . . Jonathan Mitchell." *Magnalia Christi Americana.* By Cotton Mather. IV: 158–65.

―――. *An Essay for the Recording of Illustrious Providences.* 1684. London, 1890.

―――. *The First Principles of New-England, Concerning the Subject of Baptisme and Communion of Churches.* Cambridge, 1675.

———. *A Further Vindication of New-England.* London, 1689.

———. *Heaven's Alarm to the World.* Boston, 1682.

———. *An Historical Discourse Concerning the Prevalency of Prayer.* Boston, 1677.

———. *Ichabod or, A Discourse showing what Cause there is to Fear that the Glory of the Lord, is Departing from New England.* Boston, 1702.

———. *The Life and Death of that Reverend Man of God, Mr. Richard Mather, Teacher of the Church in Dorchester in New England.* Cambridge, 1670.

———. *The Mystery of Israel's Salvation.* London, 1669.

———. *A Narrative of the Miseries of New-England, By Reason of the Arbitrary Government Erected there.* London, 1688.

———. *New England Vindicated.* London, 1689.

———. *The Present State of the New-English Affairs.* Boston, 1689.

———. *Reasons for the Confirmation of the Charter Belonging to the Massachusetts Colony.* [England]: n.p, n.d.

———. *A Relation of the Troubles which have hapned in New-England, By reason of the Indians there.* Boston, 1677.

———. *Renewal of Covenant the great Duty incumbent on decaying or distressed Churches.* Boston, 1677.

———. *Returning Unto God the great concernment of a Covenant People.* Boston, 1680.

———. *The Times of Men are in the hand of God.* Boston, 1675.

Meserole, Harrison T., ed. *American Poetry of the Seventeenth Century.* University Park: Pennsylvania State UP, 1985.

Michaelsen, Scott. "John Winthrop's 'Modell' Covenant and the Company Way." *Early American Literature* 27 (1991): 85–100.

Middlekauff, Robert. *The Mathers: Three Generations of Puritan Intellectuals, 1596–1728.* New York: Oxford UP, 1971.

Miller, J. Hillis. "Narrative." *Critical Terms for Literary Study.* Ed. Frank Lentricchia and Thomas McLaughlin. Chicago: U of Chicago P, 1990. 66–79.

Miller, Perry. *Errand Into the Wilderness.* Cambridge: Harvard UP, 1956.

———. *The New England Mind: From Colony to Province.* Cambridge: Harvard UP, 1953.

———. *The New England Mind: The Seventeenth Century.* Cambridge: Harvard UP, 1939.

———. "Solomon Stoddard, 1643–1729." *Harvard Theological Review* 34 (1941): 277–320.

Miller, Perry, and Thomas H. Johnson. *The Puritans: A Sourcebook of Their Writings.* 1938. 2 Vols. New York: Harper and Row, 1963.

Mink, Louis. "Everyman His or Her Own Annalist." *On Narrative.* Ed. W. J. T. Mitchell. Chicago: U of Chicago P, 1981. 233–39.

———. "Narrative Form as Cognitive Instrument." *The Writing of History.* Ed. Robert H. Canary and Henry Kozicki. Madison: U of Wisconsin P, 1978. 129–49.

Morgan, Edmund. "John Winthrop's 'Modell of Christian Charity' in a Wider Context." *Huntington Library Quarterly* 50: 145–51.

——. *The Puritan Dilemma: The Story of John Winthrop.* Boston: Little, Brown, 1958.

——. *Visible Saints: The History of a Puritan Idea.* New York: New York UP, 1963.

Morton, Nathaniel. *New Englands Memoriall.* Ed. Howard J. Hall. New York: Scholar's Facsimiles and Reprints, 1937.

Morton, Thomas. *New English Canaan.* Ed. Charles Francis Adams. Boston: Prince Society, 1883.

Moseley, James G. *John Winthrop's World: History as a Story, the Story as History.* Madison: U of Wisconsin P, 1992.

[*Mourt's Relation.*] *Journal of the English Plantation at Plimouth.* Ann Arbor: University Microfilms, 1966.

Murdock, Kenneth B. "Colonial Historians." *American Writers on American Literature.* Ed. John Macy. New York: Liveright, 1931. 3–12.

——. *Increase Mather: The Foremost American Puritan.* Cambridge: Harvard UP, 1926.

——. "William Hubbard and the Providential Interpretation of History." *Proceedings of the American Antiquarian Society* 52 (1941): 15–37.

The Necessity for Reformation. Creeds and Platforms of Congregationalism. Ed. Williston Walker. 1893. Philadelphia: Pilgrim, 1960. 423–39.

Nelsen, Anne Kuesner. "King Philip's War and the Hubbard-Mather Rivalry." *William and Mary Quarterly* 3rd ser. 27 (1970): 615–29.

Nelson, Raymond. *Van Wyck Brooks: A Writer's Life.* New York: Dutton, 1981.

Norton, John. *Abel Being Dead, Yet Speaketh; or, The Life and Death of . . . John Cotton.* London, 1658.

——. "Sion the Outcast Healed of Her Wounds." *Three Choice and Profitable Sermons.* Cambridge, 1664.

Noyes, Nicholas. *New England's Duty.* Boston, 1698.

Olsen, V. N. *John Foxe and the Elizabethan Church.* Berkeley: U of California P, 1973.

Oxford Latin Dictionary. Ed. P. G. W. Glare. Oxford: Clarendon, 1982.

Parrington, Vernon. *The Colonial Mind: 1620–1800.* Vol. 1. *Main Currents in American Thought.* New York: Harcourt, Brace, 1959.

Partner, Nancy. "Making Up Lost Time: Writing on the Writing of History." *Speculum* 61 (1986): 90–118.

Pearce, Roy Harvey. *Savagism and Civilization: A Study of the Indian and the American Mind.* Baltimore: Johns Hopkins UP, 1953.

Pease, Donald. *Visionary Compacts: American Renaissance Writings in Cultural Context.* Madison: U of Wisconsin P, 1987.

Perry, Dennis R. "Autobiographical Role-Playing in Edward Johnson's *Wonder-Working Providence.*" *Early American Literature* 22 (1987): 291–305.

———. "Autobiographical Structures in Seventeenth-Century Histories." Diss. U of Wisconsin-Madison, 1986.

Poole, William F., ed. and intro. *Wonder-Working Providence of Sion's Saviour in New England.* By Edward Johnson. Andover: Draper, 1867.

Pynchon, William. *The Meritorious Price of Man's Redemption, or Christ's Satisfaction Discussed and Explained.* London, 1655.

Rahe, Paul. *Republics Ancient and Modern: Classical Republicanism and the American Revolution.* Chapel Hill: U of North Carolina P, 1992.

Rawson, Grindal. "To the Learned and Reverend Cotton Mather." In *Magnalia Christi Americana.* By Cotton Mather. [xvi].

Reagan, Ronald. Speech. July 4, 1984. *Weekly Compilation of Presidential Documents.* Vol. 20. No. 27. 978–81.

Ricoeur, Paul. *Time and Narrative.* Vol. 1. Trans. Kathleen McLaughlin and David Pellauer. Chicago: U of Chicago P, 1984.

Rorty, Richard. *Irony, Contingency, and Solidarity.* Cambridge: Cambridge UP, 1989.

Rosenmeier, Jesper. " 'They Shall No Longer Grieve': The Song of Songs and Edward Johnson's *Wonder-Working Providence.*" *Early American Literature* 26 (1991): 1–20.

———. " 'With My Owne Eyes': William Bradford's *Of Plymouth Plantation.*" *Typology and Early American Literature.* Ed. Sacvan Bercovitch. Amherst: U of Massachusetts P, 1972. 69–105.

Rowlandson, Mary. *A True History of the Captivity and Restoration of Mrs. Mary Rowlandson. Journeys in New Worlds: Early American Women's Narratives.* Ed. William Andrews et al. Madison: U of Wisconsin P, 1990. 27–65.

Sachse, William L. "The Migration of New Englanders to England, 1640–1660." *American Historical Review* 53 (1948): 251–78.

Sargent, Mark L. "William Bradford's 'Dialogue' with History." *New England Quarterly* 65 (1992): 389–421.

Scheick, William, ed. *Two Mather Biographies:* Life and Death *and* Parentator. Bethlehem: Lehigh UP, 1989.

Schweninger, Lee. *John Winthrop.* Boston: Twayne, 1990.

Scottow, Joshua. *A Narrative of the Planting of the Massachusetts Bay Colony. Collections of the Massachusetts Historical Society.* Boston: Little, Brown, 1858. 4th ser. IV: 279–332.

Seavey, Ormond. "Edward Johnson and the American Puritan Sense of History." *Prospects* 14 (1978): 1–29.

Silverman, Kenneth. *The Life and Times of Cotton Mather.* New York: Columbia UP, 1985.

Simmons, Richard C. "The Founding of the Third Church in Boston." *William and Mary Quarterly* 3rd ser. 26 (1969): 241–52.

Slotkin, Richard, and James K. Folsom, ed. and intro. *So Dreadfull a Judgement: Puritan Responses to King Philip's War.* Middletown: Wesleyan UP, 1978.

Smith, John. *The Complete Works of John Smith.* 3 vols. Ed. Philip L. Barbour. Chapel Hill: U of North Carolina P, 1985.

Stoddard, Solomon. *The Safety of Appearing at the Day of Judgment in the Righteousness of Christ, Opened and Applied.* 1687. Edinburgh, 1792.

Stoever, William K. B. *"A Faire and Easie Way to Heaven": Covenant Theology and Antinomianism in Early Massachusetts.* Middletown: Wesleyan UP, 1978.

Taylor, Edward. *The Poems of Edward Taylor.* Ed. Donald Stanford. 1960. Chapel Hill: U of North Carolina P, 1989.

Thompson, Benjamin. "Celeberrimi: Cottoni Matheri Celebratio." In *Magnalia Christi Americana.* By Cotton Mather. [xiv].

Tichi, Cecelia. *New World, New Earth: Environmental Reform in American Literature from the Puritans through Whitman.* New Haven: Yale UP, 1979.

Todorov, Tzvetan. *The Conquest of America: The Question of the Other.* Trans. Richard Howard. New York: Harper and Row, 1984.

Underhill, John. *Newes From America.* London, 1638.

Wall, Robert Emmet. *Massachusetts Bay: The Crucial Decade, 1640–1650.* New Haven: Yale UP, 1972.

Ward, Nathaniel. *The Simple Cobler of Aggawam in America.* Ed. P. M. Zall. Lincoln: U of Nebraska P, 1969.

Watters, David. "The Spectral Identity of Sir William Phips." *Early American Literature* 18 (1983/84): 219–32.

Weber, Donald. *Rhetoric and History in Revolutionary New England.* New York: Oxford UP, 1988.

Wenska, Walter. "Bradford's Two Histories: Pattern and Paradigm in *Of Plymouth Plantation.*" *Early American Literature* 13 (1978): 151–64.

Wheelwright, John. *John Wheelwright: His Writings.* Ed. Charles H. Bell. 1876. Freeport: Books for Libraries, 1970.

White, Hayden. *The Content of the Form.* Baltimore: Johns Hopkins UP, 1987.

———. *Metahistory: The Historical Imagination in Nineteenth-Century Europe.* Baltimore: Johns Hopkins UP, 1973.

———. *Tropics of Discourse: Essays in Cultural Criticism.* Baltimore: Johns Hopkins UP, 1985.

———. "The Value of Narrativity in the Representation of Reality." *On Narrative.* Ed. W. J. T. Mitchell. Chicago: U of Chicago P, 1981. 1–23.

Wigglesworth, Michael. "God's Controversy with New England." *American Poetry of the Seventeenth Century.* Ed. Harrison T. Meserole. 42–54.

Williams, Raymond. *Marxism and Literature.* New York: Oxford UP, 1977.

Williams, Roger. *Experiments of Spiritual Life and Health.* Ed. Winthrop S. Hudson. Philadelphia: Westminster, 1951.

Winslow, Edward. *Good Newes from New England.* London, 1624.

———. *Hypocrisie Unmasked.* Providence: Club for Colonial Reprints, 1916.

Winthrop, John. *The History of New England from 1630 to 1649.* 2 vols. Ed. James Savage. Boston: Phelps and Farnham, 1825–1826.

―――. "A Model of Christian Charity." *Winthrop Papers*. II: 282–95.

―――. *A Short Story of the Rise, reign, and ruine of the Antinomians, Familists, and Libertines that infected the Churches of New England*. London, 1644.

―――. *Winthrop Papers*. 6 vols. Boston: Massachusetts Historical Society, 1929–1992.

Wise, Gene. *American Historical Explanations: A Strategy for Grounded Inquiry*. 2d. ed. rev. Minneapolis: U of Minnesota P, 1980.

Wood, William. *New England's Prospect*. London, 1634.

Ziff, Larzer. *Puritanism in America: New Culture in a New World*. New York: Viking, 1973.

Index

1. danger of individual interpretation of Bible

2. centrality of language / linguistic disputes in 17ᵗʰ century NE
   controversies (40)

3. idea of "providential historians" (68) → 125

4. authority of historian (recurrent theme ?) — authority
   (eg. 78   162-63

5. good example of idiomatic shift (129)

6. history and sense of purpose (147)

7. find the threads of identity construction (e.g. 150

8. past illustrates compromise (109) ~ ala Clay

9. idioms in conflict (Increase Mather) - p.131